Sephardic Women's Voices
Out of North Africa

Nina B. Lichtenstein

Sephardic Women's Voices
Out of North Africa

Gaon Books
www.gaonbooks.com

Sephardic Women's Voices: Out of North Africa. Nina B. Lichtenstein. Copyright 2017. All rights reserved. This publication is in copyright. Subject to statutory exception and to the provisions of relevant collective licensing agreements, no reproduction of any part may be made without the written permission of Gaon Books, except for brief quotations included in analytical articles, chapters, and reviews.

For permissions, group pricing, and other information contact Gaon Books, P.O. Box 23924, Santa Fe, NM 87502 or write (gaonbooks@gmail.com). Gaon Books is an imprint of Gaon Institute for Tolerance Studies, a 501-c-3 non-profit organization.

Manufactured in the United States of America.

The paper used in this publication is acid free and meets all ANSI (American National Standards for Information Sciences) standards for archival quality paper. All wood product components used in this book are Sustainable Forest Initiative (SFI) certified.

First edition
Library of Congress Cataloging-in-Publication Data

Names: Lichtenstein, Nina B. author.
Title: *Sephardic women's voices: out of North Africa* / Nina B. Lichtenstein. Description: First edition. | Santa Fe, NM : Gaon Books, 2016. | Includes bibliographical references and index.
Identifiers: LCCN 2016017330 (print) | LCCN 2016030192 (ebook) | ISBN 9781935604884 (pbk. : alk. paper) | ISBN 9781935604891 (ebook) Subjects: LCSH: French literature--North African authors--history and criticism. | French literature--Jewish authors--History and criticism. | French literature--Women authors--History and criticism. | French literature--20th century--History and criticism. | Jewish women in literature. | Sephardim in literature.
Classification: LCC PQ150.N67 L53 2016 (print) | LCC PQ150.N67 (ebook) | DDC 840.9/9287089924061--dc23
LC record available at https://lccn.loc.gov/2016017330

All translations are by Nina Lichtenstein unless otherwise noted.

Table of Contents

Acknowledgments 9
Introduction 11

Part I: Historical Context
The Jews of the Maghreb: Belonging and Marginalization
Chapter 1. The Narrative of Loss 23
    i. Recapturing Sephardic History in the Maghreb 26
    ii. Jewish Women in the Historical Context 39
Chapter 2. The Jews in Colonial Maghreb: Between a Rock and a Hard Place 45
    i. Cultural and Social Change 47
    ii. The Loss of Language and Amnesia 60
    iii. A New Schism 72

Part II: Literary Considerations
Chapter 3. History and Writing 79
    i. Vanishing Bodies and Voices; Repressed Identities 79
    ii. *Aliyah* or *Yeridah*? The Israel Experience 83
    iii. Arriving in the Land of *Liberté, Egalité* and *Fraternité* 88
    iv. Eclipsed Narratives 90
    v. What Makes Literature Jewish? 97
Chapter 4. The Sephardic Woman and Post-colonial Discourse 101
    i. Theoretical and Literary Reflections 101
    ii. Diasporic Voices 109
    iii. Language Matters and Sephardic Literature 115
    iv. Modes of Narrating Personal Experience 122
    v. On Loss and Memory 129
    vi. The Role of Jewish Women Voices 132
    vii. A Unique Point of View: Sephardic Women in France 136
    viii. Where Do They Fit In? Issues of Classification 140

Part III: Voices

Chapter 5. Mothers, Fathers and Rabbis: Sephardic Traces in Writing
    Memory and Identity   147
    i. Woman as Mother, Woman as Daughter: Annie Cohen,
    Nine Moati and Gisèle Halimi   150
    ii. A Mother to Contend With in Gisèle Halimi's *Fritna*   154
    iii. Lyrical Memories of a Sephardic Mother in Annie Cohen's
    Bésame Mucho   164
    iii. Sephardic Transmission in Birth and Death in Nine Moati's
    Mon Enfant, Ma Mère   175

Chapter 6. Phantom Rabbis and Marabouts: Catalysts of Memory and
    Nostalgia in the Texts of Annie Cohen and Annie Fitoussie   185
    i. The Wisdom of the Fool in Annie Fitoussi's
    La mémoire folle de Mouchi Rabbinou   187
    ii. Faucets Unplugged in Annie Cohen's *Le Marabout de Blida*   199

Chapter 7. Rebels with a Cause: Fathers and Daughters
    in Narratives by Paule Darmon and Chochana Boukhobza   211
    i. Cultural Clashes In and Out of the Family
    in Paule Darmon's *Baisse les Yeux, Sarah*   212
    ii. Beyond Personal Confession:
    Chochana Boukhobza and *Un Eté à Jérusalem*   228

Conclusion   239
Bibliography   247
Films and Websites   260
About the Author   261
Index   263

THIS BOOK IS DEDICATED TO MY PARENTS

Acknowledgments

"Just keep at it; a little every day," a mentor once told me. Although this was when I was in graduate school writing my dissertation, I still hear those wise words. It is unquestionably all the encouragements, support and help that a writer finds herself blessed to have from mentors, colleagues, family and friends, that deserve to be acknowledged when a book is finally born.

My dissertation advisor, Lucy Stone McNeece fearlessly modeled the courage to do two things: sticking to a topic that may to some seem quite eccentric, and pursuing an advanced degree involving late hours at the library while having young kids at home. Longtime mentor and staunch supporter T. A. Perry has shown by meticulous example the writer's mantra, "just sit yourself down and do it," and the extraordinary value of quiet meditation. French-Moroccan sociologist Arrik Delouya was a tireless and selfless resource in the early days of my research, and Noam Stillman has been one of those few people I always felt comfortable asking for help, who never said no, and who has given me wonderful opportunities to share my work along the way.

Without the writers, whose shimmering works of human experiences of lives caught "in-between" profoundly moved me, there would be no incentive to write this book. Thanks to them, the urge soon developed to share with an Anglophone readership the experiences of a Jewish, female loss of North Africa as expressed in the French language. One of those writers, the prolific, passionate and brilliant Chochana Boukhobza, originally from Sfax, Tunisia, has become an invaluable friend in this process and beyond.

Thanks to the continued support of Shulamit Reinharz and the Hadassah Brandeis Institute, I have for the last six years had an academic home where great minds come together to develop fresh ideas about Jews and gender. As an independent scholar, this "home" base has proven vital.

Without the generosity of spirit that I have always been granted from my parents, my life and work would be nothing like it is today.

Finally, it is to my three sons I owe the utmost gratitude. Their love, humor and energy have sustained me every step of the way.

Introduction

> *The works of many...Jewish writers, thinkers, and historical figures from the Arab world and the Levant remain inaccessible in English, despite enormous resources, clearly defined market and wide-open space of reception available for works of Jewish interest. Deemed marginal in relation to the central narrative of modern Jewish history as it has been interpreted and appropriated... the testament and experience of these writers remains poised, like parts of messages left in many bottles, all waiting to be found and put together.*[1]

I BEGIN OUR JOURNEY WITH THIS OBSERVATION BY AMmiel Alcalay, whose ideas about the important but often neglected role of Jewish writers from the Arab world reflect the inspiration behind my project. Sephardic women's writings have proven to be such bottled messages that once found and carefully interpreted, present invaluable information about the marginalization and silencing of the Jewish experience in and out of the Maghreb, or North Africa. Over time these stories have drifted onto my shore, offering testaments of a generally excluded human experience that belongs in the diverse and hybrid collection of post-colonial stories of displaced peoples. Once their narratives are located and appreciated for their literary and historical value, it becomes clear that they need to be incorporated into a larger movement within the Jewish historical and cultural trajectory. It is a journey that you are invited to join in the following pages, where stories by seven different women afford an opportunity to (re-)discover the voices and experiences of the North African Jews.

My goal here is two-fold: First, to make accessible to the English speaking reader the many moving experiences of francophone Jewish women as expressed in their prize-winning literary works written be-

---

1   Ammiel Alcalay, *After Jews and Arabs: Remaking Levantine Culture*. London: U of Minn. P. 1993, 10.

tween 1979-1998, and that are not yet translated from French.² Second, to contextualize these voices by first placing the shared experiences of their families and communities in the historical framework as it relates to Jews from Arab lands generally, and from North Africa specifically. This is somewhat of a sweeping reconnaissance mission, which – relatively swiftly – traces the historical trajectory of the Jews of North Africa since biblical times and the first Exodus from the Land of Israel, until their arrival in France in the mid-twentieth century. After the review of Jewish history in the Maghreb, with particular focus on the colonial era and the complex social and political dynamics leading up to decolonization and its aftermath, the book transitions into a discussion about various literary considerations in the framework of post-colonial narratives.

We must ask ourselves, for example, why have the narratives by Jews from Arab lands been eclipsed? What exactly do we mean by Jewish literature, and what makes it specifically Sephardic? How are female (Jewish) identities repressed and then written? Where do Sephardic women's voices fit into these paradigms? What are diasporic voices, and in what way does language matter in these literary texts? What are the various modes of narrating personal experience, and what are the issues of classification of this hybrid literary genre, and how are they evolving? These are some of the main inquiries that will be discussed in the chapters preceding the literary analysis. There are eight different texts elucidating for us Sephardic women's experiences in and out of North Africa. In the literary analysis section of this book – the last three chapters – I introduce the various themes and narrative approaches of the novels and memoirs I have chosen to focus on, and that together give personal expressions to the unique historical experience presented in the first part of the book.

***

Post-colonial studies have enjoyed a long and fruitful tenure of articulating the devastating long-term effects of colonialism. Around the world, countries and peoples are left with profound psychological,

---

2 Chochana Boukhbza's *Pour l'amour du père/For the Love of the Father* (1996), is translated by me and is available as a free e-book from the Brandeis Institutional Repository (http://bir.brandeis.edu/handle/10192/31752).

social, economic and political scars as they grapple with recovery and attempt to become autonomous authors of their own lives. While the political and academic discourse of the "West"[3] continues to discuss what it means to be a post-colonial subject, women have also become a recurrent theme of post-colonial studies. Women's voices and testimonies not only bear unique witness to gendered human experiences in the various colonial and post-colonial histories, but also contribute to increased social and political awareness among women that ultimately begins to have an impact not only on identity, but also on policies and politics. One can say that being a writing post-colonial subject is always inscribing oneself in the specific political arena of that legacy.

This book explores writings, both memoirs and novels, by contemporary Jewish women born in North Africa roughly between the 1930s and the 1950s, making them the last generation to have experienced the ancient and diverse Jewish presence there. Their unique position in the history of North Africa as colonial subjects, yet differentiated from their Arab neighbors, lets us consider the critical contribution they make to our understanding of a distinctive Jewish memory and identity. Marked by the often-complex relationship between Jews, Arabs, and the French colonizers that was the reality in North Africa in recent history, this difficult past continues to complicate Jewish life in modern day France.[4]

Authors who have experienced colonial subjugation write of the painful and often ambiguous experiences associated with being ruled by a "promising" culture, where, as cultural critic Homi Bhabha notes,

---

3   By "West" I refer to the dominant discourse of the industrialized world, primarily that of the academy in Europe and in the U.S.
4   Two recent studies, Maud Mandel's *Muslims and Jews in France: History of a Conflict*. Princeton: Princeton UP, 2014, and Ethan B. Katz's *The Burdens of Brotherhood: Jews and Muslims From North Africa to France*. Boston: Harvard UP, 2015, both examine Muslim-Jewish relations in light of the migration of hundreds of thousands of Jews and Muslims from Algeria, Morocco and Tunisia to France in the course of the twentieth century. Both historians shed invaluable light on how a typically "reductionist-charged narrative of polarization has repeatedly hidden a more complex set of social interactions"(Mandel, 156), and it is precisely here, in that permeable and fertile space in-between historical archives, the historian's analysis and statistics, that literature can provide nuances to human experiences that resist the usual binary construction of Muslim-Jewish relations.

elements of mimicry and ambivalence represent "disabling contradictions" within colonial relationships, as well as within the post-colonial subject. The Jews of North Africa were not exempt from such disabling contradictions, as will be elaborated upon in this book. Unheard voices still remain excluded from the present "corpus" of post-colonial testimonies: there is always room for another "other" to be silenced and marginalized, and the Jew, and in our case the Oriental Jew, continues to be the epitome of that always already excluded "other." The French essayist and public intellectual Alain Finkielkraut states bluntly that "The Ashkenazim are identified with domination, and the Sephardim with exclusion,"[5] and Tunisian novelist Albert Memmi was among the first Jews from North Africa to articulate this dire discrepancy when he noted that, "Jewish history has so far been written by Western Jews; there has been no great Oriental Jewish historian. This is why the "Western" aspects of Jewish suffering are widely known."[6] The goal here then, is to open up the floor to the "Oriental Jewish" experience and in so doing look to those voices to explain why and how the North African Jewish history has remained a little known chapter. Most of all, however, the purpose of this work is for us as readers to listen to their stories.

This book thus represents the coming together of two fields of study, that of Jewish studies and French/Francophone studies, since it examines both the Jewish colonial experience in the Maghreb and also the post-colonial adjustments and challenges required by their mass-migration from North Africa to France. Literature and history will compliment each other to offer a more comprehensive approach revealing often-overlooked and complex relationships and, hopefully,

---

5   Alain Finkielkraut, *The Imaginary Jew*. London: University of Nebraska Press, 1994, 143.
6   Albert Memmi, "Who is an Arab Jew?" on www.Jimena.org. Official website of Jews indigenous to the Middle East and North Africa. Source quoted as Israel Academic Committee on the Middle East, February, 1975, 3. Since Memmi's statement several Jewish historians from North Africa, most of whom were educated in the French system often in France, have published important texts on Jewish history in Tunisia, Morocco and Algeria. Michel Abitbol, André Chouraqui, Paul Sebag, Benjamin Stora and Haim Zerfani are all "Oriental Jewish historians" as Memmi might have called them, and many of their works inform this study.

leading to a better understanding of differences and marginality within this context. The literature of Jewish women writers of Maghreb or North African origins (two terms that I will use interchangeably) will provide the reader with an increased awareness of Jewish difference as experienced by women whose identities have been shaped by the diverse historical elements in their personal, family, and community's trajectories. My goal is to direct attention to texts written by women who have not typically been included in discussions on minority or immigrant literatures in France, or in the world at large, nor in the syllabi of post-colonial (francophone) studies. Their letters have remained hitherto largely uncharted and are still unknown territory to many who profess an interest in immigrant or migrant narratives.

Historically, Jews, like women, have been defined, alienated and silenced as agents relative to social and political change. They have been designated as passive though potentially dangerous elements. As soon as they mobilize or become active and autonomous, they are perceived as threatening. After the Second World War, the realization of the horrors of the Shoah, with its near annihilation of European/Ashkenazi Jewry, obscured the destiny of North Africa's Jews as they suffered from intensifying anti-Jewish sentiments among their Arab compatriots and neighbors.

The Arabs saw the establishment of the State of Israel as part of continuous imperialist and expansionist Zionist agendas in the Middle East. The silent mass exodus and forced exile of the nearly one million Jews in North Africa and the Middle East (known as the Maghreb and the Mashreq respectively) in the years preceding and immediately following decolonization, remains a poorly explored part of world history for both anglophone and Ashkenazi Jews around the world, and by the general public as well. This history has also been largely eclipsed within the current discourse on politically exiled refugees, where the question of Palestinian refugees has become a dominant issue in the Arab-Israeli conflict.[7]

---

7   Gina Waldman, co-founder and current president of JIMENA (Jews Indigenous to the Middle East and North Africa), has helped shed light on this eclipse by testifying before the UN Human Rights Council in 2008. JMENA is dedicated to educating and advocating on behalf of the 850,000 Jewish refugees from the Middle East and North Africa. Waldman was born in Tripoli to a family that had lived in Libya for centuries, and along with her family and

The plight of European Jews in the first half of the 20th century is the defining Jewish experience, including the establishment of the (initially predominantly Ashkenazi) Jewish state, mostly because of interest on the part of America and England in the fate of European Jews. Testimonies of survivors among European Jews abound in world literature, urging younger generations to remember and to turn the knowledge of those shared memories into socio-political awareness and action, adopting the slogan "Never Again."

The drama lived by the Jews of the Islamic world, however, has remained relatively invisible in the face of their Ashkenazi brothers' and sisters' stories of gas chambers and ovens, and the silence surrounding their fate may be in part an expression of their own empathy as much as a general lack of interest, even among Jews themselves, in the fate of this non-European minority. Fortunately, during the last ten to fifteen years there has been a slow but steady growth in public awareness about the plight of Jews from Islamic lands and it is in this climate of positive change that this book seeks to offer a qualitative element to compliment what can often be heard as quantitative statistics.[8] Knowledge of the Jews of the Maghreb can lessen the tendency to amalgamate all Jews into one homogeneous and reductive "other." Anthropologist and ethnographer Jonathan Boyarin suggests that, "The silencing of discourse about Jewish difference is generally accomplished through the subordination or assimilation of Jews in categories presumed to be dominant."[9] This might be one reason that Jews have become a "forgotten minority" since the Second World War because they are often indistinguishable from their non-Jewish neighbors, as exemplified by the French republic's efforts

---

most Jews in Libya she was persecuted, nearly murdered and brutally expelled from her homeland in 1967. Source: Jimena.org.

8   As recently as on June 23, 2014 the Government of Israel adopted a law to designate November 30th as the annual national Day of Commemoration for the Jewish refugees who were displaced from Arab countries and Iran in the 20th century. The law, which is the culmination of several years of hard work and dedication by an international team of *Mizrahi* Justice advocates, legislates commemoration events and the inclusion of *Mizrahi* history into Israeli schools' curriculum. Source: Jimena.org.

9   Jonathan Boyarin, *Storm from Paradise. The Politics of Jewish Memory*. Minneapolis: U of Minnesota P, 1992, 101.

to remove identification in religious appearance among immigrants and minorities in the modern secular state.

Professor and literary critic Thomas Nolden has pointed out that contemporary Jewish literature has come to represent "one of the most exciting developments in France's recent cultural scene."[10] The authors discussed in this book contribute to a re-imagining, a redefining of what it means, not only to be French and a French writer, but also a French Jewish woman writer of North African origins, by introducing notions of difference into their writings. How do they help shape the current debates about French national and cultural identity, and at the same time that which is specifically Sephardic?

Jewish writer Hélène Cixous, who was born in Algeria in 1937 and raised there under French colonial rule, is particularly helpful here. Informed from a Jewish woman's perspective and an indispensable resource for both these debates and the ongoing discussions on colonialism, her voice is invaluable to the area of post-colonial women's studies, and specifically to the unique place held by the Jewish experience of marginality and non-belonging, considering her very public and significant influence in French literary, academic, cultural and political arena. In much of her own autobiographically inspired writing, Cixous deals with questions of her own (Jewish) history of identity formation and of belonging (or not) in both Algeria and France.

After a traumatic childhood experience in Algeria under the Vichy regime of the Second World War, and with the laws of *Numerus Clausus* (the fixed number severely restricting admission of Jews to schools and universities, but also to professions) refusing her entry into the public school where she was a student, she would be forever scarred by the experience of arbitrary exclusion. She has the following observation about being a French Jew born in Algeria (Jews in Algeria under French rule gained French citizenship with the famous Crémieux decree in 1870): "To be French, and not a single French person on the genealogical tree, admittedly it is a fine miracle, but it clings to the tree like a leaf menaced by the wind."[11] She thus under-

---

10   Thomas Nolden, *In Lieu of Memory. Contemporary Jewish Writing in France*. New York: Syracuse UP, 2006, xii.
11   Hélène Cixous, "My Algériance. In other words to Depart not to arrive from Algeria." Translated by Eric Prenowitz. *Tri-quarterly* 100 (1997): 260.

scores an undeniable Jewish conscience testifying to a Jewish subconscious premonition that when the next storm hits, no matter how solidly rooted a family might feel, the fear of being carried away by the gusts from the stormy winds remains deeply ingrained. In writing about this awareness of vulnerability, which she ultimately turns into strength and rootedness in and through her writing, she further notes: "I don't have a legitimate language. I sing in German, I disguise myself in English, I fly in French, I am a thief, where would my text belong? ... I don't have any roots: from what sources could I feed a text. A diasporic effect."[12] A continually "diasporic" text, in a borrowed language, transforming it through the use of linguistic particularisms and, as Françoise Lionnet notes, "rendering it porous and open to what was once its other,"[13] Cixous knows from experience the difficulties and the delights in this freedom. When she was eighteen-years-old, she left Algeria: "From 1955 on, I adopted an imaginary nationality which is literary nationality."[14] Cixous' reflexions on the various aspects of her experience of marginality both as a Jew and a woman, are highlighted in the word she coined - *juifemme* (a wordplay including the identifiers "*je*/I," "*juif*/Jew" and "*femme*/woman" suggesting that each element carry their own significance, and together they represent her inescapable reality: "I am a Jewish Woman"). This word, *juifemme*, will emphasize the different dimensions of the challenges of the Jewish experience in and after North Africa. Because of her spearheading the development of *écriture féminine* or feminine writing as developed within feminist and women's studies, Cixous has been the subject of innumerable studies, and her more recent focus on her complex childhood in Algeria – juggling an extremely hybrid identity due to her family's diverse background – makes her a valuable inclusion here. But rather than as the subject

---

[12] "Je n'ai pas de langue légitime. En allmand je chante, en anglais je me déguise, en français je vole, je suis voleuse, où déposerais-je un texte ?... Je n'ai pas de racines : à quelles sources pourrais-je prendre de quoi nourrir un texte. Effet de diaspora." Hélène Cixous, *Entre l'Ecriture*. Paris: Des Femmes, 1986, 2.
[13] Françoise Lionnet, *Post-colonial Representations. Women, Literature and Identity*. Ithaca: Cornell UP, 1995, 172. Lionnet is a professor at UCLA in Comparative Literature, French and Francophone studies, and gender studies, as well as the current director of the African Studies Center.
[14] Cixous, Hélène, *Rootprints*. New York: Routledge, 1997, 204.

of a separate textual analysis in the literary section below, her voice and ideas of the writing woman are instead braided into the fabric of the book, functioning as a *fil d'Ariadne,* or connective thread of inspiration and a reminder of the female Jewish consciousness that is omnipresent here.

One writer who examines the challenges of the Jewish experience is French and Moroccan-born psychiatrist Daniel Sibony. His concept of *entre-deux,* or in-between, informs my own inquiry since I use this idea to describe the complex but fertile place of existing in-between (cultures, languages, identities) occupied by Jews of the Maghreb. Suggesting a force of difference and a process of possibilities rather than a paralyzing predicament of fixed notions, the concept of *entre-deux* opens the complex lived experience to yielding creative and dynamic cultural and literary manifestations.[15]

Cultural critic Edward Said has noted that such manifestations should not only be sought out in traditional literary or historical genres since, as he suggests, "More reliable now are the reports from the front line…hybrid combinations of realism and fantasy…explorations of mixed forms (essay, video and film, photography, memoir, story, aphorism) of unhoused exilic experiences".[16] Considering the benefit to my project in exploring other media, I will also bring into the discussion two "autobiographical" films depicting the stories of Jews exiled from Arab lands in forms of interviews, memoirs, documentary footage and pictures, *The Forgotten Refugees* (2005) by the David Project and *The Silent Exodus* (2002) by Pierre Rochov. I also consider the seminal photographic collection by French photographer Frédéric Brenner entitled *Diaspora: Homelands in Exile* (2003), composed of two volumes, one entitled "*Photographs*" and the other "*Voices*." Brenner says himself that, as he was "gathering and assembling the multiple fragments of exile," by taking the photographs over a time span of twenty five years, "I was trying to restore to each Jew his or her own face, to return to each his or her own memory – the memory of these fragments that have survived in the margins of history."[17]

---

15 See Daniel Sibony, *L'Entre-Deux. L'Origine en Partage.* Paris: Seuil, 1991.
16 Edward Said, *Culture and Imperialism.* New York: Vintage Books, 1994, 330.
17 Frédéric Brenner, "Photographs," *Diaspora: Homelands in Exile.*

There are certain themes that recur throughout Brenner's work, as noted by Tsvi Blanchard in the introduction to *"Voices"*: "...the tension between the image and the world; the condition of exile – of not-being-at-home or even, paradoxically, not-being-oneself; the impossibility of Jewish authenticity, or at least its great difficulty."[18] These are the same tensions explored in this book, where the diverse, multi-cultural and hybrid nature of a Jewish identity of in-between will confirm its authenticity, decidedly and not at all impossibly.

So, I invite you along on this journey of reconnaissance, first tracing the historical trajectory of the Jews of North Africa with particular focus on the colonial era and the complex social and political dynamics leading up to decolonization. Then follows a discussion about various literary considerations in the framework of post-colonial narratives, and here I pay particular attention to the importance of the francophone Sephardic women's voices within this paradigm. Finally, I introduce the various themes and narrative approaches of the eight literary texts on which I have chosen to focus and that together give a voice to Sephardic women's post-colonial experiences.

All the authors considered in the literary section of this book were born in North Africa and immigrated to France as young children or young adults. Their texts were written over a span of twenty years, between 1979-1998[19], after the writers had settled in France. Each novel or piece of life writing is analyzed in light of the information provided in the previous sections, revealing narratives of

---

Photographs and Voices. New York: Harper Collins, 2003, ix.
18   Ibid., viii.
19   As is noted in the documentary *Comme un Juif en France/Being Jewish in France* (2007) by Yves Jeuland, this was a particularly fertile period (the 1980s, especially) for Jewish cultural expression/production in France, since "it was fashionable to be Jewish." The French public had grown supportive of French Jews' backing of Israel's right to exist, a sensitivity heightened by the pan-Arab aggressions threatening its existence, and subsequent Israeli victories in the Six Day War of '67, and the Yom Kippur War of '73. The French public was eagerly interested in learning about Jewish history and culture, and were practically obsessed with the burgeoning Holocaust literature. In this context, we also see many books authored by Jews from North Africa, beginning to *prendre la parole* or "take the stage" to express their difference.

uprooting, loss and migration to be added to any meaningful discussion about minorities claiming autonomous identities and a place in the ever-evolving hybrid and heterogeneous literary production we see in the world. Ultimately, it is my hope to make accessible the messages of these award-winning literary treasures to an anglophone audience who would otherwise not be able to hear their powerful testimonies.

Beruchim Haba'im!
Welcome!

Part I: Historical Context
The Jews of the Maghreb:
Belonging and Marginalization

CHAPTER 1

THE NARRATIVE OF LOSS

IN ORDER TO UNDERSTAND THE SCOPE OF A LOSS, IT IS HELP-
ful to go back and look at the history of one's relationship to that which
has been lost. It could be an object, a relationship, a home or a country,
but regardless of what is lost, the perception of one's connection to it
will influence the mourning and the memory of that loss. For the Jews
who have lost their homelands in North Africa, one way of coping with
the demise of their Maghreb Jewish civilization has been through writing it, writing it out, creating something that fills the void of not only a
place of belonging, a family heritage and of childhood memories, but
also of what inscribes the individual in her personal history, and that
of a people living in history, making history.

Hélène Cixous, born and raised in Algeria, and who has written
extensively on the formative experiences in childhood of being a despised minority and never fully fitting in, has talked about the function
of writing as a means to define one's identity, saying that when writing
about loss becomes necessary and possible, one has to "…lose everything, to have lost everything once."[20] Some of Cixous' more recent
autobiographical writings can be understood as a desire to place her
marginalized Algerian-Jewish self into her own story as an attempt at
re-writing herself back into the history that has excluded her. It is as
an act of dynamically inscribing oneself, rather than passively being
inscribed/scripted in or out of history, that we can view the strategy of
historical re-inscription as it has affirmed itself among Jews of North
African origin in the last three decades. Historically, while living in
diaspora, the Jews have often been perceived as living/falling outside
of history, that is, not as agents of history, but as driving forces only
within their own insular communities or ghettos. This is of course a

---

20   "…tout perdre, avoir une fois tout perdu." Hélène Cixous, *Entre
l'Ecriture*. Paris: Des Femmes, 1986, 48.

simplistic view of Jews as historical beings, and a product of the politically charged narratives of the conquerors, or the ones in power. The Jews have come to occupy the space of myth, as a static, essentialized and a-historic other, one that, until the establishment of the State of Israel, had little chance of de-mythifying itself.

As minority narratives claim the relevance to which they are entitled, we realize with renewed acuteness that the stories of those excluded from history are indeed just as critical, if not more so, to our understanding of the various histories that make up the greater human endeavor. We need to revisit our constructed knowledge and the basis for our understanding of inter-human and international relations as they have formed history, so that the human lives that shape them are recognized as making a difference.

Looking closer at the issues surrounding the exiled Jews of North Africa, we should bear in mind that in this inquiry we are not "simply" referring to a few individuals who for political reasons were exiled from their homelands, but of an entire people, a complete civilization, which was displaced *en tout* (completely), unable to return again as the thriving communities they once were. Whispers bearing witness to and leaving traces of a lost world are what is explored in the following chapters. This becomes an imperative contribution to what needs to be taken into account as the world continues to name, judge, remember and justify according to the narrative of those in power, and hence, forget the other's truth. In the analysis of the importance of Jewish memory, the ideas of Alain Finkielkraut are helpful. Following in the footsteps of his predecessor, philosopher and cultural critic Walter Benjamin (1892-1940), Finkielkraut has defined the political importance of memory, and in *The Imaginary Jew*[21] he points out that, although memories may be personal, what is remembered is above all else a political question. Political in that even the narratives of memory represent a battle ground whose winnings are appropriated and used for political purposes.

To ensure that the memories of the Jews of the Maghreb are remembered and included not only in North African history and Jewish history but also in the post-colonial discourse as well as in the rapidly

---

21 Alain Finkielkraut, *The Imaginary Jew*. London: University of Nebraska Press, 1994.

evolving contemporary French corpus of a more hybrid "national" literature, we need to be reminded that this is indeed a highly politicized act.[22] In his seminal book *Zakhor: Jewish History and Jewish Memory* (1982), Yosef H. Yerushalmi alludes to the complicated relationship between (Jewish) history and (Jewish) memory. While he notes that, "memory is always problematic, usually deceptive, sometimes treacherous,"[23] he goes on to validate its selective nature as determining the content of what defines a person, a community or a people. There is a graceful admittance in his work that what offers people a sense of transcendence is always affected by us, by the material act of remembering.

Where Yerushalmi takes issue with modern historiography is when "[w]ith unprecedented energy it continually recreates an ever more detailed past whose shapes and textures memory does not recognize. But that is not all. The historian does not simply come in to replenish the gaps of memory. He constantly challenges even those memories that have survived intact."[24] Hence, as we embark on a study of some selected Jewish women's memories and try to understand how they place themselves in history or express their experience through writing, we will first consider the history of the Jews' relationship to the Maghreb with an acute awareness of the constant bargaining between history and memory. "Certain memories live on," Yerushalmi reminds us, and the others "are winnowed out, repressed, or simply discarded by a process of natural selection which the historian, uninvited, disturbs and reverses."[25] Despite his own vocation as a historian, he admits to and underlines the complicated rapport between the historian's role as "disturber of memories" and that of his human and Jewish need to remember group as well as individual memories. It seems that the

---

22   For an important study of Muslim memorialization of Jews, see Aomar Boum's *Memories of Absence: How Muslims Remember Jews in Morocco* (Stanford, CA: Stanford UP, 2013). Boum seeks to reveal lesser known counternarratives to the nationally promoted concept of 'ayn mika– that "... things that might be important should be ignored because of the trouble the observer can experience if he notices them" as he interviews three generations of Moroccans about their memories of their former Jewish neighbors.
23   Yosef Hayim, Yerushalmi, Zakhor, *Jewish History and Jewish Memory*. Seattle: University of Washington Press, 1982, 5.
24   Ibid., 94.
25   Ibid., 95.

Biblical imperative and cultural obsession to "Remember!" as experienced by Jews, can be fulfilled in its most rewarding way by allowing memory and life to converge, communicate, enrich and even modify each other, in a symbiotic relationship whose ultimate purpose should be to inform us of the intrinsic value of both.

The retrospective examination of the Jewish presence in the Maghreb that follows is at once necessary and relative. Necessary for the quest to understand the relationship of the Jewish people to this region of the world, and relative as we analyze the personal memories expressed in literature by Jewish women writers of North African origins. It would be my hope that "modern historiography" and literary memory together will enhance our appreciation of this unique Jewish story and hence bring our understanding of "the Jewish experience" beyond the monochromatic prism in which it is often understood.

RECAPTURING SEPHARDIC HISTORY IN THE MAGHREB

It is important to bear in mind that in modern Jewish history, *Sephardim* and *Mizrahim* (Jews in Islamic lands whose trajectory did not go via Spain and the Iberian Peninsula) have become the Jews' "other," since in both European/American (Jewish) and Israeli society their experiences have only been marginally included in the understanding of a "Greater Jewish Narrative" until in more recent years. European Jews have examined their own history from a eurocentric perspective, and thereby marginalized the other (non-European) Jews like *Sephardim* and *Mizrahim* by scrutinizing them in all their otherness and exoticism, as noted by Spector, Laskier and Reguer.[26] They go on to explain, "This lacuna in both Jewish and Middle Eastern studies is partly because general histories of the region write Jews out of the standard narrative."[27] As

---

26   *The Jews of the Middle East and North Africa in Modern Time.* New York: Columbia UP, 2003, vii-viii. The need to address this politically charged "omission" has been recognized and is beginning to be rectified, as historians such as Norman Stillman, Michael M. Laskier and Zion Zohar have contributed significantly to filling this void. Historian Bernard Lewis is of an earlier generation and has dedicated much of his career to the study of the history of Arabs, Islam and Jews living in Muslim countries.
27   Ibid., vii.

part of the religious and ethnic mosaic that was traditional Islamic society, Jews were but one of many minorities; a minority easily relegated to the margins, or simply ignored altogether both by Muslim pre-colonial and colonials societies, and altogether repressed and eliminated in the narrative of most Islamic post-colonial societies. The time has come for the Jews of North Africa and the Middle East to write themselves back into the history of Arab lands to reclaim a narrative space in the historical text and context; a self-affirming and necessary undertaking, given their significant historical presence in these regions.

A large part of Jewish presence that evolved over thousands of years of cultural, religious and economic embedding in the countries of Morocco, Tunisia and Algeria is indigenous to the region. These early indigenous Jewish communities were strengthened by the arrival of the Jews from the Iberian Peninsula in the late 1400s, and together they formed a diverse and vivid North African Jewish heritage, drawing its cultural and religious resources from varied milieus and backgrounds. The Jewish presence in the Maghreb was also one marked by the ambiguities of simultaneously being seen as a native and a stranger. Consequently, the Jews had to manage the identity of being Maghreb's "other" even in a place they had called home for many generations.

To help us gain a relative perspective, let us turn to the most important historical considerations concerning the Jews in North Africa. The recorded history of North Africa begins with the founding of Carthage in 813 B.C.E. For 667 years until its fall to the Romans in 146 B.C.E., Carthage came under the influence of the Jews and Phoenicians of Palestine. The Romans were succeeded by the Vandals, the Vandals by the Byzantines, and the Byzantines by the Arabs in A.D. 642.[28]

We can go all the way back to 721 B.C.E. in Jewish history to find the first "official" exile of Jews from what today is considered Israel. The "Jews" which then consisted of Ten Tribes making up the total of the first, defining, Jewish generations as history knows them, were dispersed by the Assyrians who conquered the land, and consequently some fractions of Jews, with Phoenicians by their side, arrived in Af-

---

28   Michael Laskier, *North African Jewry in the Twentieth Century. The Jews of Morocco, Tunisia and Algeria*. New York: NYUP, 1994, 5.

rica and began to settle. Jews have lived and thrived, also periodically suffered, within the different cultures and under the various rulers throughout the typically pluralistic cultures of Mashreq (the Middle East) and the Maghreb (North Africa) for over twenty-five hundred years, and one can trace a more encompassing thrust into exile or diasporic existence to the destruction of the First Temple in 586 B.C.E when the Jews were officially dispersed from the defined geographic space then called Palestine.

The Jewish population in the Maghreb was strengthened even more after 70 C.E, when the second Temple fell to the Romans. There is a documented Jewish presence among the early Berber settlements in North Africa (the Berbers being the oldest ethnic group indigenous to North Africa), to the extent that a non-negligible part of the present day Berber population can trace their roots back to a Jewish lineage. The Jews that arrived after 70 C.E. were mostly peaceful Jews, city dwellers who would live under Roman rule.[29] The Jews that had been exiled earlier to the Sub-Saharan steppes were mostly warrior nomadic tribes. By the end of the Roman Empire (476 C.E), two very different kinds of Jewish populations could be distinguished in North Africa: one consisting of Judeo-Berber nomadic tribes who were pagan and lived beyond the control of the Romans, and the other consisting of the more sedentary Jews of the cities, living under Roman influence peacefully engaging in agriculture and commerce. By the time the Vandals arrived and assumed power around 500 C.E., the Jewish influence was growing in the region, and Jews and Berbers were culturally and politically closely linked together. The region was then pursued by the Byzantines who harassed the city-dwelling Talmud-teaching Jews enough to cause them to flee toward the interior of the region and join forces with the Judeo-Berber tribes who now practiced a more primitive form of monotheism.

When the Arab conquest of the Maghreb took place between 642 and 900 C.E., it was the Jews and the Berbers who fought side by side in resistance. Indeed, many Berber tribes had become Jewish, and from them some of the most fierce opponents to the Islamization of the African continent. The heroine and incarnation of this resistance became known as

---

29   Didier Nebot, *Les Tribus oubliées d'Israël L'Afrique judéo-berbère, des origines aux Almohades.* Paris: Éditions Romillat, 1999, 37.

the Kahena, a priestess said to possess supernatural powers and whose heroic leadership has reached mythic proportions in Judeo-Arabic folklore. Arab historians unanimously declare her ruthless leadership as one of the most unifying forces in Maghreb history. But most of the Berbers eventually embraced (i.e. were forced to convert to) Islam following the Arab conquest, and have since undergone linguistic and cultural Arabization much more so than their Jewish compatriots, who due to their monotheistic faith and Abrahamic tradition, were often left by the Muslim invading forces to practice their religion under certain restrictions.

The defeat of the Judeo-Berber strongholds in the Aurès mountains (to the east of the Saharan Atlas in northeastern Algeria) signals the end of a political and "warrior" Judaism in North Africa, and the Jews were to become a more passive and submissive people developing instead religiously and commercially. Over time, Jews were naturally also influenced by the Arab presence, and in his address entitled "Who is an Arab Jew?" Albert Memmi points out, "I simply wish to underline that as natives of those countries called Arab and indigenous to those lands well before the arrival of the Arabs, we shared with them, to a great extent, languages, traditions and cultures."[30]

For about five centuries Islam's control over the region was to last more or less undisturbed, and from a Jewish perspective this era is remembered as "the obscure centuries," partly due to the fact that little recorded history exists from the period. During this time, the Jews lived in unpredictable conditions under the various Arab rulers of the Islamic dynasties that controlled the region, and the quality of their existence depended heavily on the favor of the specific sovereign at the given time. There was no unifying or formalized Judaism in the Maghreb then, and the many Jewish communities in the region became immersed in local spiritual practices, often creating a hybridization of Jewish and Berber traditions.

The most violent blow to the Jews, Berbers and Christians came with the reign of the Almohades in the 1200's, who both in Spain and in North Africa would use the sword to impose the ideals of their faith. This ended any form of Berber Judaism because of the zero-tolerance

---

30   Memmi, "Who is an Arab Jew?" As posted on www.jimena.org. Official website of Jews Indigenous to the Middle East and North Africa. Source quoted as Israel Committee on the Middle East, February, 1975.

of anyone not practicing Islam in its strictest, most orthodox form. There was no choice to live peacefully according to one's own monotheistic practice, but "simply" the choice of conversion or death, and Almohade-led mass exterminations and mass conversions of Jews, Berbers and Christians radically changed forever not only the political map but also the population map of the Maghreb. Consequently, Jewish sources fell quiet for some time, mostly as secretly practicing Jews had publicly accepted Islam.[31] In order to find information on the Jewish communities from this time period, the most reliable option is to turn to diplomatic archives for historical research. The rumblings of what was to become the Inquisition and expulsion of the Jews from the Iberian Peninsula had began already in 1391, with the first massacres taking place in Castile, when a few hundred survivors managed to flee and reach the African coast on the other side of the Strait of Gibraltar.

Naturally, there were also Muslims among those fleeing the Christianizing of the newly united kingdom of Aragon and Castile. It was between 1482 and 1496 that the Sephardic Jewish population (lit: "Jews from the Iberian Peninsula" i.e. Spain) arrived *en masse*, fleeing the cruel edict of King Ferdinand and Queen Isabelle to expel all Jews from the land of the cross. Steeped in culture, education, religious, scientific and philosophic training in the tradition of the Jewish-Andalusian "Golden Age" of Al-Andalus (roughly 950-1150), these *Sephardim* brought with them a "blood transfusion" of new hope and strength to their fellow Jews already living in North Africa. The number of Jews in the Maghreb was therefore greatly reinforced by these *Megorashim* (the ones expelled) from Spain and Portugal, so much so that over time indigenous Jews in North Africa, or *Toshavim*, would become more or less absorbed by them, especially in Morocco where the *Megorashim* arrived in overwhelming numbers. Much to the awe and disbelief of most of the indigenous Jewish population who had rarely if ever seen Jews with such a high level of refinement, these newly arrived Jews would come to represent the cultural, religious and political elite among the Jews of North Africa. Between them, the *Megorashim* and the *Toshavim* would disagree for quite some time on issues relating

---

31   Jacques Taïeb, *Etre Juif au Maghreb à la veille de la colonisation.* Paris: Albin Michel, 1994, 19-20.

to liturgy and ritual slaughter, differences of practice and rabbinic interpretations that had developed within each group as they had existed and evolved in two distinct cultural societies on either side of the Gibraltar. As we will see later, it was also the *Sephardim/Megorashim* who most naturally and fervently embraced European and "Western" traditions once France, Italy, Spain and Portugal started to influence more profoundly and forcefully the cultures of especially urban places within North Africa.

There is a tendency in Jewish as well as secular scholarship, and also in my own work, to blend together the identity of the "true" *Sephardim* (those whose ancestry is Iberian) with the indigenous Jews of North Africa whose ancestry never went via Iberia but came directly from Judea or Ancient Palestine, and to call them all Sephardic Jews. This can in part be understood by the (Jewish) historical tendency to divide the greater Jewish "people" into a seemingly simplified dichotomy of *Ashkenazim* and *Sephardim*, to distinguish between Jews with a cultural heritage from Eastern Europe and "the rest," whose cultural heritage can be as diverse as from anywhere within the Levant, that is, the greater Mediterranean basin, including areas as far West as Morocco, and as far East as Syria, Iran and Iraq.

Mizrahi is another term we will use, and which refers specifically to Jews who lived in Islamic lands to the east of Africa and whose heritage did not include Spain. In Israel today for example, the distinction is made more acutely between the different kinds of Oriental or *Mizrahi* Jews that make up the non-European population. Jews from Yemen, Iran and Iraq, North Africa or Egypt, are just a few of these sub-groups, and clearly Jews from the three countries of the Maghreb (Tunisia, Algeria and Morocco) are quick to distinguish themselves from each other. Aside from designating the region from whence they came, grouping Jewish cultural differences this way also helps emphasize to the outsider that within the term "Jewish," there is great diversity.

Different cultural, linguistic as well as religious traditions have formed the various Jewish populations into uniquely distinctive groups over time. The linguistic differences between the two major Jewish cultural groups are of course of utmost importance since like the Yiddish language of Eastern European Jews those of North Africa also had their own culturally specific languages. Ladino/Judezmo or Judeo-Spanish (the version that developed in Morocco was named Haketía) as well as Judeo-Arabic were the languages spoken by the Jews of the Maghreb, in addition to Arabic used as a daily vernacular, especially in exchanges with their Arab neighbors.

The Jews that arrived in Tunisia from Italy (called the Grana) continued using Italian as their *lingua franca*. However, it was primarily Judo-Arabic that was used among North African Jews since the 1500's until the advent of modernization brought in with the colonizers and their European languages. It should be noted also that of all Jewish languages of the post-Talmudic period, Judeo-Arabic is unique in that it has had the longest recorded history from the ninth century to the present, extending across three continents during the Middle Ages.[32] Linguistically, Judeo-Arabic is composed of a vocabulary and grammar that is Arabic, enriched by Hebrew and Aramaic.[33] It is written using Hebrew letters, as Yiddish was when it was the major and daily language of Ashkenazi Jews in Eastern Europe. Judeo-Arabic varied from place to place and was affected by geographical, economic, and historical circumstances.

As French Moroccan historian Joseph Chetrit points out, the Hebrew and Aramaic components of a more high-leveled Judeo-Arabic played a significant role, since this would allow the rabbi to transmit information and tradition to his congregation during sermons, or it would allow Jews to have access to a "secret argot" with which to speak in the presence of Muslim Arab speakers.[34] When the *Megorashim* arrived from Spain and Portugal and the Livornese Jews from Italy, Judeo-Arabic met Ladino and Judeo-Italian and many blended languages evolved as they absorbed lexical terms from each other. As colonialism and emerging Zionism began to influence North African Jewish societies, new challenges were given on the local language. Newspapers published in Judeo-Arabic at the end of the nineteenth century soon lost their readership to the French press diffused throughout the colonies. Change was in the air, and the pull from the West and all the

---

32   Alcalay, *After Jews and Arabs*, 19.
33   Joseph Chetrit, "Judeo-Arabic," in *The Jews of the Middle East and North Africa of Modern Times,* Reeva Spector Simon, Michael Menachem Laskier and Sara Reguer, eds. New York: Columbia UP, 2003, 128.
34   Ibid., 129.

promising possibilities that came along with the French educational system proved effective.

Dissatisfaction with the status quo made the young generally open to change, and the message transmitted in the new, Western-style schools – that the languages and cultures developed over the centuries by Jews under Islam were "inferior" to those of the West – led young people to view their own traditions with disdain. These schools taught their students, who now included girls, that their traditional vernaculars were not "Jewish languages" at all, but corrupt jargons.[35]

Hebrew, which remained mostly a liturgical language used in synagogue and personal prayers, religious studies and learning, was not the secular lingo of everyday communication. Modern Hebrew became a daily spoken official language only when the State of Israel was established in 1948.

Although the status and quality of life enjoyed by the Jews under Islam, or the Jews of *Dar-al-Islam* (Islamic territories, or "world of the fidels"), had varied greatly from generation to generation (and sometimes within a generation), they mostly lived under the status of the *dhimmi* (lit: "people of the book"), an officially inferior but protected status ascribed to Jews and Christians by Muslims. Living under *"dhimmitude"* was not simply a matter of being subservient to remain protected, since a special tax – *jizya* – had to be paid in order for this compensation to be granted.[36] As "protected" subjects, the Jews were able to maintain a relatively substantial amount of freedom in religious leadership within their communities, and although they were subjected to many practical ordinances aimed at assuring their inferiority in greater Muslim society, among themselves they organized and maintained well-run communally administered systems bringing great religious stability traditionally headed by charismatic rabbis. According to Lucette Valensi:

---

35   Alcalay, "Intellectual Life" in *The Jews of the Middle East and North Africa of Modern Times* Reeva Spector Simon, Michael Menachem Laskier and Sara Reguer, eds. New York: Columbia UP, 2003, 116.
36   For authoritative studies and details on the lives of Jews in the Arab world see Norman Stillman *The Jews of Arab Lands in Modern Times*. Philadelphia: JPS, 1991 and *The Jews of Arab Lands. A History and Source Book*. Philadelphia: JPS, 1979.

> In the Maghreb, as in the rest of the Muslim world, Jewish communities were equipped to maintain and transmit the religious scholarly tradition. Muslim authorities allowed them, as People of the Book, to practice their religion, to organize their systems of education and social assistance, to maintain their religious buildings and cemeteries, to distribute their prayer books and ritual objects, and, finally, to dispense justice. As a matter of fact, from Morocco to Libya the intellectual leadership of the rabbis remained remarkably powerful in the larger communities; some of the most famous were teachers, judges, and authors and, posthumously (if not during their life times) were considered saints who had worked miracles for their congregants.[37]

The many practical and often humiliating *dhimmi* laws outside the Jewish community curbed the relative freedom within. For example, Jews were not allowed to build synagogues taller than mosques, or to pray in a loud manner that might overpower the sound of Muslim prayers. They could not hold public office, in some time periods were not permitted to wear shoes, or ride camels. Jews always had to give way to a passing Muslim by ceding the road, and were sometimes ordered to wear specific clothing to help (the Arabs) distinguish them from the general Arabo-Muslim population, with whom they shared many external similarities. Furthermore, a Jew could never marry a Muslim woman, although a Muslim man was allowed to marry a Jewish woman. Though they had relative autonomy in governing their own internal affairs such as legal or criminal issues arising within the Jewish community, they could not be witnesses in Muslim court, nor were their laws considered in legal cases involving a Muslim.

There were sporadic outbursts of violence toward Jews where typically the Muslim governing powers (as later would be the case also with the colonial French powers) did not make much or any effort to stop, curb or investigate the crimes. These incidents that could be single occurrences or pogrom-like riots aimed to destroy Jewish prop-

---

37   Lucette Valensi, "Multicultural Visions: The Cultural Tapestry of the Jews of North Africa" in *Cultures of the Jews: A New History*, David Biale, ed. New York: Schocken Books, 2002, 893.

erties and businesses, often involved violence toward men, women and children indiscriminately and frequently left many dead.[38] Albert Memmi clearly remembers the uncertainties of this life: "The Jewish communities lived in the shadow of history, under arbitrary rule and the fear of all-powerful monarchs whose decisions could not be rescinded or even questioned. But the Jews were at the mercy not only of the monarchs but also of the man in the street."[39] He goes on to recount memories of his grandfather and father's hasty returns home after having boarded up their shops in preparations for attacks, and how his parents stocked food in expectation of a siege.

Later, colonization would replace the Shari'a law of *dhimmitude* with European legislation, something the Jews and Christians living in Arab lands would welcome, especially since Jews had equal rights in France as citizens based on the principles of the French Revolution and with the enactment of the Crémieux decree dating from 1870. This change of status among the Jewish population, historically and traditionally perceived by the Arabs as inferior, would have great impact on many levels in the colonial dynamics. As Egyptian-born British writer and political commentator Bat Ye'or notes in her extensive

---

[38] These include anti-Semitic uprisings in Algers in 1897-1898 during the Dreyfus Affair, where synagogues were profaned and Jewish owned stores were looted. In Constantine Riots in 1934 stores are pillaged, with a certain number of Jews injured and 25 men, women and children killed as a result of a Jew having urinated on a Mosque wall, but most likely influenced by Nazi propaganda which by then made its way to North Africa. In 1938 in Sidi-Bel-Abbes the anti-Semitic mayor eliminated the names of 300 Jews from the list of voters. In Morocco the Jews of Essaouira and Tangiers suffered attacks during the Franco-Moroccan war since they were accused of supporting the enemy. Before the protectorate began in 1912 there were attacks on Jews in the *mellah* of Fez with more than 60 dead. Tunisia seems to be the exception since this was a place the least affected by Arab led violence toward Jews, and not until the Germans occupied the country for six months during the Second World War did anti-Semitism become an overt and manifested problem. Haim Saadoun notes: "In the reported collective memory of Tunisia's Jewry, Muslim-Jewish coexistence was both practical and tranquil. This is not an idyllic, nostalgic point of view. Most Tunisian Jews do not remember any violent outbreaks in Tunisia, apart form the three-day violence in 1917." Haim Saadoun, "Tunisia," in *The Jews of the Middle East and North Africa in Modern Times*, New York: Columbia UP, 2003, 450.
[39] Memmi, "Who is an Arab Jew?" 2.

study on the *dhimmi*, "The loss of former privileges, particularly the privilege of humiliating the *dhimmi*, nourished the persistent [Arabo-Muslim] bitterness and hostility toward Europe."[40] This situation of embitterment of the Arab population due to their dis-empowerment under colonial rule will be an important point to consider in the section to follow, where I will shed light on the reasons why the Jews were increasingly stuck between a rock and a hard place in the Maghreb during colonial times.

During the Muslim rule of Spain, also known as a period of Jewish Renaissance (roughly 950-1150 C.E), Jews lived in freedom and religious tolerance as they could enter the fields of government, science, medicine and literature. Although the time of Muslim Al-Andalus was occasionally marked by periods of conflict – one should be careful not to subscribe to the myth of a constant and perfectly peaceful coexistence – there has been no equivalent time in history of an extended period of nonviolent and close relationship between the two religions. The unique rapport between Jews and Muslims at the time was dominated by great collaborations within the sciences and literatures, even if, as literary historian Ross Brann is quick to point out, there was a great ambivalence in the way Muslim and Jewish intellectuals imagined one another.

Analyzing this much-explored field of Muslim-Jewish relations in the Al-Andalus, Brann deftly brings historical analysis to literature while analyzing history with literary tools. What he sees as the ambivalent perceptions of the other, the Muslims express this more explicitly and verbally, whereas the Jews express theirs more implicitly and reluctantly. He suggests that the asymmetry is "stressing the inherent difference between the way a majority and a minority culture represent each other."[41] We may keep this observation in mind when we look at the many early literary expressions by Jews from North Africa that tended to depict life among Arabs as overwhelmingly positive, frequently describing what in retrospect seem as rather glorified relations

---

40 Ye'or, Bat. *The Dhimmi. Jews and Christians under Islam*. London: Associated UP, 1985, 343.
41 Ross Brann, "Specular Images: Jews and Muslims in Al-Andalus," *Prooftexts* 24 (2004): 209.

between the two relatively insular and often suspicious communities.⁴² However, after the mass exodus in the mid 1900s, in the literature, memoirs and testimonies we have seen appearing over the past sixty years (basically since the establishment of the State of Israel in '48), and specifically in the last ten to fifteen years as *Mizrah*i and Sephardic studies are growing and gaining momentum, the picture looks quite different.⁴³ One decisive voice regarding the ambivalent Judeo-Arabic relationship comes from Albert Memmi, who at no point in his literary career has veiled the complicated and often hostile existence he, his family and friends have endured before, during and especially following the French presence in North Africa.⁴⁴

According to Memmi, the so called "peaceful co-existence" of Jews and Arabs in Muslim lands is mostly a myth, one shaped by the Arabs in order to create a historic memory of Arab benevolence and generosity, especially in the wake of the establishment of the State of Israel and the wars that ensued in the nascent state. This myth has been maintained by some Jews who have repressed, forgotten, or chosen to only remember the positive aspects of life under Arab rule. We may be reminded again of Yerushalmi's observation regarding memory and history. He speaks of the time in Jewish history, in the 1800's, when Jews were moving out of the ghetto and striving for acceptance and assimilation into the greater German society, and having lost their traditional form of memory, they had to turn toward a "Western defined" manner of recording memory, which was modern historiography. "The modern effort to reconstruct the Jewish past

---

42   Blanche Bendahan, Elissa Chimenti, Maximilienne Heller and Elissa Rhais are the most significant of the early Judeo-Maghrebian women authors whose texts often told stories of Jewish life and struggles/poverty, inter-faith love dramas, and accounts of Muslim women's condition in the harem.
43   In part VI of Julia Philips Cohen and Sarah Abrevaya Stein's *Sephardi Lives: A Documentary History, 1700-1950*, we find a rich archive of documents that testify to the emergence of Sephardic studies. Although their ground-breaking work focuses on the Ottoman Judeo-Spanish world, the chapter attests to the presence of eighteen important scholarly texts by Ladino speaking Jews dating as far back as 1787 through 1952.
44   Albert Memmi's autobiographical *Le Statut de Sel* (1957) as well as his *Portrait du Colonisé* (1985), preceded by *Portrait du Colonisateur* (1957) and *Juifs et Arabes* (1974) present his most candid writings about this experience.

begins at a time that witnessed a sharp break in the continuity of Jewish living and hence also an ever-growing decay of Jewish group memory."[45]

A parallel can be drawn here between the great changes in the (Western) European Jewish communities of the 1800's, and the radical transformations and breaks in continuity witnessed in the Jewish communities of the Maghreb as the French arrived and policies, opportunities and challenges changed. The new hierarchy imposed by the colonial power brought new modes of self-definition that in turn changed forever the way Jewish Maghrebi memory defined Jewish Maghrebi history.

Although some historians tend to view the Jews as having lived harmoniously within Muslim society, Bat Ye'or reminds us of what could hardly be considered "symptoms of benign Muslim-Jewish symbiosis": "Islamic law governed the appearance of non-Muslims from head to toe, their headgear, disparate shoes, shoelaces, the style and color of their clothing, the little bells they had to wear in bathhouses and in the street, the rules concerning mounts, saddles, stirrups, houses, the segregation in separate districts with closed doors."[46] In her opinion, Muslim politicians have recently discovered the usefulness of teaching Christian anti-Judaism and critiquing European colonialism in order to glorify Islamic goodness and tolerance and thereby claim moral superiority over Europe. For Ye'or, it is problematic that Muslims now use Jewish history in this context.

In the Mashreq and the Maghreb, the condition of the Jews' existence was typically dictated by the level of generosity of the head of state and the political, economic or religious climate at a given time. It was particularly since the arrival of the Sephardic Jews in North Africa that the Jewish communities there contributed significantly not only in the economy of the region, but also in the domain of culture, science and politics. The expansion of the Ottoman Empire into North Africa in the 1500's brought yet another predicament to the Jews of Egypt, Libya, Algeria and Tunisia; however the failure of the Turks to conquer Morocco would lead to a significantly different history of its Jewish community than that of

---

45   Yerushalmi, *Zakhor*, 86.
46   Bat Ye'or, *Islam and Dhimmitude*, 349.

the other North African countries. There the Alaouites still reigned supreme, and Morocco remained isolated from the Turkish conquest and the subsequent early settlement of the French in Algeria (1830) and Tunisia (1881). Also, Morocco was geographically a far more isolated country, shielded from Western civilization, and the Jews there were additionally sheltered within the walls of the Moroccan Jewish ghetto or *mellah*.

Jewish Women in the Historical Context

Since this book's initial proposal is to shed light on Jewish women writers, it may be useful at this point to look briefly into the world of Jewish women as they lived in Arab countries and specifically in the Maghreb. This will add to our understanding of the particular historical evolution of their roles and places in society, and how it differed from that of Arab women. Similarly to their Muslim sisters, Jewish women were part of all social classes, but the majority typically lived in modest to poor circumstances. Jewish women traditionally did not wear a veil in North Africa, although once married they covered their hair in public.

However, some Jewish women did veil themselves as a sign of accommodation to the dominant Muslim culture. As for Jewish women and marriage, according to Jewish law the bride to be had to consent. Although parents and professional matchmakers made it their business to find a suitable match for the families, non-consensual marriages were less the norm than it was among the Muslims. In North Africa there were instances of young Jewish girls being abducted, converted to Islam and wed to Muslim men, and the Jewish communities did their best to deter such occurrences by marrying their girls off at a very young age, especially in Morocco where brides were often as young as thirteen-years-old. The Alliance Israélite Universelle[47] would also have

---

[47] The Alliance Israélite Universelle is a Paris-based international Jewish organization founded in 1860 by the French statesman Adolphe Crémieux (of the Crémieux decree, granting citizenship to French Jews) to safeguard the human rights of Jews around the world. The organization promotes the ideal of Jewish self-defense and self-sufficency through education and professional development and played an instrumental role in the

as one of its chief goals to enroll and educate girls in order to prevent child marriages. In Morocco by 1948 the minimum age for young girls to marry was set at fifteen.

As Sara Reuger notes in her chapter on "The World of Women" in *The Jews of the Middle East* (2003), in premodern or traditional times Jewish women, even as *dhimmi*, were part of a multi-ethnic, pluralistic and diverse world and had a strong religious identity. Even as members of many different social categories, their lives were alike enough to "permit generalization."[48] In many towns and cities, Jewish women could mix with Muslim and Christian women, especially on the bathhouse ladies' day, in those places where the *dhimmi* was not excluded from such use, in order to not have undue influence on the Muslim women.[49] Although there had been Jewish women involved in trade and politics in pre-modern times, on the eve of the colonization public life was a male province, and a "non-too-comfortable one" for *dhimmis* in general.[50] Reuger further notes that although change was quick to come with modernization, rapidly changing all aspects of life, the world of women was not affected as rapidly as that of men. The majority of the Jews lived as poor lower classes, and many young girls were sent away as maids working for the newly arrived Europeans. Soon the Jewish communities reluctantly agreed to provide vocational education to the Jewish women of poor background, and slowly but surely an economic need gave way to the idea that education was the key to the new world.[51]

Having daughters attend colonial European schools was of course the height of status (typically for the family/father and more than for the young woman!), and often this was done with the hopes that she would consequently socialize with the daughters of the Europeans and increase her chances and opportunities at "arriving." In North Africa, the degree of advancement for women was the greatest where French

---

westernization of North African Jewry.
48   Sara Reuger, "The World of Women," *The Jews of the Middle East and North Africa of Modern Times*. Reeva Spector Simon, Michael Menachem Laskier and Sara Reguer, eds. New York: Columbia UP, 2003, 235.
49   Ibid., 240.
50   Ibid., 241.
51   Ibid., 242.

influence was the "deepest and the most prolonged,"[52] and as a result northern Algeria led the way, followed by northern Tunisia, and then only much later did these opportunities brought on by the French presence arrive in Morocco.

The first modern school opened in Algiers in 1832 and Jewish girls could attend as well as boys. In Tunisia, girls could first attend modern schools when the schools run by the Alliance (AIU) opened to them in 1882, four years after it had opened to boys. By 1945 half the student body was filled with girls at the government funded Alliance schools. In Morocco there were never enough facilities for all Moroccan Jewish children, and it was not until 1950, only a few years prior to the mass emigration of the Jewish community, that education was available to all.[53] This may help explain the large discrepancy of Jewish women writers of Moroccan origin (one that has influenced the choices of works analyzed here), since few Moroccan emigrants had a strong elementary education before leaving, and as the majority of the Jews from Morocco migrated to Israel and not to France. The experience of the exodus from the Maghreb and subsequent arrival in France by Moroccan women is therefore not well documented in any literary form, although interviews exist from first-hand witnesses.

The Jewish women of the Maghreb who were educated during the colonial period were all deprived of learning about the Arab and Muslim world around them in school. Morocco and Tunisia were protectorates, not full fledged colonies like Algeria, and it was the AIU that was in charge there of the content of education, as they ran the schools that Jewish children attended. Albeit a Jewish school system, since it was based on models of "enlightened" Jewish schools from France, they would copy an assimilationist approach and strongly promote the culture of the Jews of France. Tunisian author Annie Goldman, who writes about the emancipation of the women in her family in *Les Filles de Mardochée: Histoire d'une Emancipation* (1979)[54] notes that "Culture was provided by the Alliance Française...not a word about Arab cul-

---

52   Ibid.
53   Ibid., 266.
54   Annie Goldman. *Les Filles de Mardochée: Histoire d'une émancipation*. Paris: Denoël et Gonthier, 1979.

ture, neither at school nor in any cultural context."[55] Similarly, Hélène Cixous, who was a product of the French public schools that were secular and obligatory in Algeria, had the same experience of absence of the other's narrative in school, her own being one of them: "There were only invisible signs: absence of Jews, absence of Muslims. Brilliant absences that dazzled me and took my breath away. How can one make people see the invisible?"[56]

As a young teenager Cixous reacted to this false identity that France forced onto its colony: "Never at the white Lycée, never was the Algerian mentioned. The word Algeria never enters here. In this Lycée, here, it's France, but it was a huge crazy lie that had taken all the place of truth, and that had thus become the truth."[57] This "great lie" and erasing of the other would in turn only intensify the widening gap between Muslim and Jewish women, who had lived with more awareness of each other before the French arrived, and young Jewish girls were schooled to become ignorant of their compatriots of many generations.

Modernization brought an increase in the role Jewish women played in public life and was often a factor in their jobs. According to Reguer, the sudden breaking of traditional society produced a mass of unfortunate Jews who lost their jobs and trades. To avoid being reduced to begging, many fathers looked the other way as their daughters took paying jobs, taking them away from the traditional women's role in the home. Prostitution, although morally objectionable in Judaism, was not punishable by death as in Islam, and so some young women turned to it in order to help support their families.[58]

Traditionally, in pre-colonial and pre-modern Arab societies, Jewish and Arab women had much in common, a situation that would be-

---

55   "*La culture était véhiculée par l'Alliance Française...pas un mot de la culture arabe, ni à l'école ni dans les manifestations culturelles,*" Ibid., 117.
56   Cixous, "Letter to Zhora Drif," *Parallax* 4 (1998): 192.
57   "Jamais dans le Lycée poudre jamais il ne fut question de l'être algérien. Jamais le mot Algérie n'entre ici. Dans le Lycée, ici, c'est la France, or ce n'était qu'un immense mensonge délirant qui avait pris toute la place de la vérité, et qui donc était devenu la vérité." Cixous, *Les Rêveries de la Femme Sauvage*. Paris: Galilée, 2000, 150.
58   Reguer, "The World of Women," Reeva Spector Simon, Michael Menachem Laskier and Sara Reguer, eds. New York: Columbia UP, 2003, 249.

gin to change as North Africa was subjected to colonialism, and when most urban Jewish families embraced, although reluctantly, the social advances offered to their daughters via Western education, vocational training and a much less insular existence.

Contrary to their Muslim peers, Jewish women were given opportunities that were withheld from the majority indigenous Arab population, and although their parents saw such openings as potentially threatening to traditional Jewish family values, the desire coupled with the opportunity to receive Western education would only increase the disparity between Jews and Arabs. Young Jewish women thus began their westernization and education several decades before their Muslim peers, and as a result Jewish families had more time to become accustomed to the new Western lifestyle awaiting them in France. Culture shock among Jewish women arriving in the big cities of Paris or Marseilles was therefore generally less traumatic, and rejection and discrimination by French society was far less overt and aggressive than that experienced by their Arab sisters.

We will see further on in this study that the Jewish woman writer is not necessarily concerned with all the same issues as her Arab contemporary and peer, and although exiled or emigrated Maghrebi women authors share many concerns such as the balance between tradition and modernity, family and careers, internal conflicts between their Maghrebi and European cultural identities and affinities, just to name a few, the Jewish women have not been as categorically excluded and erased from a male dominated patriarchal world as has her Arab-Muslim sisters. We can say without danger of misrepresentation that in literature by Jewish women, there is less anger, less hopelessness, less signs of misogyny, abuse, violence and repudiation than that often depicted in the literature of their Muslim contemporaries.

Chapter 2

The Jews in Colonial Maghreb:
Between a Rock and a Hard Place

At the dawn of French colonization and protectorate in North Africa, there were barely 200,000 Jews living there, with Morocco having the largest community at 100,000 in 1912, followed by Tunisia with 50,000 in 1881, and Algeria with a mere 30-35,000 in 1830. These numbers were to increase substantially during the time of France's presence in the Maghreb, due in part to increased birthrates, improved living conditions such as sanitation and medicine that modernization would bring, but also in large part because of the amelioration in the status of the Jews now relieved of the burden of the centuries old yoke of living under the discriminating laws of dhimmitude, such as having been restricted to living in overpopulated Jewish quarters or ghettos – *harat al-yehud*.

By the end of the colonial era (Algeria became independent in 1962), Algeria had seen the most profound population growth in its Jewish communities numbering by then 140,000, which was an increase of almost 400%. On the eve of Moroccan independence in 1956 the Jewish population there had increased with 150% totaling 250,000, and finally Tunisian Jewry's more modest growth at less than 100%, reaching 95,000 Jewish souls by the end of the protectorate, also in 1956. These numbers tell us a lot about life under French rule, despite the more ambiguous and complicated picture reflected in the pages to follow. Clearly, these were times that, although placing the Jews in a complex position between colonizer and colonized, brought promises of a better life with more opportunities and less oppression. This alone was an enormously hopeful ground upon which the Jews, in the majority, planted their feet and walked on with great hopes and aspirations. Especially in Algeria, where the Jewish population almost quadrupled in three generations, the prospects for the Jews gaining citizenship linked to the French mainland were clearly a monumental draw.

They most likely did not anticipate the desperate conflicts and disparate interests that would ensue as the French presence drew to a close, after a grueling and long-drawn war, and once the wheels of Franco-Arabo-Judeo history were set in motion, exterior as well as interior forces shaped the eventual culmination of a unique Jewish civilization. It is easy to assume that the Jewish existence in the Maghreb must have been more or less the same in the three countries we are considering. After all, the countries have long shared a common Arab culture and the religion of Islam, in addition to being neighbors and all with vibrant ports opening up to the commerce of the Mediterranean. But history tells us otherwise, as each of the countries developed and took shape according to different historical events specific to its place, as noted above. This in turn naturally affected the Jewish communities whose livelihood and viability evolved in close but differentiated ways as generations passed. Although Jews from the Maghreb were clearly marked by their shared experience of Arab culture, Moroccan Jews had a specific *patrimoine* or heritage, differentiated from that of Algerian Jews and Tunisian Jews, and this in turn affected differently their memory and cultural identity as they emigrated to new countries and had to re-establish their lives.

Within each country there were also differences among the various Jewish communities, as for example in Tunisia, where the Jews that had arrived from Livorno, Italy in the late 1600s, the Grana, distinguished themselves from the indigenous Jews, the Touansa. Not only did the Grana remain Italian citizens and were therefore exempt from the laws of the *dhimmi*, but they lived in the European quarters and not in the *hara* or the Jewish ghetto. They even had a wall at the cemetery separating their graves from those of the indigenous Jews. Eventually, by the time the Tunisian Jewish community began to dissolve, there were three distinctive Jewish communities: those with French citizenship, Tunisian subjects, and Italians. The Algerian Jewish society had been deeply religious until the arrival of the French, something one is quick to forget considering how assimilated the great majority had become by the time the French withdrew in 1962.

In Morocco, as much as 40% of the Jews were Berbers, living primarily in the South within the valleys of the Atlas Mountains and also in the North, around the Rif mountains. Another uniqueness about Morocco was that the French, Spanish and British were all heavily involved there, and there continued to be a significant Spanish Colonial presence in the North including in the Rif mountains, maintaining a strong connection to Iberian culture and language in that region, affecting the Jewish cultural evolution. Annie Cohen's *Bésame Mucho* (1998)[59] is a literary example of this Hispano-Andalusian influence that will be explored later in the literature section of the book.

In this chapter we will look closer at how the Jews were caught in a precarious situation as the French moved in to the Maghreb and the colonial powers manipulated societies that would react to this presence. We will examine how the Jewish communities were affected by France's presence and how they lived in this newly divided world where society became polarized by "us," the Arabs, a new "them," the French, and where the Jews were neither. Hélène Cixous remembers what that felt like in her essay "My Algériance" (1997): "The Cixous children, those not really Jewish false French odd inadequate people who loved Algerians who spurned us as enemy Françaouis, Roumis and Jews."[60] The memory of this childhood rejection was to leave an indelible mark on the future writer.

Cultural and Social Change

During the long historical co-existence of Arabs and Jews in the Maghreb there was always a clear demarcation between "us" and "them." Despite this acute sense of the other, and notwithstanding the official inferior status of the Jew as *dhimmi* that lasted until the French arrived, there was also a more than two millennia-old cultural confluence that had brought the two people close on many levels. Although often challenged for its accuracy, the Jews from Arab lands have at times identified themselves, or been identified by Ashkenazi Jews, as "Arab Jews," symbolizing thus their ethnic (vs. religious) sameness with the Arabs with whom they shared distinct cultures tied to

---

59   Annie Cohen, *Bésame Mucho*. Paris: Gallimard, 1998.
60   "My Algériance. In other words to Depart not to arrive from Algeria". Trans. Eric Prenowitz. *Tri-quarterly*. 100 (1997): 267.

their Algerian, Tunisian and Moroccan specificities. While the Jews in North Africa suffered greatly from time to time, this was more typically in isolated (but not exclusively) cases of clashes between Arabs and Jews, and rarely well organized or unified attacks from the surrounding Arab neighbors, like those endured by Jews in the Mashreq or the East, where hostilities were not uncommon due to less open societies, and where pan-Arab nationalisms later began to develop more intensely. When riots or clashes happened in the Maghreb, it was often the result of some outside incitement in the Eastern parts of the Levant, and especially seen after 1948, causing ripple effects to North Africa.

Similar but different, then, is how the Jews saw themselves, and to the outsider they were often not differentiated at all, sharing many exterior traits, as well as language, culinary and cultural traditions. The major difference was their belief system defined by the Jewish religion, and sometimes even that would converge as Arabs made pilgrimages to Rabbis' graves, seen by both groups as saintly and a source of miracles, or Arabs would come to hear certain prayers during the Jewish High Holidays to benefit from the rabbinic or priestly blessings seen as dating back to Abrahamic times when a shared lineage had defined Jews and Muslims as brothers.[61]

The memories that seem to repress or forget the painful chapters or episodes, are often filled with reminiscences of working and professional relationships, neighborly rapport, shared recipes, stories, and even mutual assistance in times of need or emergencies. We will later look at how Jewish women authors express this Judeo-Arabic identity, where elements of both their Jewish and their Arab/Maghreb identity come together to express a cultural *métissage* – or mix – with deep roots resonating in their writings. Differentiation from the Arab other, as well as expressions of unity (or desires of unity) is present in the narratives, and as Daniel Sibony, psychoanalyst, writer and social critic suggests[62] the dynamic space of possibilities that he calls the *entre-deux*, or the in-between, is where we can see the Jew as existing in colonial Maghreb. This space of *entre-deux* can be paralyzing but

---

61   This symbiosis of customs and beliefs is especially well evoked in the French animated film *The Rabbi's Cat* (2011) written and directed by Joann Sfar, of Algerian Jewish background.
62   Sibony, *L'Entre-Deux. L'Origine en Partage*. Paris: Seuil, 1991.

at the same time a place of great opportunities, since it can limit but also open the subject's potential for change. Another *entre deux* can be seen in the experience of a colonial subject and a hybrid Jew with roots in exile, such as Cixous, for whom "…being abroad at home is what I call *entre deux*…always in the passage. In the passage from one to the other…"[63] For Cixous, being in perpetual passage gives way to more freedom, even though she would experience the non-belonging as painful when she was a child in Algeria.

It is no coincidence, then, that with the entry on the scene of the French colonial powers, interjecting full force into the region from 1830 until 1962 when France finally withdrew from Algeria, a colossal change occurred in the relationship between the Jews and the Arabs. The French knew that the Jews would be eager to embrace everything French since the Jews of Western Europe had already come a long way on the path to social advancement and more privileged lives, and were a show of example for what was seen as the mostly "backward" Jews of the Orient. The French also knew that a substantial number of the Jews in coastal commerce centers and towns in North Africa had historically maintained robust business relations with cities in Europe such as London, Amsterdam, Livorno and Paris and hence would be extremely useful as liaisons between the Jewish, the European and the Arab communities, since they were able to maneuver in all three communities based on their linguistic and professional background.

Jews were thereby seen as a tool, useful for facilitating entry into areas where the French would find it otherwise difficult to gain access, to understand, and most of all to be trusted. The assigned person for this place of in-between, a position that the Jews in North Africa and as minorities in the whole region of the Muslim Mediterranean have always occupied, was that of the *drogman* (intermediary), the mediator between two worlds, and this was most common in the realm of commerce. Historian Lucette Valensi has studied the changes that occurred in North Africa as Europeans introduced Western modernization and imposed societal change, and she notes that when "A sizable Christian population coming from every port of Mediterranean Europe superimposed itself on the local population of Muslims and

---

63   Cixous, *Rootprints*, 10.

Jews,"⁶⁴ one could only begin to imagine the effect this would have on the existing hierarchy and social and political system. Jews would often be "favored" over Arabs for purely utilitarian reasons, and their status would thus change to one of superiority over Arabs, which was considered a great humiliation especially by those Arabs who saw the Jews as belonging to the inferior *dhimmi*, a status assigned to them, in their eyes, according to religious authorities as dictated by divine decree.

As Ye'or remarks, Muslims were "...revolted by the abolition of Shari'a, colonization, and the emancipation of the infidels."⁶⁵ Yet, paradoxically, the political emancipation that was bestowed upon the Jews by the colonial powers made relative and "camouflaged" the domination they experienced during colonial times.⁶⁶ The fact is that the Jews were just as dominated by the French as were the Arabs, and lived at the grace of the imposed colonial policy, arbitrarily implemented among the Jews as colonized sub-groups, and often discriminatory in its views of the different Jewish communities. Historian Michel Abitbol remarks that the French government would deal with the Jewish population differently in each country. In Algeria they favored assimilation, in Tunisia reform, whereas in Morocco France preferred to keep the status quo.⁶⁷

Although Jews in Algeria were granted French citizenship in 1870, in Morocco the authorities almost categorically rejected all Jewish applications for naturalization. There were exceptions both in Tunisia and Morocco if the subject was able to prove an extraordinary commitment to France, which usually required the person to be convincingly "Westernized," well-traveled, financially independent and culturally French "enough"; in other words, more of an elitist opportunity and not a realistic possibility for the average Moroccan or Tunisian Jew. Colonial policies in the Maghreb also divided the Jews, as for example in Oran, Algeria, where the Hispanicized and Frenchified Jews scorned those who spoke Arabic, or the Jews from the southern part of

---

64   Lucette Valensi, "Multicultural Visions," 892.
65   Bat Ye'or, *The Dhimmi*, 353.
66   Shmuel Trigano, "La Mémoire du Peuple Disparu." *Pardès* 28: *La mémoire sépharade*. Paris: In Presse Editions, 2000, 41.
67   Michel Abitbol, "The Integration of North African Jews." Translated by Alan Astro. *Yale French Studies*. 85 (1994): 250.

the country, always arabophone, looked with contempt on their francophone fellow Jews in the North.

When France entered North Africa in the 1800s, it was not only one singular Jewish presence they found, but Jewish communities throughout Algeria, Tunisia and Morocco who had developed differently according to the distinct historic events as they marked the region. When France subsequently colonized Algeria in 1830 and made Tunisia and Morocco protectorates in 1881 and 1912 respectively, the status of the Jews would shift again. Since Jews in France were citizens, French dominance and presence in North Africa opened up the door between two dramatically different cultures; the French Jews, who were typically better educated, more assimilated and constitutionally empowered, and those of the Maghreb who were mostly separated and differentiated from the Arab population by discriminatory laws (dhimmitude) and living generally in ghettoized communities.

Although the Jews of the Maghreb had enjoyed relative autonomy and participated in the economy, there were few opportunities beyond traditional trades, and the French Jews saw it as a duty and great opportunity to bring enlightenment to their North African "family." Now, the Jews who under Islam had been living under the *dhimmi* status welcomed with guarded enthusiasm the ideal of *"liberté, égalité, et fraternité."* France had the appeal of a secular country, where freedom and democracy seemed to promise greater self-determination and possibilities. They expected that their commitment to *"la Patrie"* would guarantee respect, tolerance and protection of their differences in the tradition of the principles of the French Revolution. As noted, with France's entry into the Maghreb came the well established and politically charged Jewish organization Alliance Israélite Universelle (AIU) which offered much hope of advancements and improvements in the lives of the Jews of North Africa through the channels of education, vocational training, various Jewish organizations and community outreach.

The original aims of the AIU when it was founded in Paris in 1860 as a response to increasing anti-Semitism in Eastern communities, and particularly after the Damascus Affair in 1840,[68] were to work toward the emancipation and moral progress of Oriental Jews and to assist those suffering from repercussions of anti-Semitism. However, the major tool of AIU outreach was the establishing of French language schools throughout the Middle East and in North Africa, which were in essence secular in nature. With this came the colonial and eurocentric vision of the exotic "other" as inferior, primitive and in need of Western defined enlightenment and redemption. "Assuming that their Oriental brethren were living in abject conditions of subjugation and ignorance, they aimed to spread enlightenment...A regeneration of the Jews was at stake, by which Oriental Jews would be technically and intellectually prepared for modern times. Western gods were thus shaping Oriental man in their own image."[69]

Although many Jewish families were wary of losing children to the "westernizing agenda" of the AIU and skeptical toward what seemed foreign and threatening in the proposed process of frenchification, most Jews, especially among the city dwellers, made an irreversible and ultimately political choice by welcoming what France and their Franco-Jewish brothers had to offer in hopes of improving the lives of their children and generations to come. This sudden alliance between the French Jews and those in the Maghreb would only further complicate the historically strained relationship between Jews and Arabs, as many of the opportunities offered the indigenous Jews would never or rarely be available to Arabs, hence fostering yet more resentment. The laws of the *dhimmi* revoked, there were now new prospects for the Jews to make changes in their lives, leading to differences that gave the impression of French favoritism on behalf of the Jews.

Michael M. Laskier, who has written extensively about the role of the AIU during the French occupation, explains well the ambiguity that surrounds the positive or negative role of the AIU:

---

68   A blood libel where Jews were accused of ritually murdering a Franciscan superior and later executed for the crime. Some of the repercussions were when 60 children were arrested and starved in order to convince their parents to confess to the crime.
69   Valensi, "Multicultural Visions," 912.

> *It would be difficult...to deny that the AIU guided the Jews in the path of French culture, and from the late 1940's, in the direction of Hebrew culture, hence aggravating the already existing Judeo-Muslim tensions, cultivating a French-educated elite, and facilitating* aliyah *[immigration to Israel/Palestine]. The AIU then, sharpened divisions culturally, but was not the root of the conflict, for the Jews were separated from the Muslims in* mellahs *and* haraht al-Yahud *long predating the arrival of the AIU and European colonialism, in the accordance with [Sharia] legislation. Only under European presence and the oeuvre of the AIU did the Jews begin to leave the ghettos for the new, integrated urban neighborhoods, built in the early twentieth century.*[70]

The Jews were free to move out of the *mellahs* and the *harahs*, and many chose to live in the European or French quarters. However, neighborhoods more or less exclusively inhabited by Jews remained a distinctive part of urban demographic patterns in colonial Maghreb. The historical tendency of Jews had always been to live in close proximity of the synagogues, schools (often housed in the synagogues), kosher markets and other communal support networks, and this tradition did not change for most Jews in colonial North Africa. Accessing social mobility, however, meant leaving the familiarity of the Jewish neighborhood, and soon the once familiar-ness of the ghetto would become an element of embarrassment as the ideals and appeals of everything French gained popularity and became accessible through both French schools and the education provided for free by the AIU. Valensi notes, "The Alliance network of schools became a refuge of children from the poorest arabophone neighborhoods, whereas those who could afford them preferred the French middle schools and high schools as a safer avenue for social mobility, by way of access to further studies and hence to the liberal professions."[71] Under pressure from the rising tide and trend of westernized educational choices, many Jewish families experienced difficult decisions, and communities saw great shifts in the ways their children were to be educated.

---

[70] Laskier, *North African Jewry in the Twentieth Century*, 347.
[71] Valensi, "Multicultural Visions," 913.

The AIU also helped facilitate making *aliyah* (immigration to Israel) and because of its stronger presence in Morocco than in Tunisia and Algeria (where every Algerian community was directed by a consistory directly from France), a much larger percentage of the Jewish Moroccan population emigrated to Israel instead of to France or other destinations like Canada and South America. It offers an interesting study in itself to consider to which part of the world the different North African Jewish communities emigrated. Suffice it to say here that the more influenced by France a community was, the more likely were they to go to France primarily, and francophone Canada secondarily.

The more religious and less Westernized Jews (such as those living in remote regions separated geographically from direct French influence), typically found in Morocco – although by no means exclusively there – immigrated to Israel. The draw of the "New World" that South America represented in the middle of the 1900s seems to have attracted the more adventurous business minded Jew, who had maintained Judeo-Spanish or Ladino as his *lingua franca*, the case of many Jews from the northern part of Morocco, the *Megorashim*, that had retained close connections with their Hispanic heritage from generations in al-Andalus.

This slightly generalized overview, however, does not mean that Israel did not receive any "westernized" or educated Jews, or that France in turn did not become the homeland to Jews with little or no education. Part of the difficulties that Moroccan Jewry experienced as they arrived in Israel in terms of discrimination and problematic integration into a then predominantly euro- and Ashkenaz-centric society, has been seen in part as a result of a lack of communal leaders and intellectuals that defined the new Moroccan community in Israel as a whole. They thus had fewer voices that would and could publicly and pragmatically argue for their rightful place and fair treatment as new immigrants from Arab lands.

Algeria's Jews were the first to feel both the "blessings and the curses" of the French colonial presence, since their life was turned upside down from a social as well as a religious point of view by the Crémieux decree of 1870, which, after the fall of France's Second Empire and with advent of the Third Republic, granted French citizenship to the Jews of Algeria overnight. This clearly opened up doors for these Jews professionally and socially, mainly through access to education not available to Arabs or their fellow Jews in Tunisia and Morocco.

The Jews of Algeria would now automatically be able to attend French schools, serve in the French army and have to answer to French civil courts and no longer to their traditional rabbinical courts. These were changes that, over two or three generations, would contribute to forging a deep (French) national conscience among the Algerian Jewish population, and a profoundly earnest French identity. Despite the French civil opportunities, rights and responsibilities, a feeling of being second-class citizens nevertheless prevailed, and especially on a social level many did feel discriminated against. With the arrival of the French in 1830 the social structure in Algerian society had completely changed, as David Cohen notes, and the structure of the new social hierarchy did not bring the positive changes one might have expected with "emancipation." Cohen has the following pertinent observation regarding this complex situation:

At the top of the social hierarchy were the French colons who never wanted to give Algerian Jews citizenship. Below them were the Jews who had served in the French army. Foreign Europeans, established in Algeria since the 1860's, came next. They included Italians, the Maltese, and the Spaniards, who did not look favorably on the higher status of Jews in Algerian society. Finally, at the bottom of the social ladder were the Arabs, who did not understand how Jews, who were dhimmi, *could attain a social status higher than theirs. Ironically, this meant that Jewish success led to political, administrative, and economic anti-Semitism.*[72]

Thus, in addition to an often oppressive and repressive system, the colonists brought with them a new hierarchical structure that was superimposed onto the already existing social hierarchy. This, as we see in passages as the one above, greatly increases the tension between

---

[72] David Cohen, "Algeria," *The Jews of the Middle East and North Africa of Modern Times*, 460-461.

cultural groups. In their study and collection of first hand experiences and memories from life in Algeria, Joëlle Allouche-Benayoun and Doris Bensimon have interviewed many Jews who lived in Algeria during colonial times. From their subjects they learned among other things that the Jewish bourgeoisie followed by parts of the middle class wanted to assimilate into French society at all costs. According to one interviewee, Eliane B.:

> *The Jews always copied the civilization where they lived, and the more this civilization was flourishing, the more they copied it. In Alger, the French had a lot of splendor. They were very racist, but they had brilliance when it came to refinement, good taste in couture, in their homes, in order, in cuisine, and receptions. On all these levels, they were a people who knew the way! And so, the Jewish community, with its ease of adaptation and its need to always do its best, became a refined, intellectual, fine, distinguished community based on the model of the French community.*[73]

With observations like these, we can appreciate the ambiguous experience of wanting to belong, to be like those in power, to have the same possibilities and opportunities, but at the same time be well aware of the conflict this "mimicry" represents toward your own heritage and traditions. Homi Bhabha sees these elements of mimicry and ambivalence as representing disabling contradictions within colonial relationships, as well as within the post-colonial subject.[74] The Jew lives this "disabling contradiction" not only as a post-colonial subject, but lived it also as a colonial subject, since he, as opposed to the Arab, was

---

[73] "Les Juifs, dit Eliane B, ont toujours copié la civilization dans laquelle ils vivaient et plus la civilization était florissante, plus ils la copiaient. A Alger, les Français avaient beaucoup d'éclat. C'étaient des gens très racistes, mais qui avaient de l'éclat au point de vue raffinement, délicatesse pour la couture, pour la maison, l'ordre, la cuisine, les réceptions. Sur tout ces plans, c'étaient des gens qui tenaient le haut de pavé ! Et alors, la communauté juive, avec sa facilité d'adaptation et son besoin de faire toujours mieux, était devenue une communauté raffinée, intellectuelle, fine, distinguée, sur le modèle de la communauté française," Joëlle Allouche-Benayoun and Doris Bensimon, *Les Juifs d'Algérie. Mémoires et identités plurielles*. Paris: Editions Stavit, 1999, 112.
[74] Homi Bhabha, *The Location of Culture*. London: Routledge, 1994.

more precariously engulfed into an abyss of ambiguity because of his "easy" access to that which was mimicked/mimickable. This dynamic would leave its marks on Jewish identity and memory, and make language and writing all the more hybrid and eventually less distinctively Jewish. For the Jews of North Africa, the fusion of the new French culture – so desired and so promising – with their Jewish identity rarely happened easily, since a substantial part of it had to be repressed, abandoned and rejected in order that the Jew be able to assume the new majority identity, associated as it was with the ruling class and not with the minority culture of which the Jews had thus far been part. Historian Danielle Levy-Mongelli also elaborates on this "colonial project" and calls it the Jews' "deceptive alternative:"

> *For its intrinsic needs, for its success, the colonial project brought a caricatural image, incomplete, of the western model, and kept the minority cultures suppressed. It addressed the Jews in a seductive manner, taking advantage of the Jews' need to lose themselves in the desire to be like the majority, and in forcing them to take sides in a deceptive alternative: the fusion in an abstract universe, access to the others through assimilation, or the conservation of their differential originality, but that on the eve of the decolonization was reduced, mutilated, stained with humiliations. As for the memory of Israel, two thousand years of distancing had relegated it to the level of myth.*[75]

As French as the naturalized Algerian Jews would eventually feel, and even the non-naturalized Tunisian and Moroccan Jews who were prod-

---

[75] "Pour ses besoins intrinsèques, pour sa réussite, le projet colonial transportait une image caricaturale, incomplète, du modèle occidental, et tendait à la suppression des cultures minoritaires. Il s'est adressé aux Juifs sur le mode de la séduction, en agissant sur la nécessité du Juif de se perdre dans la manière d'être des majoritaires, et en le forçant à prendre partie dans une alternative trompeuse : la fusion dans l'univers abstrait, l'accès aux autres par l'assimilation, ou la conservation de l'originalité différentielle, mais qui était à la veille de la décolonisation, réduite, mutilée, entachée d'humiliations. Quant au souvenir d'Israël, deux mille ans d'éloignement le reléguaient au rang du mythe." Danielle Levy-Mongelli, "Un cas particulier d'aliénation culturelle: les Juifs d'Afrique du Nord dans l'Aventure Coloniale Française." In *Juifs du Maroc. Identité et Dialogue*. Grenoble: Sauvage, 1980, 252.

ucts of the AIU schools and all the culturally French indoctrination surrounding them, they were invariably reminded of their non-belonging, their alterity, or as Julia Kristeva would name it, their abject status in the eyes of the "real" French. The colonizers and French settlers would easily and happily remind the Jews of their belonging always, already to the realm of the *unheimliche*: un-at-home; non-at-home; among the Arabs as among the French, there would be little opportunity to be fully at home.

Although the Jews of Algeria wanted to be like the French in many ways, and strived to become frenchified, the perception of this "other" that the French represented in their eyes was tainted by outbursts of anti-Semitism recurring throughout the colonial empire. Some instances were isolated, quiet and a sign of a more latent anti-Semitic attitude, others were provoked by occurrences in the *métropole* such as the hate speeches of Edouard Drumont, the notorious French anti-Semite and most strident accuser of Dreyfus in the affair that shook the French nation. Max Regis, a student of Drumont, who was well received by the European settlers in Algeria, dispersed his diatribes successfully in North Africa. However, despite this latent and sometimes overt anti-Semitism, many of the Jews in North Africa seemed eager and willing to assimilate. The later question became how much they gave up in doing this, and for what, and at what price?

For Hélène Cixous, the consequence was upsetting, especially during the Second World War when their French citizenship was revoked:

> *The extent to which the Jews of Algeria, save exception, were altered, amnesiated of their own culture, illiterate in their own language Hebrew was always a painful experience... While the Jewish community of Algeria seemed to have sold its soul to France for nothing, no longer being either this or that and living in its majority of cultural makeshifts and of simulations.*[76]

Consequently, while many North African Jews, especially the educated and professional, would feel well adjusted once they immigrated

---

[76] Cixous, "My Algériance. In other words to Depart not to arrive from Algeria." Translated by Eric Prenowitz. *Tri-quarterly* 100 (1997): 265.

to France and their lives in the *métropole* stabilized, the regret of having turned away from Judeo-Arabic or Judeo-Maghrebian traditions and heritage became more acutely felt as the loss of the Maghreb was realized.

When they further realized that the knowledge they would like to transmit to their children (especially as these asked questions about their heritage) was limited and often nil after years and generations of assimilation, a sense of remorse and guilt of abandonment occurred. This is a regret that French Sephardic Jews are working to come to terms with and rectify through various movements that focus on "*le sauvetage de nôtre patrimoine Judéo-Maghrebin*" or "the conservation of our Judeo-Maghrebian heritage," through the efforts of individuals like sociologist Arrik Delouya, who has written an extensive bibliography on all existing literature concerning Moroccan Jewry, and is among the many who organize heritage tours for Jews to his native Morocco, as well as spearheading humanitarian projects in Morocco bringing Jews and Muslims together for a common cause.[77]

Many web sites have been created to encourage and facilitate the dispersion and accessibility of information about North African Jewish culture, history, recipes and travels, as well as providing help finding genealogies, and as forums for discussions on topics relating to the rights, memories and goals of the exiled Jewish communities from the Maghreb[78]. Sephardic Jews in France are looking for their authentic, real roots and the heritage that will re-connect them to the reality of their identities. For as Levy-Mogelly states, "The Jew of colonialization becomes a synthetic Frenchman, a product of the laboratory, who, affirming himself as uniquely French, assimilates into a non-reality."[79] According to this historian, in other words this Jew, that

---

77   Delouya is president of Permanences du Judaïsme Marocain / APJM - Paris, and founder of Association Israélienne pour la Préservation, la Diffusion & le Rayonnement du Judaïsme Marocain.
78   The web sites are created specifically for each country: for Jews from Morocco: www.dafina.com, Tunisia: www.harissa.com, and Algeria: www.zlabia.com. There is also www.diarna.org, "The Geo-Museum of North African and Middle Eastern Jewish Life," which pioneers the synthesis of digital mapping, scholarship, field research trove of multi-media documentation.
79   "Le Juif de la colonisation devient un Français de synthèse, un produit de laboratoire, qui, s'affirmant comme uniquement français, s'assimilait à une non-réalité." Levy-Mogelli, "*Un cas particulier*," 252.

could not retain his "real" minority culture in order to become the new *Juif-Français de synthèse* (integrated or blended French Jew, but also meaning manufactured) was really becoming a synthetic, non-authentic persona, identifying with something that was an illusion. She became an empty man-made product where nothingness now existed where the once precious collective memory of Israel as The Holy Land, the Maghreb and a rich Jewish heritage had occupied a principal part of communal memory and imagination.

The Loss of Language and Amnesia

When famed French philosopher of Judeo-Algerian heritage, Jacques Derrida, said "Yes, I have but one language, and it isn't mine," we can only understand this realization as going back to the day when he was sent home from school, excluded from a childhood garden of Eden, and stripped of his citizenship, as happened to him during the Second World War, similarly to Cixous' experience.[80] It was then that his memory was scarred, since he was an impressionable young boy at the time. This wounding happened much later than what Derrida himself sees as the "original scar," that of his circumcision, as he elaborates upon at length in his essay "*Circumfession*."

Gideon Ofrat, author of an intriguing book on the Jewish elements in Derrida's philosophy and writings, notes that "A social entity whose civil identity is arbitrarily taken or restored by the dominant society remains condemned to eternal exile from its identity, and therefore, too, from its language."[81] Ofrat further identifies Derrida's amnesia and consciousness of estrangement from roots and tradition with deconstruction.[82] "The eternal estrangement between writing and origin is a person's sentence of estrangement between his culture and its source."[83] The estrangement between writing and origin, culture and its source, is not simply a reference to Derrida's and the other Jewish and Arab children's estrangement from their native source and origin.

---
80   "Oui, je n'ai qu'une langue, or, ce n'est pas la mienne." Jaques Derrida, *Le Monolinguisme de l'Autre*. Paris: Editions Galilée, 1996,15.
81   Gideon Ofrat, *The Jewish Derrida*. Syracuse UP: Syracuse, 2001, 16.
82   Ibid., 17.
83   Ibid., 18.

Being schooled under the French meant a total eclipsing of not just any Jewish cultural or religious heritage, but also of North Africa as a primary source of cultural pride, belonging, and knowledge. Similar to Cixous' remembrance of the "absence" at school of all things Jewish and Muslim, Derrida remembers well his days in school in Algeria: "Not one word about Algeria, not one about her history and her geography, all the while we were able to draw the coast of Bretagne or the estuary of the Gironde with our eyes closed."[84] The colonial agenda cast a shadow on any ethnic, religious or cultural heritage the natives of the land may have had, and Jews and Arabs alike experienced devastatingly the foundation of their identities slipping into obscurity.

According to Ammiel Alcalay's observation of the French educational system in the Levant, the complete suppression of Arabic culture, language, history and geography from school agendas is the most glaring example of disenfranchisement. Derrida and Cixous, the two most famous French-Algerian Jews in modern French society, were no exceptions to this experience, as Alcalay notes:

French education came to the Middle East [and North Africa] hand in hand with the kind of imperial ventures that disenfranchised native populations paid for with their blood. Clearly, the effect of this "civilizing mission" was to ally certain classes within Middle Eastern [and North African] Jewish communities to the movement of European expansion and detach them from the concerns of the local populations with and among whom they lived.[85]

In her childhood exile in Algeria, Cixous would experience the agonizing difficulty of alienation by not being able to befriend the only three Arab girls in her French school, who would not reciprocate Cixous' attempts to reach out to them as colonized and marginal (Jew, Arabs and girls) in the French system. She recalls in her *Letter to Zohra Drif*:

---

84   "…pas un mot sur l'Algérie, pas un seul sur son histoire et sur sa géographie, alors que nous pouvons dessiner les yeux fermés les côtes de Bretagne ou l'estuaire de la Gironde." Derrida, *Le Monilinguisme de l'Autre*, 76.
85   Alcalay, "Intellectual Life", in *The Jews of the Middle East and North Africa of Modern Times*, 90.

> *I had a feeling of community. With them. But to say so was hopeless and senseless...I also needed in an indefinable way a discovery, a reunion, an alliance, because with them I made sense to myself...For them, surely I was what I was not: a French girl. My ancient desire for them, my desire for innocence, for purification, inaudible. There was no us.*[86]

To the Arab girls, Cixous represented the incarnation of the despised colonizer. The Jews of Algeria remember that the relationship between Arabs and Jews was experienced differently based on the city you lived in and the social class you were part of. It was more common among the bourgeoisie, the merchants and shop owners etc. to have a cordial relationship with the Arabs, guarded but relatively friendly. Among the lower working classes of Jews, however, the Arab stirs worries based on vivid memories of violence and clashes throughout the 1800s, the pogrom of Constantine in 1934, and the violent riots in Oujda, Morocco, in 1948. Contrary to Cixous' childhood experience of desiring to become closer with the Arabs, indeed to be *inséparabe*, for most Jews the Arab remains the "other," the one she tries to distance herself from in order to integrate into the French civilization.

This was problematic for the Arabs since they saw both peoples as indigenous, and the Jew as inferior. But the Jews' newfound connection to France made the Arabs realize that they now held a position of superiority in their changing colonial society, where they, the Arabs, no longer were in charge. Also, in their process of westernization, the Jews often left their native language of Judeo-Arabic in favor of French, a linguistic element that would alienate the Jews even further from the Arabs.

The other "other" for the Jews in Algeria were the people with whom they were in competition since they were often of the same social working and middle classes. They were the "neo-French": the Spanish, Maltese and Italians who had been naturalized since 1889 and who would compete economically and socially with the Jews. For the Jews, this group of "others" was also where they would see Christian anti-Sem-

---

[86] Hélène Cixous, "Letter to Zora Drif." *Parallax* 4 (1998): 193.

itism imported from France beginning in the 19th century. *Les vrais Français* (the real French) vs. *les Français d'ici* (pied-noirs) was a distinction that the Jews were aware of among themselves, since the pied-noirs were perceived as more aggressively competitive and *"arriviste"* and also more intensely anti-Semitic. Despite the Jews' efforts to assimilate into the Christian French society, Jews would continue to be reminded of their otherness by the anti-Semitisms of everyday life. Historian Michel Abitbol remarks:

> *The anti-Jewish legislation of the Pétain government was part of the dynamics of the "Pétain-mystique," which spread like wildfire across North Africa. This legislation drew the sympathy from the European population of the Maghreb, which on various occasions asked for the "correction" and adjustment of some clauses that were thought to be too soft or not rigorous enough. Letting the Jews alone believe that this legislation was imposed on France by the "enemy," the pied-noirs saw in it, on the contrary, a golden opportunity to settle their accounts with a Jewish population who for three-quarters of a century had troubled the privileged sleep of their dominant social caste.*[87]

The pied-noirs would point to the Jews and note that they were Jews and not one of them. In turn, the Jews did not want to be associated with the pied-noirs who saw themselves as superior to the Jews, even though there were Jews who by their own definition saw themselves as pied-noirs. One example of this ambiguous labeling and what can be understood as a desperate attempt at belonging is found on the website for Algerian Jews, www.Zlabia.com (a site offering a "virtual" cultural home and information base for Jews of Algerian origins). Here the editor/creator of the site, Jaco Halfon (who lives in California), has written an article about his experience with his father's adamant insistency on the family's pied-noir identity. He writes:

---

[87] Abitbol, *The Jews of North Africa during the Second World War*. Detroit: Wayne State UP, 1989, 168.

> *Since our immigration to France, every time I heard my father talk about our life in Algeria to those who would listen, I felt pretty uncomfortable when he pronounced the word "pied-noir." Perhaps it was the exaggerated pride that he put in it, or the fact that he was so set on being accepted among the French of the* métropole *as one of them, and he used this argument in order to convince above all himself. If I ever dared to bring up the debate, my father would always repeat with force that we were surely pieds-noirs and that our family had been French for many generations.*[88]

Halfon points out that there were probably only a few French Jews who followed in the footsteps of the French colons and settled in the colonies, and this would by definition make them pied-noirs. However, in his eyes this would hardly be a status of which to be proud, contrary to his father's fervent assertion. He also regrets the fact that despite the over two thousand year old Jewish heritage and roots in Algeria, during their four generations of life under the French, the Algerian Jews became completely assimilated into French culture and lost their own indigenous Algerian-Jewish culture.

This unique culture the French-Algerian Jews have begun to seek out in order to teach it and pass it on to their own children, by now far removed from their ancestral North African heritage. Anthropologist Joëlle Bahloul notes that one of the errors of historical reconstitution (in France) resulted in the classification of Jews from Algeria in the category of "returning people" and the consequent designation of these communities as "colonists" or "settlers." The settlers were in reality those with real origins in France (as opposed to imagined origins, as experienced by assimilated and frenchified Algerian Jews) who im-

---

[88]   "Depuis notre immigration vers la France, chaque fois que j'entendais mon père raconter notre vie en Algérie à qui voulait l'écouter, je me sentais plutôt inconfortable quand il prononçait le mot 'pied-noir'. Peut-être était-ce la fierté exagérée qu'il mettait ou alors le fait qu'il était si acharné à être accepté par les Français de métropole comme un des leurs et utilisait cet argument pour s'en convaincre surtout lui-même. Si jamais j'osais soulever le débat, mon père ne manquait jamais de répéter avec force que nous étions bien des pied-noirs et que nôtre famille était Française depuis plusieurs générations." Halfon, "Pied Noir," 1.

migrated to Algeria during the colonial period.[89] With this distinction in mind, it seems that historian Abitbol is not distinguishing accurately between the actual *gaule* ancestry of the pied-noirs, despite several generations in Algeria, and the Algerian Jewish ancestry that did not change magically after they were naturalized, even after several generations of being French citizens. He makes the following statement in his article entitled "The Integration of North African Jews in France" regarding repatriation:

> *With respect to the Algerian Jews in particular, we should not so much speak of immigration to France as of repatriation, as we do when referring to the 800,000 pieds-noirs who arrived [in France] in July 1962. Touched by the grace of the Crémieux decree, the ancestors of the Algerian Jews had ceased being "Jewish Natives" and had become French citizens. Their descendants, like all pieds-noirs, were able to benefit from the many services provided for repatriated Frenchmen by the government.*[90]

One might suggest that these two disparate statements indicate the difficulty in "categorizing" both the Jewish and the pied-noir Algerian/French, the identities becoming blurred in history both within and without the group, highlighting one aspect of colonialism's complex consequences.

In considering the push me-pull me relationship of the Algerian Jew and the pied-noir, we see that the stereotype of the pied-noir in the eyes of the Jew, is as colonizer, racist and reactionary, but he was also perceived as exuberant, a talker and picturesque. As noted earlier, there are Jews who lived in Algeria who wanted to identify with the pieds-noirs, since they hoped and wanted to be viewed as authentically French as possible. Chantal Benayoun, in her essay "Entre Hier et Aujourd'hui: Regards et Images des Pieds-Noirs"[91] raises the important issue of the ambiguity within the pied-noir identity. Imagining the

---

89   Bahloul, "La Rentrée en France des Juifs d'Algérie" in *La mémoire sépharade. Pardès.* 28 (2000): 179-186.
90   Abitbol, *Yale French Studies* 85 (1994): 183.
91   In *Les Juifs dans le regard de l'Autre*. Presses Universitaires du Mirail/Editions Vent Terral, 1988, 127-143.

ambiguity of the Jews toward an already confusing identity, it becomes like a destabilizing palimpsest or layering of ambiguities, showing the many levels of the effects of colonialism:

> *But from the background and the memory of the Algerian war, the alterisation of the Pieds-Noirs takes on a whole other form, which will give this population an image of a paradoxical and ambiguous character. In effect, all the while being in some views assimilated to the ex-colonized Arab by an imaginary that associates the proletarianisation with the physical stereotype, the Pieds-Noirs were elsewhere supposed to incarnate the ex-settler-colonizer, exploiter and rich, racist and reactionary. Thus is played the double face with which the Pieds-Noirs will have to come to terms from the beginning.*[92]

The years passed with the French presence in North Africa as part of everyday life, and French culture became increasingly more "normal" among most Jews and many Arabs too, whose own indigenous Arab culture and language were forcefully repressed from their lives. Colonialisms were by now spread to all corners of the world, and the Arabs' brothers in the Mashreq were beginning to rouse the oppositional stirrings later to be known as the great Pan-Arabic and Pan-Muslim movements. Historian Norman Stillman notes that "The French authorities tried to limit direct contacts between the local Arab population and the Middle East, but they could not cut off news from the region or keep out its ideological and political currents,"[93] and as Pan Islamic, Pan-Arab, and pro-Palestinian sentiment increased throughout the Arab world in the early 1930s,

---

[92] "Mais sur fond et mémoire de guerre d'Algérie, l'altérisation des Pieds-Noirs prend une toute autre forme qui va donner à l'image de cette population un caractère paradoxal et ambigu. En effet, tout en étant à certains égards assimilés à l'ex-colonisé arabe par une imaginaire associant la prolétarisation et le stéréotype physique, les Pieds-Noirs sont par ailleurs sensés incarner l'ex-colon-colonisateur, exploiteur et riche, raciste et réactionnaire. Ainsi fait jouer le double visage avec lequel les Pieds-Noirs vont devoir d'entrée composer." Benayoun, in *Les Juifs dans le regard de l'Autre*, 137.
[93] Stillman, *The Jews of Arab Lands*, 97.

"anti-Zionism was, of course, an important corollary."[94] It should be noted that the Grand Mufti of Jerusalem, Hajj Amin al-Husayni, was a friend and ally of Hitler, and visited Germany several times in the years leading up to and during the Second World War. He was to become the founder and president of the Arab League in 1944, and acted as the president of the World Islamic Congress in 1951 and also as the leader of Muslim Brotherhood. His popularity was tremendous in Egypt, Syria, Jordan, Iraq and Palestine, among other countries. Al-Husayni's building relationship with Hitler and the Nazi agenda, and his subsequent use of Nazi propaganda and organization of Nazi-Muslim armies throughout the Middle East, is by now a documented fact.[95]

The Mufti's fascist affiliations as well as adaptation of Nazi policies did not help Arab-Jewish relations, and he is also known to have called upon the Muslim world to kill all Jews. Much of the language of jihad continues to use the Nazi and fascist terminology introduced in the Arab world by al-Husayni during his forty years of influence and leadership in the region. After the Second World War he worked closely with leaders like Yasser Arafat (a nephew of the Mufti) and President Nasser of Egypt. In 1962 he proposed to make all Arab lands *"Judenrein,"* cleansed of all Jews, using the very term employed by the Nazi regime in their genocide of the Jews in Europe. With this violent influence growing and gaining momentum in the Mashreq, it would only be a matter of time until the Jews of the Maghreb would begin to hear the rumblings of dangerous anti-Semitic propaganda as the Second World War approached.

Norman Stillman further notes, "During the 1930s, there was a virulent revival of pied-noir anti-Semitism. For the right-wing French colonists, the Nazis were natural allies against the Jews and the Bolsheviks."[96] Later, as North African Arab nationalists began to organize against their colonial oppressors, they were not as "germanophile" as their Middle

---
94   Ibid.
95   See Michel Abitbol "The Diverse Reactions to Nazism by Leaders in the Muslim Countries," in A. Meddeb and B. Stora, eds., *The History of Jewish-Muslim Relations: From the Origins to the Present Day.* Princeton and Oxford: Princeton UP, 2013, 349-359, and Henry Laurens "The Mufti of Jerusalem, Opportunism and Anti-Semitism," in Ibid., 360-361.
96   *Jews of Arab Lands in Modern Times,* 111.

Eastern counterparts, but as Stillman points out, "...in North African eyes, Germany was free from the taint of colonialism and was the historic enemy of the French oppressors."[97] German ships docking in the Canary Islands were bringing ballots and tractates written in Arabic that were destined for dispersal in Algeria and Morocco. In them France was designated as "a Jewish nation" and the following is an example of the kind of inflammatory text intended for the general Arab population in North Africa: "The Jew eats into you like the vermin gnaws at the sheep...France protects him. He is her agent...Germany locks the Jews up and chases them and confiscates their goods. If you were not the slaves of France you could act in the same manner."[98]

The Second World War was a time of great differentiation in the three North African countries with regards to the Jews. Since Algeria was a full-fledged colony, the Vichy regime was able to more easily impose their discriminatory and anti-Semitic laws on the Jews, including the *numerus clausus*. Michel Abitbol notes:

The Number of people affected by the clauses of the Jewish Statute varied from one North African country to another. But, whether they were Moroccan, Tunisian, or Algerian, the Jewish victims all had in common their adaptation of the "French Ideal." Having gone through the French educational system and often being the brilliant products of France's "civilizing mission," these men and women were sent back to their prior status of "natives" and were, as well, deprived of their means of livelihood. This happened because they had reached out to France and its culture. It is not surprising, then, that the Jews least affected by the Jewish Statutes were those – more numerous in Morocco than in Tunisia and Algeria – who had distanced themselves from Western civilization or had ignored it, in short, those whose way of life and behavior had remained the most traditional.[99]

---

97 Ibid., 106.
98 "Le Juif vous ronge comme la vermine ronge la brebis...La France le protège. Il est (son) agent...L'Allemagne enferme et pourchasse les Juifs et confisque leurs biens. Si vous n'étiez pas les esclaves de la France vous pourriez agir de même." Mohammed Kenbib, *Juifs et Musulmans au Maroc 1859-1948*. Publications de la Faculté des Lettres et des Sciences Humaines-Rabat, 1994, 596.
99 *The Jews of North Africa During the Second World War*, 68.

With the revocation of the Crémieux decree in Algeria, the Jews lost all their political rights and protection, and thus began to be seen as more alien and threatening by both right-wing French, especially among the settlers and functionaries, as well as by Arabs who became influenced by the anti-Semitic propaganda seeping in from the East and the North. Vichy was especially invested in taking full advantage of Nazi policies to help separate the Jews from the Arabs. Jewish children were banned from their French schools, Jewish employees from jobs, and Jewish businesses were "aryanized" and confiscated. Cixous remembers her father losing not just the right to practice medicine, since it was much more than his job that was arbitrarily ripped away: "It was 1941, my father was no longer either doctor or officer or French or anything."[100] He was rejected just a year after he had served in the war as a doctor and officer in the Tunisian army. Words that recur throughout Cixous' writings that relate to her experiences in Algeria speak for themselves: admitted-reached-rejected-received-rejected-admitted-banned-incorporated-excorporated-inscribed-crossed out. [101]

There were also labor camps established in Algeria where, in addition to opponents to Vichy from various origins, Jews from France and Algeria were sent since they were branded systematically as "suspects." Tunisia was occupied by Germany for a period of six months between 1942-43 and, in addition to the anti-Jewish decrees affecting the Jews in areas such as legal status and access to education and level of economic influence/possibilities, some 5000 Jewish men were sent to forced labor camps established in Tunisia by the Germans. Jewish property (homes, cars, blankets, radios and public buildings) was also confiscated as soon as the Germans arrived.[102]

In Morocco, the Jews fared much better during the Second World War than their fellow Jews in Algeria, and during the two years of Vichy reign in the region (from July 1940 until November 8, 1942 when the Allies landed in North Africa), they were protected by the Sultan Mohamed V who refused to differentiate between his subjects and thereby protected the Jews against requests from France to implement

---

100   Cixous, "My Algériance," 272.
101   "Admis-atteint-rejetait-reçus-rejetées-admis-interdits-incorporés-excorporés-inscrits-rayés"
102   Saadoun, "Tunisia," 450.

discriminatory laws aimed at excluding Jews from public education and economy, as well as confiscation of Jewish properties. In addition to the measures taken by the Sultan, the Spanish Zone did not issue any discriminatory laws against Jews under Franco.

Historian Henry Abramson notes the following the Second World War period in North Africa: "…in the case of Algeria and Morocco, the occupation was actually by Vichy France rather than by the Nazis directly. Whereas Vichy France did not waste any time in sending Jews from France to the gas chambers, there was far more hesitation to implement these policies in North Africa, where colonial French had so many other issues to contend with."[103]

Tunisia fell under German occupation quite late – November of 1942 – and because of the allied invasion, was liberated some six months later.[104] Although the Jews in North Africa did not suffer many deaths during the Second World War, relative to their European counterparts, the well-organized increase in "ideological mobilization" inspired by anti-Semitic models alien to the Maghreb, would cause much pain, humiliation and real reasons for concern. Use of vocabulary and methods that across the Mediterranean were tools leading to the implementation of the Final Solution were widespread, pointing to the intended reach of Hitler's long-term plans.[105]

The anti-Jewish policies of the French government also served to satisfy interests and wishes of a segment of the local population, who were only too happy to see the Jewish population stripped of their rights.[106] However, large-scale expulsions, sequestration or confiscation of assets (as seen in Egypt and Syria in the 50s, for example) were never implemented in the Maghreb.

In Casablanca, for example, in the beginning of November 1942, there were open preparations for a pogrom against the Jewish quar-

---

[103] "A Double Occlusion: *Sephardim* and the Holocaust" in *Sephardic and Mizrahi Jewry. From the Golden Age of Spain to Modern Times*. Edited by Zion Zohar. New York: NYUP, 2005, 289.
[104] Ibid., 289.
[105] Hitler's Wannsee Conference held in January 1942, which announced the implementation of the Final Solution, lists the numbers of Jews in each country to be made *judenrein* and shows revealing figures: France is noted as having 700,000 Jews, a number that included Jews in all French territories.
[106] Abitbol, *The Jews of North Africa*, 12.

ters, or the *mellahs*. Haim Zafrani recollects anti-Jewish posters on the walls in the big cities, as well as vehemently anti-Semitic newspaper articles in the major press.[107] Fortunately for the Jews, the Allies arrived in the nick of time, preventing any major incidents aside from a few riots encouraged by the remaining French administration not yet rid of its Vichy policies and supporters. Despite the so called "dark period" of Vichy-laws in Morocco, from July 1940 until November 1942, and notwithstanding the open incitements by European fascist groups, Jews did not experience much violence, and the attitude of Sultan Mohammed V is said to have played a significant role in this situation. He refused to sign anything barring Jews from public life or schools, and even went "as far as" to grant them equal rights before the law and access to citizenship with the same rights and obligations as the Muslim Moroccan.[108]

After the war ended, most Jews as a group did not cling to unpleasant memories regarding their treatment by the French during those particularly difficult years. Writing about this trying time, Abitbol notes that the Jews generally emphasized their loyalty and attachment to France by not dwelling on the painful experiences of 1940-43 and that they wished "…to perceive them only as the consequences of the 'betrayal' of one man – Pétain – and the pressure exerted on the 'Vichy-Berlin regime' by the German occupant."[109] I believe this willingness to repress can be understood better in the light of what followed historically in the region after the Second World War, which was the more open manifestation of anti-colonial and nationalist movements among the Arab population, and the clearly difficult position in which Jews found themselves as the voices against the French presence grew stronger. Abitbol continues: "Swallowed up soon after [the Second World War] by events that were to put back into question their very presence, as well as the presence of France, in Maghreb lands the Jews of North Africa obstinately chose to blot out of their memories this brief span of their history."[110]

---

107 Zafrani, *Deux mille ans de vie juive au Maroc*. Paris: Maison Neuve & Larose, 1998, 294.
108 Ibid., 299.
109 Abitbol, "The Integration of North African Jews in France." 170.
110 Ibid.

In the bleak reality of events, it was a fact that the Jews needed the French now, since they had become too French to share the same fate and the same needs as their Arab landsmen and would not, as a collective group, take up the nationalist battle cry for independence. Unless you were an Algerian Jew, and even then, you were typically seen as too Arab of a Jew to be accepted among the French, and even among the Jews of Israel who at the time were mostly of European background, did a discriminatory anti-Arab sentiment bleed over on the reception and perception of Jews from Arab lands. The Jews of the Maghreb had to fend with the inevitable alienating experience of being stranded on an island of in-between-ness, causing them much uncertainty and pain.

A New Schism

By the time the State of Israel was established in 1948, and as the Israeli-Arab conflict became a full fledged war, the feeling of insecurity and fear among Jews living in Arab cultures was greatly intensified. As a result, the Jews of the Maghreb did not as a rule follow their Arab countrymen in their surge in national identity and consciousness as the Arab population began to mobilize for their struggle toward eventual independence, and French presence in North Africa became more precarious. Albert Memmi notes on the issue of the non-involvement of the Jewish communities in the nationalist movements:

> *We must, nonetheless, remember a most significant fact: the situation of the Jews during the colonial period was more secure, because it was legalized. This explains the prudence, the hesitation between political options of the majority of Jews in Arab lands. I have not always agreed with these choices, but one cannot reproach the responsible leaders of the communities for this ambivalence – they were only reflecting the inborn fear of their co-religionists.*[111]

As a result, when the Algerian war broke out in 1954, the Jews did not automatically take the side of their Arabo-Berber neighbors,

---

111   Memmi, "Who is an Arab Jew?" 2.

since they had, since 1870, been increasingly frenchified, in addition to holding French citizenship. During the first 2-3 years of the war of independence, Jews remained more or less neutral. Some who were sensitive to injustice toward Muslims, were for reforms and supported the FLN (National Liberation Front), others openly supported a French Algeria and worked with the pieds-noirs.[112]

Abitbol also notes, "There had been some Jewish militants in the Algerian national movement, but their numbers decreased significantly in the last years of the war of independence, when terrorists targeted synagogues and other Jewish sites."[113] After these incidents, not only did the number of Jews supporting the national movement decline, but research shows that more or less the entire Jewish community sided with the European extremists represented by the OAS[114] (Organization of the Secret Army) and some even joined in the fight against the FLN.[115]

The division between the two indigenous populations of the Maghreb became deeper as each day passed, and every Arab-Israeli event in the Middle East would spark further tensions and more aggressions toward the North African Jewish communities. Alcalay, quoting Stillman, underlines the naked truth about the destructive nature of colonial presence for the Judeo-Arabic relationship in that region: "Unquestionably, [though,] the inroads, conflicts, and pressures superimposed by colonial rule upset the traditional forms of confessional autonomy and went into creating 'an unequal process which linked the Jewry of the Mediterranean Islamic countries to the movement of European expansion, and detached it from the fate of the Arab peoples.'"[116]

When Morocco and Tunisia were liberated from their status as protectorates in 1956, and Algeria claimed their independence from France after the grueling and bloody war of independence that lasted

---

112 David Cohen, "Algeria" in *The Jews of the Middle East and North Africa*, 467.
113 Abitbol, "The Integration of North African Jews in France," 248.
114 A short-lived French far-right dissident organization during the Algerian War (1954–62), the OAS used armed struggle in their attempt to prevent Algeria's independence from French colonial rule. Its motto was *L'Algérie est française et le restera* ("Algeria is French and will remain so").
115 See David Cohen, "Algeria," in *The Jews of the Middle East and North Africa of Modern Times*, 467.
116 Alcalay, *After Jews and Arabs*, 45.

until 1962, the Jews of North Africa were in a difficult and perilous predicament. The Jewish position of *entre-deux*, of existing in an ambiguous space between the former occupier and the occupied and fully accepted neither among the French nor among the Arabs, would eventually make life intolerable for Jews in the region. It is as if they lived in a suspended space, one that only complicated the already compromised issue of belonging and non-belonging. From 1948 until 1962, when the last departure *en masse* of Jews took place, the Jewish communities lived under constant fear of attacks. Several civilian-operated riots ended in bloody massacres of entire families or small villages, synagogues were desecrated, and Jewish shops and businesses looted all with little effective interference by the French police.

The increasingly marginal existence of the Jews was felt in the most acute way, as they were left to fend for themselves without assistance from those who could have stopped or at the very least curbed the violence. The final result of this increasingly difficult existence was a silent mass exodus that ensued, as entire Jewish communities uprooted and vanished from North African soil in a matter of months. A total of approximately 500,000 Jews lived in the Maghreb as independence from France was achieved. When all is told, only between 1- 2 percent of the total Jewish populations in the Maghreb remain there today; almost nil in Algeria, where post-independence tolerance of minorities has been the lowest. Morocco is where tolerance has remained the official policy of the Monarch, making it the only place in the Maghreb where Jews feel they can safely visit and organize heritage-tours, although with the increasing spread of terrorism targeting tourists in Arab countries, even Morocco has seen a sharp decline in Jewish tourism.

The most obvious choices of emigration were these: immigrate to Israel, the nascent but struggling nation where all Jews were welcome to a homeland of their own (this became the typical choice of the more religious families, the poorer and less educated who often lived outside of larger towns, cities, and remote areas who were thus less frenchified), or, immigrate to France, where they would be at least linguistically and culturally "prepared." Although the Algerian Jews already had French citizenship, this was not as easy or automatic for the Jews from Tunisia and

Morocco, where permits to travel and emigrate as well as the acquisition of passports (be it Israeli or French) were regulated by strict quotas. The Jews from the Maghreb were generally faced with both a difficult period of acculturation and an emotional challenge that we will examine in the literature evoking these immigrant experiences.

As we have seen from this historical overview of Jewish life in the Maghreb, the loss of this place does not represent for the Jew a loss of unity, or a new fragmentation of identity that was not already familiar. The Jew, even after generations of living in the region, had always existed with a recurrent reminder of her difference and her otherness. On the same note, the historical "symbiosis" between Jew and Arab, whether harmonious or not, by mere virtue of having lived in the same geographical area under shared historical events for centuries, sometimes millennial, also came to an end with the departure of the Jewish communities.

As literary critic Ronnie Scharfman notes in her essay on Moroccan-Jewish writer Edmond Amran El Maleh: "The hyphen, the 'trait d'union' that designated this bicultural, diglossic Maghreb subject as 'judéo-arabe' or 'arabo-juif,' has been severed by the departure and dispersal of this ancient Jewish community from Morocco."[117] The earlier hyphenated identity was broken apart and never to be brought together again in the "new diaspora" as anything but an antonym of its parts.[118] Anthropologist Joelle Bahloul points out that the Jewish colonial experience developed in the framework of a triangular relationship, placing the Jew in a status of in-between. On the one side was the Franco-European community with the political and cultural power it represented, and on the other side was the indigenous Arabo-Muslim society.[119] With the French leaving the area and the Arabs regaining independence, that triangle collapsed into an even more painful dichotomy or

---

117 Ronnie Scharfman. "The Other's Other: The Moroccan-Jewish Trajectory of Edmond Amran El Maleh," *Yale French Studies* 82 (1993): 136.
118 For a poignant essay on the trauma experienced by Arab Jews in this forced re-formatting of their identity, see Iraqi born Ella Shohat "Reflections of an Arab Jew," in *The Flying Camel. Essays on Identity by Women of North African and Middle Eastern Jewish Heritage*. Loolwa Khazzoom, ed. New York: Seal Press, 2003, 115-121.
119 Bahloul. "La Rentreé en France des Juifs d'Algérie," 183.

opposition; the Jew and the Arab in their newly historically carved out roles could no longer easily find a way to coexist. Their relationship would cease to be determined by their shared history and commonality, but rather be defined by the newer and distressing developments of partitions and separations in nation building, surrounded by more resentfulness, hateful speech and actions than opportunities for dialogue and coexistence.

The Jews lived with a problematic and ambiguous status and identity under the French in the Maghreb, and by looking closer at the various complications that arose in inter-relations between Arabs, French and Jews during that time, we may begin to see wounds that will not be easily healed over time. The awkward position of the colonized Jew, between a rock and a hard place, has only compounded more deeply an identity of in-between.

For this study, however, it is the lasting impressions of the Maghreb over many generations, as developed both before and after the colonial period, that will inform the literary study of Jewish texts by women carrying the Maghreb within them as they continue to live their lives, some more, some less Jewishly, but all as authors proudly and profoundly marked by their own experiences of the Jewish culture in a homeland that would not and could not remain the same. The new Franco-Sephardic "essence," transposed and blossoming in new territories across the Mediterranean, cannot be essentialized in its intensely hybrid and often-diverse forms. Nevertheless, we will become acquainted with narrative voices and themes that remember their origins, although they may be heard as faint whispers of a dreamlike past, or as the cries from wounds yet to heal. As difficult as these voices can be to classify, they yearn to see themselves as participants and actors in a world moving beyond post-colonial traumas and painful exiles, into, perhaps, an increasingly diasporic world where humanity listens compassionately to the Other among itself.

Part II

Literary Considerations

Chapter 3

History and Writing:
A Silent Exodus and Suppressed Sephardic Voices

I have lost everything in this collapse, but not my memory.
Albert Bensoussan

Language is the exile's true homeland.
Edmond Jabès

As a Jew is about to depart from Algeria for good, an Arab approaches and offers a departing gift: "Don't leave. It is the French who will bring you unhappiness…We were born together, we lived together, we fed from our mothers together…why are you leaving? The war is over…"[120]

Vanishing Bodies and Voices: Repressed Identities

Indeed, the Arab was the other, but an other with whom a profound memory is attached. Shared Jewish-Muslim memories and intersections, both historical, religious, political and personal, have recently been collected and published in a new and groundbreaking work, *A History of Jewish-Muslim Relations: From the Origins to the Present Day* (2013), and in it, co-editor Abdelwahab Meddeb, a Muslim from Tunisia, recalls warmheartedly:

> *Through them [the Jews], I saw fulfilled the possibility of being in the world and of still perpetuating what resists and what remains of the origin. In short, I told myself that, whether one is a Jew or a*

---

[120] "Ne partez pas. Les malheurs vous viendront des Français…On est né ensemble, on a vécu ensemble, on a tété nos mères ensemble…pourquoi partez-vous? La guerre est finie…" *Les Juifs dans le regard de l'autre*, 124.

Muslim, it is possible to be Tunisian and modern. Evolution was not mere betrayal. That is what the Jews' presence evoked for me in Tunis, where moreover, they exemplified join de vivre, *hedonism, a positive diversity.*[121]

Even though these memories are usually nonviolent, and not infrequently, even fond memories, they are often ambiguous for the Jews, because of the recurring and intermittent humiliations, attacks and later anti-Semitic overtures. Hélène Cixous has narrated many such sorrowful memories of the impossibility of becoming close to, or even being understood by, her Arab neighbors, because of the perception that the Jews were also part of the colonizers:

The most unbearable is, beyond the battles and the humiliations, that we were assaulted in Clos-Salembier by the actual people we so wanted to love, with whom we were lamentably in love, with whom we thought we were attached by all the relationships and communities of our shared origin, of destiny, of states of mind, of the memory of touch, of taste, our enemies were our friends, there were mistakes and confusion...I wanted to be on their side but it was a desire on my part for their side...I am inseparabe.[122]

Young Cixous sought closeness and contact, and desired deeply to connect with her Arab classmates and neighbors in a way that was experienced as difficult and impossible. French and Arab writer Leila

---

121   Abdelwahab Meddeb. *A History of Jewish-Muslim Relations: From the Origins to the Present Day.* Abdelwahab Meddeb and Benjamin Stora, eds. Trans. Jane Marie Todd and Michael B. Smith. Princeton: Princeton UP, 2013, 14.
122   "Le plus insupportable c'est, par-dessus les combats et les humiliations, que nous étions assaillis au Clos-Salembier par les êtres mêmes que nous voulions aimer, dont nous étions lamentablement amoureux, auxquels nous étions liés pensions-nous par toutes les parentés et communautés d'origine, de destin, d'états d'esprits, de mémoire de toucher, de goût, nos ennemis étaient nos amis, il y avait erreur et confusion...je voulais être de leur côté mais c'était un désir de mon côté de leur côté...je ne désirais que leur Ville et leur Algérie, je voulais à toutes forces y arriver...Moi, pensais-je je suis inséparabe." Cixous, *Les Rêveries de la femme sauvage.* Paris: Galilée, 2000, 44-45.

Sebbar has edited a collection of childhood memories by more than thirty Jewish authors from Muslim lands in *Une enfance juive en Méditerranée musulmane* (2013), where she sees childhood memories as a form of collective creative archeology to remember what was. Here we find an exploration "of a Southern Mediterranean that was cosmopolitan, a Jewish and Muslim Mediterranean, now orphaned by its Jews who inhabited it before Islam. A perfectly joyful, sometimes cruel history recounts it. Individual stories remember another time."[123]

Sebbar, herself an exiled Algerian writer, sees this past as part of her own story, her own loss, as she notes, "Lost native country. The voice of the languages spoken recited sung dreamed, the voice of letters and books, we think they are forgotten, they are there, these voices, on the pages of writers in exile and the childhood of the last generation of this story. Mine as well."[124] In the collective memory of the Algerian Jews, it does happen that this other becomes the enemy. But she becomes the enemy first and foremost because of a third other, namely the French colonizer. However, blaming the increasingly intolerable relations between Jews and Arabs in the Maghreb only on the French would be an oversimplification. Michel Abitbol has articulated some of the additional considerations we should bear in mind:

> *The alienation was political and not solely cultural. The colonial situation had caused insuperable rifts among various religious and ethnic groups, as they adopted different strategies vis-à-vis the French. This meant that the rate of the North African Jews' departure reflected not only the course of Arab-Israeli relations, but the specific vicissitudes of decolonization in their countries of origin. The Jewish exodus from North Africa was thus hastened by*

---

[123] "…une Méditerranée du Sud qui fut cosmopolite, une Méditerranée juive et musulmane, aujourd'hui orpheline des Juifs qui l'ont habitée avant l'Islam. Une Histoire parfois joyeuse parfois cruelle raconte cela. Des histoires individuelles se souviennent d'une autre fois." Leïla Sebbar. Une enfance juive en Méditerranée musulmane. Saint-Pourçain-sur-Sioule: Bleu Autour, 2012, 12.
[124] "Pays natal quitté perdu. La voix des langues parlées récitées chantées rêvées, la voix des lettres et des livres, on croit les avoir oubliées, elles sont là, ces voix, dans les pages des écrivains en exil et l'enfance de la dernière génération de cette histoire-là. La mienne aussi." Ibid.,13.

such events as Tunisia's accession to internal autonomy in 1954, Morocco's proclamation of independence in 1955, the Suez campaign of 1956, the 1962 conflict between Tunisia and France over the military base at Bizerte, the March 1962 signing of the Evian agreements that put en end to the Algerian war, and the independence of Algeria in July of the same year.[125]

To these catalysts of the Jewish exodus from Arab lands, it is necessary to also add the establishment of the State of Israel in 1948, with the subsequent Israeli-Arab war; a situation only magnified in gravity and intensity during and after the Sinai Campaign in 1956, and also the Six Day War of 1967, when Israel preempted Arab aggression with a humiliating defeat of the Egyptian and Syrian Air Forces and consequently annexed the Sinai Peninsula, Jerusalem, Gaza and parts of the West Bank. These crushing Arab losses only deepened feelings of Arab distrust and resentment toward the Jews.

The silent exodus of the Jews from Arab countries can be so called because much of it happened quietly and clandestinely, since Jews were often not allowed to emigrate, many not holding passports and being denied citizenship in the country they lived. Memories of this quiet vanishing are sometimes traced back to school, where children had the alarming experience of friends disappearing without notice, as entire Jewish communities silently shriveled up and left towns with gaping voids as Jewish families made the difficult decision to leave. Ruth Tolédano Attias recounts that she and her friends would come to school in the mornings and find the seats of their classmates empty, and the teacher would say nothing of the departures. Their houses were vacant, everything gone, and the children had noticed nothing leading up to this sudden departure, being protected by the adults from the tragic unfolding of events: "Little by little, emptiness happened around us. The world unraveled around us."[126]

In those countries in the Middle East where the Jews were expelled, such as Syria, Iraq and Egypt, the departures happened more dramatically, and the Jews had to leave all their property and valuables behind, not being permitted to take anything with them except what

---

125   Abitbol, "The Integration of North African Jews in France," 249.
126   See *La mémoire sépharade*, 148.

they could carry. Many Jewish families in North Africa had similar experiences, and family heirlooms and personal valuables were hidden in clothing, sewn into fabrics in a desperate attempt at saving memories, significance and traces of a life in the Maghreb. There are memories of wedding rings being slipped off fingers at the customs, of articles from the baggage being ruined or torn, as a last "jab" to ensure they really did leave without anything of significant value. To a child the experience of seeing his or her parents being humiliated officially, as often happened at the port customs as families migrated, would leave behind indelible marks in memories. In some of the writing by the authors included in this study, the actual moment of departure becomes a point of recovery, a point of reference for the fictional character or the auto-fictional narrator, full of a significance that needs to be revisited and recounted.

ALIYAH OR YERIDAH? THE ISRAEL EXPERIENCE

The Jews in North Africa were not forcefully expelled, but it became more and more difficult to live there as Jews, and thus eventually they decided that there was no viable future for their families among the Arabs. The Jews from Algeria went in an overwhelming majority to France, and just between 1962 and 1963 over 100,000 arrived in the *métropole*. Unlike the emigration from many Middle Eastern countries that had Jewish communities nearly obliterated, the Algerian Jewish departure was not a frantic escape, but occurred through well-organized emigration.[127] As mentioned earlier, the majority of the Jews from Morocco emigrated to Israel rather than France, and this was initially an emigration organized clandestinely, with the help of Zionist organizations such as the United Jewish Appeal. In 1944 only 44 Jews left, and by 1949 10,000 had gone, quietly. The semi-legal emigration organization called Kadima opened in 1949, and from '49 to '56, when Morocco became independent, 90,000 Jews emigrated through this operation. Between 1961-1964, an additional 80,000 Moroccan Jews left for *Eretz Israel*, the Land of Israel, but this time it was through legal means.

---

127   Cohen, "Algeria," 469.

As Michael M. Laskier notes, the Moroccan Jews were granted Moroccan citizenship after the independence in 1956, but many remained fearful and skeptical of accepting the obligation to be conscripted in the army and the possibility of having one day to fight against Israel.[128] One AIU teacher in Morocco expressed the complex web of his conflicted interests since he was torn between three major forces: "First, there was Morocco, his *patrie*. Second, there was the newly established State of Israel, the cradle of his religion. Finally there was France, the source of his culture and emancipation."[129]

Leaving the Maghreb behind was not an easy transition for the majority of these Jews, since all things familiar were abandoned. Cultural locations that had given Jews their bearings for centuries were no longer there, and the required assimilation would leave the immigrants and their offspring with a challenging emptiness. In his book *La mémoire sépharade* Shmuel Trigano asks, "What do they have left of permanence, of constancy, of concrete, when their entire world had disappeared and sunk forever, leaving them in a radical nakedness? From what can their identity be made up of when they have lost the material basis normally essential to culture and identity: their territory, language, human environment?"[130] With their Judeo-Arab and sometimes-Berber language and cultural customs, they were met with open, public and government endorsed discrimination in Israel, despite the call – loud and clear – for new Jewish immigrants in the nascent years of the State.

Many immigrants from the Maghreb and the Mashreq would talk about their immigration experience to Israel not as *aliyah* (literally "go up" or "ascend") but rather as a *yeridah* ("going down" or "descent," referring this way to their decline in social standing and spiritual experience – not as expected or dreamed of – implicitly presented as positive and uplifting in Zionist discourse). This is a sore and shameful point

---

128   Laskier, *North African Jewry in the Twentieth Century*, 187.
129   Ibid., 188.
130   "Que leur reste-t-il de permanent; de constant; de solide alors que tout leur monde a disparu et sombré à jamais, les laissant dans une nudité radicale? De quoi peut être faite leur identité alors qu'ils ont perdu les bases matérielles habituellement essentielles à une culture et à une identité : le territoire, la langue, l'environnement humain?" Trigano, *La mémoire sépharade*, 43.

in Israel's history and continues to be at the core of many controversial social and political issues today. Even the prime minister at the time of the mass immigration of Jews from Arab Lands, Ben Gurion, saw the "Arab Jews" as "afflicted with slave mentality" and of no positive value since the early Israeli nation-builders did not want any Arab or Levantine influence in Israel. In effect, Moroccan Jewry became a symbol in Israel of all the social and cultural "illness" of Oriental Jewry as a whole.[131] Israel was at the time heavily involved in what is known as "Operation Kibbutz Galuyyot," or "The Ingathering of Exiles", and the vastness of this population migration surrounding the newborn State is demonstrated by the fact that about 600,000 people arrived in Israel between 1949 and '51, a period when immigration was at its height. Many were survivors of the death camps in Europe, but the majority were Jews from various Arab lands, and as Alcalay notes, they had been "…drawn step by step into a tangled net of circumstances they could no longer find a way out of, [and] had been expelled – more or less brutally – from countries they and their families had lived in for thousands of years."[132]

Once arrived in Israel, they again became marginalized as an abject other. Zohar continues:

> *Ironically, though possessing many of the Oriental characteristics admired in the Arabs [by the early Zionist settlers], Oriental Jews were deemed too traditionally Jewish, which diminished their status in the eyes of the early European settlers, who perceived religiosity as a remnant of the hated exile.*[133]

Indeed, writer Cynthia Ozik sees the common dispraise of diasporic/exilic traditions in Zionism as an inspiration with two parents: the memory of home, its warm mother, and the revulsion of Exile, its stern father.[134] The adherence to religious traditions, or/and to the

---

131   See Zion Zohar, "Sephardim and Oriental Jews in Israel" in *Sephardic and Mizrahi Jewry. From the Golden Age of Spain to Modern Times.* New York: NYUP, 2005, 305.
132   Alcalay, *After Jews*, 221.
133   Zohar, "Sephardim and Oriental Jews in Israel," 304.
134   Ozick, "America: Toward Yavneh", in *What is Jewish Literature?* Hanna Wirth-Nesher, ed. Philadelphia: JPS, 1994, 21.

patriarchal cultural traditions typifying Arab cultures and common among *Mizrahi* Jews, was therefore judged as non-desirable in this newfound country created to finally end centuries of lamented existence in an exile defined by repression and submission to the dominant culture. One may even argue that the Zionist narrative has been so repulsed by the notion of exile that it has repressed altogether memories of coming from somewhere else, as Jonathan Boyarin has suggested.[135]

Those Jews who arrived in Israel, initially more or less euphorically, would find that they had to repress their Oriental, Arab culture, and were often made to feel ashamed to speak their native Judeo-Arabic language in public, being told they looked too Arab. Ella Shohat speaks about this repression of her family's Arabness when they arrived in Israel, and how it lead to a "profound and visceral schizophrenia." She notes that their identity as Arab Jews was understood as an ontological subversion and that being forced to assume a homogeneous European Jewish identity was "an exercise in self-devastation."[136] Just as the Jews from Eastern Europe who came to France fleeing the Russian pogroms of the 1880's were seen as a disgrace by their frenchified and assimilated co-religionists because of their "bad" manners, "primitive" clothing, and Yiddish language, so were the Jews from North Africa and the Middle East an embarrassment to the Eurocentric Jewish establishment in Israel. This points to the fact that the Jew has his "other" too; the Jews are "strangers to themselves" and suffer from what Daniel Sibony will call *"la haine de soi,"* a self hatred which becomes an uncompromising *"haine de l'autre,"* a hatred of the other.[137]

Eli Yassif points out in "The 'Other' Israel" that the heavy pressure of the official educational system, the radio and the newspapers led

---

135 Boyarin, "Diaspora: Generation and the Ground of Jewish Identity" in *Theorizing Diaspora*, Jana Evans Braziel and Anita Mannur, eds. Malden: Blackwell Publishing, 2003, 104.
136 Shohat, "Reflections of an Arab Jew," in *The Flying Camel. Essays on Identity by Women of North African and Middle Eastern Jewish Heritage.* Loolwa Khazzoom, ed. New York: Seal Press, 2003, 117.
137 For an intriguing discussion about the psychoanalysis of cultural conflicts in Israel, see Sibony, *L'Entre-Deux. L'Origine en Partage.* Paris: Seuil, 1991 and *Proche-Orient. Psychanalyse d'un Conflit.* Paris: Seuil, 2003.

"Diaspora Culture" to become de-legitimized in Israeli Society.[138] The new immigrants, the Jews from Arab lands, had difficulty finding jobs and were encouraged on all levels to hide their cultural uniqueness and seek acculturation to the prevailing norms, which were Eurocentric, Ashkenazi-centric and, as revealed in many studies on Israeli society and politics, discriminatory toward and Sephardic immigrants. Some traditions of Moroccan Jews such as veneration of saints and the spring festival Mimouna, celebrated at the conclusion of the eight days of Passover, have seen a rebirth in Israel after an initial period of repression and suppression in the years following the immigration of Moroccan Jews.

Today, as North African Jews are slowly moving from the margins toward the center, and have proved their influence in Israeli culture and politics, members of the Knesset, the Israeli parliament, attend yearly Mimouna festivities. Slowly but surely, the non-European Oriental cultural traditions of Sephardic Jews are becoming part of a larger and less narrow Israeli-Jewish identity. For a long time since its inception, Israel perceived Oriental music, for instance, as inferior, and it was banned from the radio, and mainstream media would ignore singers whose music reflected an Oriental style, even though sung in Hebrew.[139] Being Israeli meant being European, until eventually Jews from Arab lands, who comprise more than half of Israeli society, began to claim their part of mainstream Israeli culture.

A deep feeling of victimization is still present today among *Mizrahim/Sephardim* in Israel. One group of intellectuals representing this disillusioned part of society is the New Historians, with whom Ella Shohat also associates. In their view, the Zionist narrative has denied, erased, and excluded the *Mizrahi* historical identity, and they argue that *Mizrahi* Jews are Zionism's "other" victims alongside the Palestinians. The post-Zionists promote the view held by many young *Mizrahim* that discrimination did not end with their parents' generation, but continues today as their children who were born in Israel continue to face discrimination and cope with social and economic handicaps.[140]

---

138 Yassif, *Cultures of the Jews*, 1073.
139 See Zohar, "Sephardim and Oriental Jews in Israel," 305.
140 See Meyrav Wurmser, "Post-Zionism and the Sephardi Question."
Middle East Quarterly online, Spring (2005), Volume XII, Number 2, 1.

According to Shohat, Zionism is a white, Ashkenazi phenomenon, based on the denial of the Orient and the rights of both *Mizrahi* Jews and Palestinians. Indeed, she argues, the conflict of East vs. West, Arab vs. Jew, and Palestinian vs. Israeli exists not only between Israelis and Arabs, but also within Israel between Ashkenazi and *Mizrahi* Jews.[141]

With the arrival of the Jewish North Africans in France, the Jewish population doubled from 235,000 to 500,000 between 1957 and 1970. The transfer of the Algerian Jewish community to France was a "total" and diversified immigration, embracing all sectors of the population. As Michel Abitbol notes, Moroccan Jewish immigration to France was much more selective than its Algerian counterpart, and it was largely made up of elements of the community who were bourgeois, "'french-ified" or in some way skilled. The Tunisian immigration resembled the Algerian one in that it included all social strata.[142] As noted earlier, Jewish life in France was greatly enhanced by the arrival of the Jewish emigrants from the Maghreb. Pre-1957 French Jewry consisted primarily of Jews from Eastern Europe and Alsace/Lorraine, and as the 1960's and 70's unfolded, its demographics shifted dramatically. Michael M. Laskier points out that "[n]ot only did the newcomers inject new stimulus into French Jewry, but they helped transform this now heterogeneous community into the second largest in the Western world."[143]

Arriving in the Land of *Liberté, Egalité* and *Fraternité*

The other large immigrant populations in France at this time were the pied-noirs who received more than a cold shoulder from the French upon their "repatriation" from Algeria in addition to an increasingly growing influx of Arab North African immigrants, settling primarily in large cities and suburbs. A great deal of attention has been given to the various problematic issues relating to immigration in France, and how the pied-noir, Arab and Beur (second generation Arab immigrants) communities have been greeted with much xenophobia and ambiguous political, social and cultural messages, despite France's official language of integration and tolerance.

---

141   Ibid.
142   Laskier, "The Integration of North African Jews in France," 253.
143   Laskier, *North African Jewry in the Twentieth Century*, 3.

Although the Jewish immigrants from North Africa were welcomed by a well-established Jewish community that "mobilized massive resources" to assist in them, historian Ethan Katz notes, "No comparable Muslim communal structure stood prepared to help integrate new arrivals."[144] The French Jewish community acutely sensed this complicated situation, and, in part because most Jews from North Africa were able to assimilate with more ease than the average Arab North African, their auto-silencing became a subconscious tool limiting the possibility of the Jews becoming targets of French xenophobia. Additionally, the Jews arriving in France experienced relief by finally feeling that they were considered equal by law to the majority population.

Hélène Cixous, who as a child with her family experienced the distressing effects of arbitrary exclusion in Algeria, expresses her relief when saying: "We were no longer those tied up scorned and misunderstood hostages of the tragic comedy of nationalities."[145] However, for Cixous, as for many of the Jews immigrating to France in the years following de-colonization, the departure from North Africa did not necessarily mean "arrival" in France. "Algeria had given me the departure. But France could not give me the arrival," she adds.[146] It is certain that Cixous' voice did not "vanish" once she came to France, quite the opposite, since she became a public and influential figure in the intellectual and cultural scenes of France post-May'68. However, the experience of marginality and exclusion would continue: "In France, what fell from me first was the obligation of the Jewish identity. On the one hand, the anti-Semitism was incomparably weaker in Paris than in Algiers. On the other hand, I abruptly learned that my unacceptable truth in this world was my being a woman. Right away, it was war."[147]

Both Cixous and the high profile human rights lawyer Gisèle Halimi, who also immigrated to France from North Africa as a young

---

144 Katz, *The Burdens of Brotherhood: Jews and Muslims From North Africa to France*. Boston: Harvard UP, 2015, 19. Both Ethan B. Katz's *Burdens* and Maud Mandel's *Muslims and Jews in France: History of a Conflict*. Princeton: Princeton UP, 2014, offer two particularly nuanced studies, that both elaborate on the asymmetrical assimilation and social inequality between Jews and Muslim immigrants from North Africa to France.
145 Cixous, "Letter to Zora Drif," 193.
146 Ibid., 190.
147 Cixous, *Rootprints*, 204.

adult about to begin university studies, spoke out loud and clear at very young ages by becoming publicly known female figures of resistance. Cixous challenged male-dominated systems of knowledge, and Halimi, who at the relatively young age of 30, defended the Arabs accused of the el-Halia massacres in Algeria during the Algerian War of Independence, thus challenging the traditional French legal system. It may be ironic to speak of "not arriving" in their cases, in the traditional sense of the word, since this would be as "*arrivée*" as one could hope to get. However, we should not forget the significance of their formative years living as Jews in Algeria and Tunisia.

The experience of the humiliating and scary years of the Second World War, as well as being faced with the clashing cultures of traditional Judaism and Europe's often progressive and politically charged influences, would lead these young women to seek out specific paths as they took full advantage of the freedom of living in Paris during a new post-colonial era. It is from her early childhood memories that much of Cixous' autobiographical writings draw, as she seeks to map out the trajectory of her own identity and writing, albeit through many years of highly successful authorship, social engagement and intellectual and academic recognition. In a sense one might view Cixous' writing of her identity as an attempt to define her own marginality and to see how it is that her thoughts and social engagement against sexism, war, repression of ethnic minorities and women, have been shaped by her early experiences. Both she and Halimi look at their identity as women and Jews, both in North Africa and in France, as critical to their self-understanding.

Eclipsed Narratives

Having now addressed the more or less total exodus of Jews from Arab lands in the twentieth century and specifically the vanishing of North Africa's Jewish population, we will turn to the issue of why the voices of these Jews became eclipsed and erased not only in the general narrative of Jewish history and literature, but also in the greater narratives of post-colonial accounts. We know historically where the "bodies" went, in which societies and countries they created new homes and new lives, but what happened to the narratives of this experience?

How did the identities and memories shaped by this sudden and complete uprooting manifest themselves, and in what ways were their expressions unique? The Jews had vanished from the Maghreb, but, once re-located, where did their voices go? Why the silence and the self-effacement? Jewish historian Shmuel Trigano speaks of "*la puissance de refoulement*" [the power of repression] and the "*blocage de la mémoire sépharade, de sa 'panne'*" [the blockage of Sephardic memory, of its breakdown.][148] Ruth Tolédano Attias recognizes a paradoxical attitude among Sephardic Jews in that they are perfectly conscious of being the "carriers" of a history, of a culture and of a civilization, while having imposed upon their memory a profound silence.[149] Attias also sees that the absence of written history can in part be explained by the fact that Sephardic Jews lived in countries where oral transmission of (hi)stories was practiced and widespread, as well as a certain "repugnance," among religious Jews, at seeing their lives, perceived as holy and spiritual, secularized in a written text (other than Holy Texts). She also suggests that the messianic hopes were so intense that to write about life in exile may have seemed superfluous.[150]

Although this could help explain the silence of those who emigrated to Israel, which for many was seen as the ultimate redemption, the final end of all exiles, what about those arriving in France, Canada or South America? How can we explain their initial silence? Here Attias suggests that the memory of the Shoah and the confrontation with its miseries, tragedies and slaughters intimidated the Jews of the Orient into silence. It was as if "writing could not be justified by anything other than misfortune."[151] Thus, although there is no exile or departure without pain – and the Jews of Arab lands certainly had their share of misfortunes – there were other Jewish narratives much more tragic than theirs, and even occasional lynchings, looting and humiliations could not compare to the

---

148		Trigano, *La mémoire sépharade*, 30.
149		Tolédano Attias, "Lumières du Passé" in *Pardès* 28 (2000): 143.
150		Ibid., 144.
151		"l'écriture ne pouvait se justifier que par le Malheur." Ibid., 145.

genocide of the European Jews. Trigano acutely describes the psyche of this dilemma:

> *The bad conscience since attached to colonialism rebounded on them. Their drama did not deserve to be considered, less so bemoaned. They were themselves often doomed to forgetting and repressing, even to contempt, by the state of mind that so inescapably brings this on, the suffering induced by the collapse of their world. In diaspora, the settling in the "métropole"...experienced as "repatriation," a "return" – where the access to the ideal France dreamed of in the colonies made imperceptible this "occultation" that could not be named.*[152]

The eventual resurgence of Jewish self-affirmation seen in writing by Jews in France from the 1980s, and particularly by Sephardic women writers (as it is from this fertile market our literary texts have been chosen), is explained by Lucille Cairns in these terms:

> *...partly fostered by France's recognition, albeit belated and incomplete, of its own anti-Semitism under Vichy, had fostered a greater willingness on the parts of Jews generally to expose and denounce their own experiences of anti-Semitism, however incommensurate with the Shoah such experiences were in the case of Sephardic Jews. Another, very different reason could be that, due to differing gendered codes of the socially acceptable, women are on the whole more likely to admit to trauma than men. Male resistance to such admission would have been particularly acute in the highly traditional, patriarchal societies of North African Jewry...*[153]

---

152   "La mauvaise conscience attachée désormais au colonialisme rejaillissait sur eux. Leur drame ne méritait pas d'être considéré, encore moins plaint. Ils furent eux-mêmes souvent emportés par cet état d'esprit qui vouait inéluctablement à l'oubli et au refoulement, voire au mépris, la souffrance induite par l'effondrement de leur monde. En diaspora, l'installation en 'métropole'...vécue comme un 'rapatriement', un 'retour' – où l'accès à la France idéale rêvée dans les colonies rendait insensible cette occultation qui ne disait pas son nom." In *La mémoire sépharade*, 25.
153   Cairns. *Post-War Jewish Women's Writing in French*. Oxford: Legenda, 2011, 145.

Hence, we can imagine the confluence of several factors that contributed to the eventual "opening of the faucet" for Jewish (women) writers from the Maghreb. As these narratives have taken longer to find their way out of obscurity, we may ask why their writing has been eclipsed particularly in the academy of international French studies (where I began my own archaeological dig in francophone literature)? Here, Cairns suggests that there has been a tendency, since 1967, to demote Jewish francophone writing relative to its Arab counterpart, due to the fact that Israel – and hence diasporic Jews who are "commonly if erroneously associated" with her – has "increasingly been condemned as a colonial power."[154]

Both the European and North African Jewish communities experienced major traumas during the twentieth century; the Shoah decimated much of European Jewish cultural life of its content, and colonialism followed by the post-colonial exodus robbed North African Jews of their homelands and ancient cultural anchors. Maghreb Jews who assimilated into French culture had lost most of their heritage and for many years repressed the voices that were authentically theirs in order to fit into a society epitomizing Western values. One well-known personality in France, the late "father of Deconstruction" and Algerian Jew, Jacques Derrida, spoke of the "amnesia" that stripped him of his Jewish cultural and religious heritage.[155]

Interestingly, the Israeli critic Gideon Ofrat posits, in his revealing study *The Jewish Derrida* (2001), that Derrida's deconstructionist philosophy grew from his early influences and the fragments of his Jewish identity: "Indeed, the assimilation of Algerian Jews, as Derrida testifies, condemns Judaism to a state of virtual death, respiratory arrest."[156] Derrida himself says "…I carry the negative heritage, if I may say so, of this amnesia, which I never had the courage, the strength, and the means to resist…This incapacity, this handicapped memory, is the subject of my lament here. That is my grievance."[157]

I see this as similar to the loss of Jewish Ashkenazi-French memory of which Alain Finkielkraut speaks, that was a result of the obsessions

---
154   Ibid., 4-5.
155   Derrida, *Le Monolinguisme de l'Autre*. Paris: Editions Galilée, 1996.
156   Ofrat, *The Jewish Derrida*, 17.
157   Derrida, *Monolingualism of the Other*, translated by Patrick Mensah. Stanford: Stanford UP, 1998, 53-54.

and phobias of the post-Shoah society in which he grew up. Repression of memory and identity sought through assimilation did not just bring relief from victimization, but rather fostered an absence so profound that (French) Jewish identity lost much of its essence. These Jews became alienated and exiled even to themselves. Finkielkraut argues for a confrontation with this absence, with the empty sense of what Jewish identity might have come to mean for Ashkenazi Jews in France. Contrary to its promises, assimilation has deprived European Jews of memory and self-understanding, he suggests, and the price for finally becoming insiders in Western culture and societies was to become outsiders to themselves.[158]

The two documentary films, *The Forgotten Refugees* (2005) and *The Silent Exodus* (2002),[159] are both productions made to bring awareness to this event that seems grossly underrepresented in terms of historical international recognition as well as more "internally" among Western Jews.[160] Both films are rich in footage documenting Jewish life and histories in the regions as well as raw footage from anti-Jewish riots, demonstrations, massacres and lynchings dating from the years between the 1930s to the 1960s. The films also show how the Jewish refugees who immigrated to Israel lived in *maʾabarot* or temporary tent-camps, in conditions similar to the oft-exposed and lamentable living conditions of Palestinian refugees.

In these films Jews who experienced the exodus from Islamic Lands are given a chance to give their testimonials recounting their memories of how they experienced the last years in their home countries, what was lost, and of how they go on living despite irreparable material and emotional damage. Among them are numerous scholars, historians, and politicians, as well as (peace) activists, musicians and artists, talking about their hopes that increased awareness of their experience may lead to recognition and better understanding of these politically and historically complex and crippling events.

---

158   See Finkielkraut, *The Imaginary Jew*, London: University of Nebraska Press, 1994.
159   Pierre Rochav, *The Silent Exodus*, ca. 2002, and Michael Grynszpan and Tommy Schwarcz. *The Forgotten Refugees*, produced by the David Project, a non-profit educational initiative, 2005.
160   See also Regina Waldman's address to the U.N. Human Rights Council in Geneva on the issue of the nearly 1 million Jewish Refugees from the Arab countries. 8 April 2008. YouTube 15 April 2008. Web. Waldman is chair of JIMENA (Jews Indigenous to the Middle East and North Africa).

The Forgotten Refugees is produced by the David Project, a non-profit organization seeking to "promote a fair and honest understanding of the Arab-Israeli conflict" (www.thedavidproject.org), and the film avoids melodramatic angles in areas such as the choice of style of accompanying music, narrator's voice or still photos and live footage. In this sense it gives what seems a less biased image and message, and aims at a more balanced socio-politico-historical understanding, as opposed to the more emotional choices in the approach of *The Silent Exodus*. My intention here is not to undertake a film analysis evaluating these films' merits or cinematic value, but rather to indicate a few relevant issues for any study of Sephardic and *Mizrahi* Jewry. First it should be noted that the films are produced relatively recently (2002 and 2005), and they are the only ones of this kind aimed at a general audience, with the hopes of having a wide appeal in raising public awareness of the issue of the historical omission or eclipse of the fate of Jews in Arab lands.[161]

They offer a "live" glimpse into what Jewish culture looked like in Arab lands and what the exiled communities hope to accomplish as they are given the opportunity to express themselves. In this way, the two films function as important locations or opportunities for Oriental Jewish voices not only to be heard, but also to hear themselves publicly enunciate their silenced history. The production of the films, (and, one may add, the establishment of organizations like JIMENA: Jews Indigenous to the Middle East and North Africa, and The David Project) is in response to what is seen from a Jewish perspective as a critical missing element in the international representations of the conflict in the Middle East, and the perceived biased focus of international organizations like the European Union and the United Nations with regards to the predicament of Palestinian refugees.

With the Palestinian refugees occupying the central stage of the Arab-Israeli drama, it is often overlooked or excluded that what took place in the years from 1948 through the 1980's is understood by some to be a "pop-

---

161   The recent French four-part art documentary *Jews and Arabs: Intimate Strangers* (2013) directed by Karim Miské, adds a valuable dimension to the understanding of the shared and divergent histories of the two peoples. It covers the length of Jewish-Muslim relations throughout the centuries, from the advent of Muhammed until recent flair-ups of violence and conflict in Europe.

ulation exchange"; approximately 540,000 Palestinian Arabs were uprooted as a result of the 1948 war, and more than 860,000 Jews fled Arab countries starting in 1948. One article supporting this view, entitled "Exchanges of Populations Worldwide," Malka Hillel Shulewitz and Raphael Israeli point out that contrary to the Jewish refugees who have been absorbed, resettled, educated and retrained in Israel, only a handful of Palestinian refugees have been accepted and absorbed by Arab lands (notably in Jordan). Rather, they remain the longest-living refugee problem since the Second World War.

By rejecting plans proposed by Israel to absorb and rehabilitate, the surrounding Arab nations are seen by these researchers as demonstrating a preference to "perpetuate the refugee problem by maintaining the refugee status."[162] Heavily aided and funded by the UNRWA, Europe and the United States, the Palestinian refugee camps have changed from a temporary situation requiring urgent solutions by all the parties involved in the conflict, to one with the potential for permanence and no immediate need to resolve. The refugee camps have also become – as the world is well aware – fertile recruiting centers for terrorists and radical factions of Islam, and Shulewitz and Israeli underline what they believe is the shared responsibility of the supporting nations to help dismantle them.[163]

The Jews with origins in the Mashreq and the Maghreb eventually decided they needed to speak out in order to ensure that their story, almost forgotten by self-imposed silence and muted all the more by the different national and international histories and agendas, would be heard. Their story is articulated and exposed, recognized and validated. Now that the memories of the Shoah, in their most raw form, have become part of the world's conscience, will it become possible for other Jewish memories to (re)claim their right to be told?[164] Malka

---

162   Malka Hillel Shulewitz, *The Forgotten Millions: The Jewish Exodus from Arab Lands*. New York: Cassell, 1999,136.
163   Ibid.
164   For a pathbreaking study on the relations between Holocaust memory and decolonization, see Michael Rothberg's *Multidirectional Memory: Remembering the Holocaust in the Age of Decolonization*. Stanford: Stanford UP, 2009. Rothberg posits a new theory of remembrance challenging the basic tenets of current thinking on cultural memory and group identity. He asks if the remembrance of one history erases others from view, and contrasts the model of "competitive memory" coining the notion of "multidirectional memory," where memories interact productively and in unexpected ways in the public sphere.

Shulewitz asks if it was because this transfer of whole communities took place when the tragedy that befell European Jewry was still fresh like a gaping wound, that the suffering of Jews in Arab lands left its imprint neither on the contemporary annals of the Jewish people nor on the consciousness of the free world.[165] Once the Jewish communities in Arab lands were permanently obliterated, the voices of these communities were also lost for several decades. However, it is more and more evident that the time has come for their voices to be heard. It is not only individual narratives we find, but there is also an increased determination among the Jews from Islamic lands to organize, materialize and publicize their own history, as exemplified by initiatives like these films and organizations.

What Makes Literature Jewish?

As we embark on the literary considerations of this inquiry into history, memory and identity of Jews from North Africa, it might be useful to reflect for a moment on the often-ambiguous question of "what is Jewish literature?" As Michael Kramer points out in his provocative essay "Race, Literary History, and the Jewish Question," such an inquiry is as problematic as the "thorny political question 'Who is a Jew.'"[166] Some of the telling words that come up in his essay (pluralism, divergent, hybrid, indeterminacy, multiple possibilities, essence, ambiguity, unique Jewish spirit, impossible to categorize, irreducible, fragmented), and the critical responses that follow the essay, give us an idea of how vague, how hybrid, and how challenging a discussion this has been, and continues to be. Especially considering that Jews have historically not been defined by a nation state, nor by a common language or even a common culture, but "only" by the problematic and now politically incorrect and ideologically dangerous intertwined terms of "race" and "religion," we might wonder what could be the unifying theme, form, or function to make this literature "Jewish." Once we consider some of these current challenges, we can

---
165   Ibid., xvi.
166   Kramer, "Race, Literary History and the 'Jewish Question," *Prooftexts* 21 (2001): 289.

add the Maghrebi dimension to "Jewish literature" to further complicate – or render interesting – the issues we are faced with relating to classification of French/francophone literature.

Kramer's observation that for Jews "...diversity was never the negation of unity" offers a salient reminder of how, historically, diversity typically becomes the negation of unity. We may suggest then, that by their intrinsically "diverse nature" (dare I use such a deterministic term?), Jewish literature and Jewish people offer a valuable example of unity in difference, the very hope we see in today's world as globalization forces us to consider unity with those different from us, people whose ideas vary from ours, and with whom we may not share much except our condition as human beings.

Jewish literature can be, but is not always, recognized as literature written by a Jew, and one might suggest that in order for the literature to be received as "Jewish" it also needs to display some sort of Jewish content or theme. We can think of many known works written by Jews (Spinoza, Freud, Marx, Bergson, Heine, Proust and even Kafka, for example) whose content for most may not invite any "Jewish" reading at all, while for others it is very possible to see traces of Jewish textual allusions in the form of an argument or other non-specific hints at the Jewishness of the author. In the end, Kramer's essay puts into perspective the various ways in which Jewish literature has been historically defined as Jewish by different critics, but he balances on a tightrope in the circus of modern academic discourse (and is aware of this) by concluding that "Without Jewish bodies, we cannot imagine Jewish souls,"[167] underlining the "racial" or religious component of what can be termed Jewish literature. Shifting this concluding quote from Kramer toward our current inquiry of vanished Sephardic women's bodies from the Maghreb, and their often missing voices in post-colonial discourse in France and Israel, we can see the importance of imagining and representing this other. We are offered glimpses into the souls of the exiled Jewish women writers thanks to the existence of their writing Jewish bodies, now transplanted to France.

By engaging in "certainties of race," Kramer is criticized for "not recognizing the many different kinds of cultural histories that make up diasporic Jewry."[168] Another issue of critique is that "One doesn't have to

---

167   Ibid., 314.
168   Bryan Cheyette, ibid., 324.

invoke a fundamentalist definition of Jewish race to see that... [many] works are viewed by their readers as making a contribution to the consciousness of the Jews as an ethnic group, although ...[they] also have a strong universal axis of meaning."[169] Kramer responds to some of his critics by noting that "Culture will always be the focus of Jewish literary studies, but race will always be its foundation."[170]

Eva Martin Sartori and Madelaine Cottenet-Hage, on the other hand, do not think that the mere fact of being Jewish makes one a Jewish writer. In deciding who to include in their anthology of Jewish women writers in France, they found that what is just as important to lend credibility to the label of Jewish writer, is rather "a writer who is writing about Jewish communities, creating Jewish characters, examining the future of Jewish exile – their relationship to Israel, to their host countries..."[171] From this perspective, theoretically any writer who engages with Jewish topics such as these could be counted as a "Jewish writer," and this would certainly avoid the sticky and related question of "who is a Jew?" Or, conversely, it would also eliminate writers who are Jewish but who do not at all engage in any topics relating to anything specifically, or particularly, of Jewish concern.

One of the most valuable lessons of post-colonial discourse has been that we are made acutely aware of how important it is for individuals and communities to have a voice, to define themselves and to write their own history rather than being passively written by those who speak for them or define them. Narratives by those who did not historically have the power to write themselves are finding their rightful place in libraries and bookstores, media and, most importantly, in classroom syllabi. We need to remain vigilant and open-eyed since there will always be unheard voices whose testimonies and narratives shed light on a part of the history of humanity (and in-humanity) often unfamiliar to us. The narrative of the marginalized or overshadowed, repressed or self-effaced can make us aware of the many shades of gray that exist where too frequently only black and white are represented. Generally speaking, the black and white

---

169   Gershon Shaked, ibid., 333-334..
170   Ibid., 346.
171   Sartori, Eva Martin and Madeleine Cottenet-Hage, eds. *Daughters of Sarah: Anthology of Jewish Women Writers in France*, Teaneck: Holes & Meier, 2006, xii.

view is an easier sell. With grey, the reader has to assume a more reflected reading, and eventually, hopefully, a similar nuanced view of the world. The story of Sephardic Jews in the post-colonial era represents one such example where there are many shades of grey. Though mostly entirely vanished from Arab lands, their voices are claiming their place in contemporary discourse on identity, memory and human rights. As Hélène Trigano notes: "By claiming the right to speak, the *Sephardim* access a representation of what happened to them, of what they were, of what they have become, and in that, finding support to give a sense to their existence."[172] The Franco-Sephardic literary contributions about to be analyzed reflect the spirit of this existence, a spirit operating in what Thomas Nolden calls the "liberating effect of displacement" experienced by Jewish women writing in renewed diasporas.[173]

---

[172] "A travers la prise de parole, les sépharades accèdent à une représentation de ce qui s'est passé, de ce qu'ils étaient, de ce qu'ils sont devenus, en y prenant appui pour donner un sens à leur existence." *Mémoire sépharade*, 247.
[173] Nolden, *Voices of the Diaspora. Jewish Women Writing in Contemporary Europe*, Evanston: Northwest UP, 2005, xxvi.

Chapter 4

The Sephardic Woman and Post-colonial Discourse

To write is to try to understand, to try to repeat the unrepeatable, to write is also to bless a life which has not been blessed.
Clarice Lispector

Perhaps the time has come to look more closely at ruptures, breaches, breaks, to identify them more precisely, to see how Jews endured them, to understand that not everything of value that existed before a break was either salvaged or metamorphosed, but was lost, and that often some of what fell by the wayside can become, through our retrieval, meaningful to us.
Y.H. Yerushalmi

Theoretical and Literary Considerations

Having considered some significant historical points of reference for Jews as they relate to the Maghreb – from the ambiguous period of colonization to the difficult event of the modern Jewish exodus – it is now possible to take a more informed approach to the development of the literary explorations of Jewish women writers of North African origins. The project to evaluate the issue of Jewish narratives of writers with Maghreb roots has been a response to a general lack of awareness of the scope of Jewish presence in the Arab world until the middle of the twentieth century, of their treatment by the dominant Muslim culture, and of the complicated colonial and post-colonial circumstances the Jews had to endure. Furthermore,

Sephardi/Mizrahi narratives have often been excluded both within the dominant Ashkenazi Jewish world view (as in Israel and the West), in the discourse on the Arab-Israeli crisis in the Middle East, and in the world in general. Since it is from my literary involvement with post-colonial Jewish women's narratives that this entire project came to be, it is especially fitting to acknowledge the importance of literature in the process of transmitting a better and fuller understanding of the human experience as it traverses, and indeed creates, history, for as literary critic and professor Françoise Lionnet points out: "...literature allows us to enter into the subjective process of writers and their characters, and thus allows us to better understand the unique perspectives of subjects who are agents of transformation and hybridization in their own narratives, as opposed to being the objects of knowledge as in the discourse of social science."[174]

Literature, then, has an important empowering function, since we as readers may come to experience the other's subjectivity in the very process of its self-fashioning. An agent is a person that exerts power or produces an effect, and it is exactly these two words – power and effect – that suggest the relevance of the production of narrative and literature in history. Although I hope that Jonathan Culler's suggestion that literature has lost its centrality is too pessimistic, I do find particularly reaffirming his statement that "...in the humanities and the social sciences everything is literature."[175] It may seem as though the traditionally strictly guarded border between sciences and the humanities is blurring, in a positive recognition that one is deeply compromised without the other in the quest for human knowledge and understanding. Our concepts of knowledge and improved understanding of world events and/in history have begun to include and make necessary – indeed critical – subjective narratives hitherto excluded. Imagine "a sociology that does not transform those studied into objects but preserves in its analytic procedures the presence of the subject as actor and experiencer," as Sandra Harding invokes in her essay "Feminist Standpoint

---

[174] Lionnet, "Logiques Métisses", "Cultural Appropriation and Post-colonial Representations," in *Post-colonial Subjects. Francophone Women Writers.* Mary Jean Green et al, eds., Minneapolis: U of Minn. P, 1996, 323.
[175] Culler, "The Literary in Theory," in *What's Left of Theory?* Judith Butler, John Guillory and Kendall Thomas, eds., New York: Routledge, 2000, 289.

Epistemologies."¹⁷⁶ As we move from the historical to the literary we can appreciate the intimacy that exists between them, and confirm that the literature of the Jews of North Africa, embedded in the narrative of their history, is invaluable in the context of evolving world narratives of marginalized, hybrid, and exiled peoples. Official discourse – and we may include here all historical discourse such as colonial, post-colonial, and those globalizing discourses in the age of information technology leading to a rapid democratization of knowledge – tends to want to create fixed identities, and especially those of the other.

Edward Said made us aware of this imbalance when he stated: "What matters a great deal more than the stable identity kept current in official discourse is the contestatory force of an interpretative method whose material is the disparate, but intertwined and interdependent, and above all overlapping streams of historical experience."¹⁷⁷ The Jewish experience in the Arab world is one such "overlapping stream of historical experience" which clearly presents itself as a "contestatory force" compared to the more commonly heard experiences, in the francophone post-colonial discourse, of colonized peoples such as Arabo-Muslim men and women.¹⁷⁸ Interestingly though, this is hardly one of the experiences Said had in mind when he speaks of, and for, "great decolonizing resistance movements" like those seen in all parts of Africa, and "mass uprisings of the 1980's"¹⁷⁹ such as the Palestinian Intifadas and the collapse of the communist regimes of Eastern Europe, as symbolized and immemorialized by the fall of the Berlin wall. We may ask why not, and offer a "contestatory force" to such selective critical narratives.

Post-colonial narratives, and the critique shaped by the same historical and cultural forces, have taken on particularly liberating forms since one of the main thrusts of post-colonial movements has been the idea of freedom of identity, and freedom in expressing these identi-

---

176   Harding, "From Feminist Empiricism to Feminist Standpoint Epistemologies" in *From Modernism to Postmodernism*. Malden, Mass: Blackwell Publishers, 1996, 629.
177   Said, *Culture and Imperialism*, 312.
178   Both Ella Shohat and Regina Waldman may represent two such "forces" giving voice to different historical experiences.
179   Ibid., 331.

ties. Most importantly, they have been fueled by the desire for self-determination, not only for nations, but also for groups within nations, individuals and, of particular interest to us, for women. Some of the important theoretical issues to bear in mind when considering the nature and impact of post-colonial discourses include, as Homi Bhabha points out, the fact that unlike Marxism (which, despite its progressive nature, has been unable to accommodate difference in its academic and theoretical manifestations), the post-colonial state of being does not have a master text, and this contributes to the plethora of possibilities in its expressions.

This can seem threatening to some, of course, and the lack of defined meanings or values in combination with the "openness" may point toward anarchism and chaos, some of the fears elaborated by the ideas of the postmodern condition. Pointing to some of the central figures and approaches in the "post-" world, Bhabha identifies the Derridean deconstructive gesture that literary and cultural scholar Gyatri Spivak speaks of as well as the "contrapuntal nature" of the post-colonial critique in relation to the West that Edward Said has developed.[180] The grand narratives of Western culture such as the Enlightenment and the universalism it boasted, have been devalued and replaced by a new appreciation of difference à la Derrida, and as we look to post-colonial narratives we can delight in the "moment" itself of *différence*, where we are encouraged and invited to undertake readings that produce meaning rather than protect the significance of imposed values and world views. This opens up the possibility of rebuilding our perceptions, not just of the so-called familiar world we think we know, but also of the other and of the other's text.

In the preface to her translation of Derrida's *De la Grammatologie*, *Of Grammtology* (1998), Spivak suggests that the deconstructive reader "…[locates] the moment in the text which harbors the unbalancing of the equation, the sleight of the hand at the limit of a text which cannot be dismissed simply as a contradiction."[181] Why not take this "textual" Derridaen view and extend it to the narrative of the Jews from Arab

---

180 See "The Post-colonial Critic: Homi Bhabha Interviewed by David Bennett and Terry Collits." *Arena* 96 (1991): 53.
181 Gayatri Spivak, "Translator's Preface," in Derrida, *Of Grammatology*. Baltimore: John Hopkins UP, 1998, xiix.

lands, which can be seen as exactly that "moment" which "harbors the unbalancing of the equation" of the official discourse on the complex and painful Israeli-Palestinian conflict, where the different historical texts have not been scrutinized sufficiently for their contradictions?

It seems too simple to blame all the ills of the Arab world (including Israel/Palestine) on colonial and imperial violations, for this is forgetting historical events and perspectives, which is a "symptomatic forgetting" very much dominating most official discourses on contemporary world conflicts today. To push the argument a bit further: where do we place the Arabo-Muslim invasions and conquest under the prophet Mohammed and in the name of Islam, if not in the same traditions as imperialism, colonialism and other "-isms" that have abused power, revolutionized, invaded, demanded, and ruled the other, and whose goals have been to impose a specific world view simultaneously demanding that this view be embraced lest you cease to exist?

The various discourses, or systems of knowledge, produced by political ideologies such as these have historically been established by those in power to produce and manage the other, as elaborated primarily by Foucault, concepts also at the basis of Said's discussion of the political, sociological, and even imaginative domination of the Orient by Western Imperialism. To the Jews in the Arab world who resisted the –ism of Islamism or Islamization of their people, the system of knowledge as defined and produced by the Muslim conquerors in power in turn managed and produced the Jews as inferior *dhimmi*, and therefore, for more than 1300 years, dominated and narrated their other in a classic example of imposed power relations.

The subaltern Jew could not speak since she was subject to the hegemony of Islam. Nor was she heard, and today her narrative is more or less completely erased from that part of the world. Thus, Jewish Maghrebi literature has been excluded from two worlds, from two canons. Speaking of the early Jewish literature in the French language in North Africa, Danielle Levy-Mongelli points out how it just didn't fit in anywhere, and here we may recognize a parallel to what we have seen earlier in this study as the Jews in colonial Maghreb felt neither here nor there. Too Jewish to feel comfortable among the French, and too French to be accepted among the Arabs: "This Jewish literature of French language in North Africa could participate neither in French literature of the *métropole*, since it referred itself to a France emptied of substance, nor in the Arab literature of the period, of Arabic or French language, since this one suffered directly from colonial oppression or has its own issues with it."[182]

Guy Dugas, who has written a seminal book dedicated to Jewish francophone authors from the Maghreb, notes that excluded from the recognized beginnings (coinciding with the awakenings of nationalist feelings and movements) of francophone literature of the Maghreb is the sixty texts or so authored by Jewish writers in the Maghreb published before 1949. He underlines the fact that the concept itself of "Littérature Maghrébine," or Maghrebi literature, is closely linked to the socio-political evolution of North Africa and is essentially forged on a national and ideological basis.[183] Now that these Jewish writers write from France, and no longer from within the Maghreb, their corpus represents a specific minority literature, but negligible neither in quantity nor in quality. "Approximately 350 books and innumerable journal and magazine articles covering various aspects of the past and the present of Judaism appear every year in France. More than three dozen Jewish writers born after the Shoah have found access to France's major publishing houses, joining the ranks of the prominent writers of the older generation."[184]

The unexpected and amazing Jewish revival in France after the Second World War is, as we have seen, due in large part to the massive arrival of Jews from the Maghreb, making French Jewish culture all the more diverse.[185] But the arrival of over 200,000 Jews from North Africa

---

182   "Cette littérature juive de langue française en Afrique du Nord ne pouvait participer, ni de la littérature française de la métropole, puisqu'elle se référait à une France vidée de substance, ni de littérature arabe de l'époque, de langue arabe ou de langue française, puisque celle-ci subissait directement l'oppression coloniale ou qu'elle réglait ses comptes avec elle." Danielle Levy-Mogelli, "Un cas particulier d'aliénation culturelle: les Juifs d'Afrique du Nord dans l'Aventure Coloniale Française." In *Juifs du Maroc. Identité et Dialogue.* Grenoble: Sauvage, 1980, 253.
183   Dugas, *La Littérature Judéo-Maghrébine d'Expression Française.* Paris: L'Harmattan, 1990, 10.
184   Nolden, *In Lieu of Memory*, 2.
185   This revitalization of the Jewish communities in France is well documented in the extraordinary and prize-winning two-part documentary on Jewish life in France, *Comme un Juif en France/Being Jewish in France* (2007), directed by Yves Jeuland.

not only diversified and rendered more heterogeneous the image of the French Jew; it also infused the very shared experience of "responding/acting as a Jews" to a new and more vibrant expression, in the face of joy as well as in the face of sadness or fear.

As noted by Ady Steg, when the Jewish community responded to the outbreak of the Six Day War in 1967: "The Jews of North Africa uninhibited us [the *Ashkenazim*]. They pushed us to scream, to cry, to sing, to invade the street. They had no complex. And France observed with curiosity the extraverted Judaism."[186] Furthermore, the Sephardic role in the literary burgeoning has been substantial. Dugas points out that this literary contribution remains profoundly Maghrebean by its rootedness in the Maghreb, by the spaces and the imagination it evokes, and by the themes that it continues to put forth.[187] The increased call to ethnic rights and expression in French society as seen in the 1970 onward, would eventually affect Jewish literary expressions as well, and on this important topic historian Michel Abitbol adds:

> *It is clear that the oft-cited "re-Judaization" of French Jewry in the 1970s and 1980s can in no way be attributed exclusively to one or the other segment of the community. It is the result of a series of historical and cultural factors affecting French society generally on the one hand, and Jewish populations throughout the world on the other. The first of these factors is the waning, as de Gaulle's legacy faded, of the so-called "Jacobin" ideology, the notion (deriving from the Jacobin party of the French Revolution) that the state must level all differences. In the 1970s, minority groups started demanding recognition of their particularities and of their "right to be different." Simultaneously, and no less importantly, universalistic ideologies such as Marxism lost their appeal. In such a climate, it is easy to see how along with regionalist groups seeking various kinds of autonomy, French Jews came to adopt a more "ethnic" posture.*[188]

---

186   Katz, *Burdens of Brotherhood*, 246, quotes from Michel Winock, *La France et les juifs*. Paris: Seuil, 2004, 323.
187   Dugas, *La Littérature Judéo-Maghrébine*, 15.
188   Abitbol, "The Integration of North African Jews in France," 257-258.

The right to be different exists together with the right to equality before the law in this difference, and that was a completely new and liberating experience for the Jews from Maghreb. As the years passed and the initial challenges of being new immigrants began to fade, a balance was increasingly struck between equality and particularism. Nolden writes that the debate in France to "define and imagine the Jew," in addition to the reaffirmation of Jewish ritual and religion called *teshuva* [literally, return, repentance], "would hardly have gained such momentum without the impact of Jewish immigrants from the Maghreb, who during the era of colonialism had retained a much stronger relationship toward the Jewish religion than had the vast majority of French-born Jews."[189]

The opportunities to express one's ethnicity and particularism have been welcomed with enthusiasm by Jews from North Africa, since they see themselves as distinctly different from their Ashkenazi compatriots. More traditionalist, the Judeo-Maghrebian community has built more synagogues, and ordained more rabbis than the *Ashkenazim*. The *Sephardim*[190] have manifested their presence in French society and the various communities where they have settled by opening religious schools, restaurants, markets, and media outlets such as radio stations, music releases specific to the Judeo-Maghrebian culture etc. Many neighborhoods in larger cities, such as Belleville and the Marais in Paris, and others in Marseille and Lyon have become gathering places and quarters to "come home to" for a feeling of "*chez soi*" in the middle of a big and often alienating city. With the particular manifestations of their cultural heritage as a "rediasporized" heritage, we can see the Jews from North Africa as contributing to the growing number of "dislocated sites of protestation to

---

189   Nolden, *In Lieu of Memory*, 23.
190   It is important to note that while French Jews from North Africa identify today as *Sephardim*, they did not see themselves as such until their arrival in France. This fact is underscored by two interviewees in Jeuland's documentary *Comme un Juif en France/Being Jewish in France* (2007). Rachel Cohen, a Moroccan Jew and now principal of a Jewish Day School in Paris, says she never identified as Sephardic until she came to France. Eva Labi, executive director of the Alliance Israélite Universelle, was born in Tunisia and states: "In my home we never used the terms Ashkenazi or Sephardic. We always said a Jew from Germany, or a Jew from Poland, or a Jew from Turkey or a Jew from Morocco."

the hegemonic, homogenizing forces of globalization,"[191] evident in France, given all her immigrant communities.

Diasporic Voices

"Diaspora" today speaks to diverse groups of displaced persons and communities moving across the globe, but originally the term had a religious significance describing the plight of Jews living outside the Land of Israel after expulsion by Roman or Babylonian conquests (587 B.C.E. and 70 C.E. respectively). In the 16th century the term was applied to that of the Black African diaspora brought on by the slave trade. Braziel and Mannur note, "Once conceptualized as an exilic or nostalgic dislocation from homeland, diaspora has attained new epistemological, political, identity-based resonances as it points of reference proliferate."[192] However, these authors caution against the uncritical application of the term to all contexts of global displacement and movement, since it is often used as a catchall phrase to speak of and for all such movements, however privileged, and for all dislocations, even symbolic ones.[193] A writer, by mere virtue of writing, can be seen as in exile, since the text itself can be a metaphor for the land to which the writer has become exiled. Or, phrased otherwise, the act of writing is "always, already" exile, the same way as exile is always, already writing. By extension, as noted by Said, exile is itself becoming a more common experience challenging the old canons of knowledge, and in this way he sees it as a positive thing that more human beings live in its condition:

> *Exile, far from being the fate of nearly forgotten unfortunates who are dispossessed and expatriated, becomes something closer to a norm, an experience of crossing boundaries and charting new territories in defiance of the classic canonic enclosures, however much its loss and sadness should be acknowledged and registered.*[194]

---

191   Braziel and Mannur, *Theorizing Diaspora*. Malden: Blackwell Publishing, 2003, 7.
192   Ibid., 4.
193   Ibid., 3.
194   Said, *Culture and Imperialism*, 317.

Diaspora and exile, these two terms have been part of the general Jewish existential awareness for centuries and, although not directly experienced by every generation, they have a predominant place in Jewish memory, narrative and cultural traditions. The traditional prayer for a return to the original home, the womb, if we might call the Land of Israel the place of conception of the Jewish people, is still recited today in Jewish daily prayers and holidays. Daniel Sibony, for one, sees this loss of the origin as a potentially positive, creative state, an eternal source of possibilities, allowing an existence in a passage in-between or *entre-deux* where life happens rather than being fixed and static, hence unnatural. "…it is necessary to have an origin that 'accepts' to become multiplied, broken into pieces, decomposed, recomposed, in short that consents to be referred to as fertile in-betweens in the form of living passages rather than fixed messages."[195] This constant movement and existence in-between is what the Jewish narrative manifests, and it is in the historically "being in passage" that this openness to creative possibilities exists.

Another distinctive feature of Jewish diaspora is the repeated experience of rediasporization. This results in a situation where, to borrow a term from Homi Bhabha, the imaginary Jewish homeland has been "less than one and double."[196] Zion is longed for and imagined through Cordoba, Cairo, or Vilna, and these frequently layered one on the other such that Cairo becomes a remembered Cordoba and the new Jerusalem a remembered Vilna.[197] For the Jews of the Maghreb, the rediasporization is a shift from living in diaspora in Morocco, Algeria or Tunisia, to living it again in France, South America or Canada. It can be Belleville as a remembered Tunis, Montréal as a remembered Blida, or Caracas as a remembered Fez, all while singing for a return to *Eretz Israel*, "Next year in Jerusalem!" But for Cixous, for example, the traditional prayer *"L'an prochain à Jérusalem"* [next

---

195 "…il faut une origine qui 'accepte' de se laisser démultiplier, mettre en morceaux, décomposer, recomposer, bref qui consente à se reporter en des entre-deux féconds en forme de passages à vivre plutôt que des messages à fixer." Sibony, *Entre-deux*, 65-66.
196 See Bhabha, *The Location of Culture*. London: Routledge, 1994.
197 Daniel and Jonathan Boyarin, *Powers of Diaspora*. Minneapolis: U of Minnesota P, 2002, 11.

year in Jerusalem] became in the mind of her young exilic self in the Maghreb: *"L'an prochain à Alger"* [Next year in Algiers.][198] In this way the story of the Jews "in passage" and "in-between" is fertile and multidirectional.

The notions of displacement and exile are also predominant in post-colonial studies, and are one of the great catalysts for creative writing. Albert Memmi reminds us of exile's redeeming quality: "Exile is painful, but through fabulation, it is also the mould/matrix of our progress...exile can be fruitful..."[199] Writing is exile, after all. For Jews, the historically perpetual existence of exile has forced them into a creatively fruitful modus operandi of survival, as suggested by Sibony. The book, the text, the Torah or Hebrew Bible, has become a way to feel at home on the road. In exile we maintain our identity differently, because of different external forces than those encountered in a homeland, or, as it may be defined in a nation-state. The boundaries between home and exile can become blurred the longer our exile subsist, and for Jews exiled from the Land of Israel in the initial expulsions of 586 B.C.E and 70 C.E respectively, coming "home" could mean a new type of exile. For as photographer Frédéric Brenner notes in the introduction to his twenty-five year long project photographing Jews around the world, only after Jews arrived as new immigrants to Israel did they realize exactly "how," for example, Moroccan they were, and that what they left behind as they were either forcefully or voluntarily exiled had actually come to define home. Feeling at home in Israel, the land from whence their ancestors had been originally dispersed into Diaspora, was not necessarily easy or natural:

> *Exile? Home? What do these words mean when the dimension of exile is omnipresent in the land of Israel? This was what I wanted to investigate: If, for two thousand years, the issue was how to remain Jewish among strangers, in Israel the issue has become how to keep one's identity among Jews. Jews had to settle in Israel in order to become Yemenite, German, Ethiopian, to understand that they had actually been at home, in exile.*[200]

---

198   Cixous, *Les Rêveries*, 126.
199   "L'exil est douloureux, mais par fabulation, c'est aussi la matrice de notre progrès...l'exil peut être fructueux..." *Postcolonialisme et Autobiographie*, 70.
200   Brenner, "Photographs," *Diaspora: Homelands in Exile*, xii.

Reflecting on the meanings of exile and home in a Jewish context makes the already fluid elements of exile and displacement more problematic. The distinction between home and exile blurs when it is experienced over and over, and the identification of exile as becoming home, only to become another place from whence to become exiled, is a dizzying concept indeed. But the displacement and reemergence brings a certain defiance that can become a source of creativity. For Algerian born historian Albert Bensoussan, "the Jewish and Sephardic diaspora has invested itself…in the voice and in writing as a mode of substitution for the impossible patch of land as reference, for the devastation of a refused identity. In the end, the book as homeland."[201] The book is thus a portable homeland, where that actual attachment to a land with national borders (to defend) becomes instead a concept of detachment, and yet in this detachment a "national" identity can be sought. We have here a paradox and a challenge. But as Daniel and Jonathan Boyarin suggest, diaspora can be "a theoretical and historical model to replace self-determination,"[202] and we can only begin to imagine a world without the need for national borders and the conflicts to maintain them. I admit that the Boyarin brothers' idealistic view of diaspora is quite appealing and, as they themselves recognize, the Jewish Diaspora, until the establishment of the modern Jewish nation state in 1948, has proven to offer to the world a fascinating possibility, a case study, for a collective identity to survive. They theorize:

> *Diaspora offers an alternative "ground" to that of the territorial state for the intricate and always contentious linkage between cultural identity and political organization. Such an alternative ground could avoid the necessarily violent ways in which states resist their own inevitable impermanence. It could also ameliorate the insistence on purity that derives from the dominant, static conception of legitimate collective identity.*[203]

---

201   "la diaspora juive et séfarade s'est investie…dans la voix et l'écrit comme mode de substitution de l'impossible lopin de référence, du ravage refusé de l'identité. En définitive, le livre comme patrie." Bensoussan, *L'Echelle Sépharade*, 24.
202   Jonathan Boyarin, *Theorizing*, 100.
203   Jonathan and Daniel Boyarin, *Powers of Diaspora*, 10.

Nevertheless, although the Jews have lived this kind of a-political existence for over two millennia, and survived, history has showed us at what price. Now that Jews have a territorial state to call home, one that has to continuously justify and defend its existence, it is safe to say that the majority of Jews would prefer to be able to have this land to which they can be attached and where they can defend themselves. However, there is an appealing quality to the Boyarin's point. They continue:

> *A fundamental divide in the contemporary debate about diaspora lies between an approach that focuses on the anamnestic powers of diaspora, creating ties through memory, and an approach that focuses on the liberatory powers of diaspora as a release from monolithic attachment.*[204]

Hélène Cixous experiences this as giving her creative freedom:

> *The possibility of living without taking root was familiar to me. I never call that exile. Some people react to expulsion with a need to belong. For me, as for my mother, the world sufficed, I never needed a terrestrial, localized country. I did not lose Algeria, because I never had it, and I never was it.*[205]

A Buddhist mantra that she came to later in life? Or can a homeland and a collective identity really be carried only in a person's mind? When will it, or will it ever, cease to be an imaginary homeland? After the Jews from the Maghreb were rediasporized out of North Africa in the 1950s and 60s, Albert Bensoussan sees the Jewish notion of homeland as redefined, and thus the literary production of "*les écrivains Judéo-Maghrébins*" – Judeo-Maghbrei writers – adds tremendous value to the concept of human belonging, identity and survival: "…the notion of homeland finds itself redefined ever more clearly, for the lack of a native ground, as homeland of the heart and of the mind…"[206]

---

204   Ibid., 24.
205   Cixous, "My Algériance," 274.
206   "…la notion de patrie s'y trouve redéfinie plus justement, à défaut de sol natal, comme patrie de cœur et d'esprit…" Bensoussan, *L'Echelle Séfarade*, 81.

For as the Jews have written their paradoxical notion of homeland during centuries of diaspora, the fact is, as Cynthia Ozik observes, "nothing thought or written in Diaspora has ever been able to last unless it has been centrally Jewish. If it is centrally Jewish it will last for Jews; if it is not centrally Jewish it will last neither for the Jews nor for the host-nations."[207] This suggests that in order to survive with a specific identity, be it religious, ethnic or national, we have to let the manifestations of that identity be central in the texts that we produce. Can a text be "centrally" Jewish and still manifest a typically hybrid, post-colonial identity? This question refers back to our earlier discussion of what defines Jewish literature.

The fact is that hybridity is not a new component in Jewish identity, since Jews have often lived at the crossroads of culturally diverse places, absorbing the heterogeneity, but at the same time maintaining their specificity. That is perhaps the strength of Jewish narrative and of Jewish existence in exile: adapting to and absorbing external forces, yet distinguishing and protective of the specific Jewish internal strength. Scholar of French and francophone culture, Alec Hargreaves notes, "International migration carries within itself a relentless dynamic of cultural change, leading to new formations that bear the indelible marks of hybridity,"[208] and we may say that the idea of hybridity is no longer an exclusive term, simply describing human identities or narratives.

Today, we see hybrid identities sought after and produced for consumers in every area in contemporary culture from vehicle production (eco-friendly hybrid cars), to films,[209] and restaurants, with their hip and colorful fusion-cuisine and décor. Contrary to these consumer hybrid productions, however, "hybridization is not some happy, consensual mix of diverse cultures," according to Bhabha, but

---

207 Ozik, *What is Jewish Literature?*, 27-28.
208 Hargreaves, *Post-colonial Cultures*, 237.
209 For example the Franco-Israeli-Ethiopian co-production *Va, Viens et Deviens (Live and Become)* (2005) exploring the hybrid identity of its main character, a young Ethiopian refugee believed to be Jewish but who in reality is Christian, and who hides his religion in order to be able to blend in with the Ethiopian Jews airlifted to Israel from dire conditions in a Sudanese refugee camp in the 1980s, to be adopted by an Israeli family comprised of a Franco-Egyptian couple.

takes on a more profound role as a "strategic, translational transfer of tone, value, signification, and position – a transfer of power – from an authoritative system of cultural hegemony to an emergent process of cultural relocation and reiteration that changes the very terms of interpretation and institutionalization, opening up contesting, opposing, innovative, 'other' grounds of subject and object formation."[210] The "othering," then, that functions as a method of preservation, of homogenizing, and of freezing for inspection in a Manichean view of opposites – such as the Western/colonial binarisms of black/white, West/Orient, primitive/cultured – is challenged by the ambiguities inherent in these hybrid identities. With the elaboration of post-colonial discourse and critique, we see an opening that invites new conditions of being, belonging and knowing the other and the self. The impact of the various cultural expressions of hybridity as found in the mundane areas of restaurants and films, for example, should perhaps not be dismissed as simply "marginally significant" in their "happy, consensual mix of diverse cultures," but perhaps rather culturally significant signs of this "opening" process affecting us at all levels: in information, in knowledge, and even in the consumers' awareness and desire to incorporate difference in our lives, albeit in an arguably superficial way.

LANGUAGE MATTERS AND SEPHARDIC LITERATURE

As we know, the question of language can be extremely politically charged, especially in the colonial situation where the colonizer's language has been imposed and has in a sense violated the language and identity of the indigenous population. The mother tongue of North African Jews, whether Arabic or Judeo-Arabic, was relegated to a non-official rank and hence generations came of age either ashamed or afraid to speak it publicly. Contrary to the Arabs, the Jews were seduced by French, since for them France was not only experienced as a colonizer in simply all its negative terms.

---

[210] See "Surviving Theory: A Conversation with Homi K. Bhabha," in *The Pre-Occupation of Post-colonial Studies*, 370.

> *Quickly the North African Jew realized that his perception of the world and his active relations to the world around him passed through a rupture with the maternal language. He was going to forget, reject and re-learn. The dominant language was going to crush and replace the fragile mother tongue; soon (and this is one of the knots of cultural mystification), the Jew would no longer perceive it as an intruder, but it was accepted, courted, respected to the detriment of the other.*[211]

This natural affiliation to the French language, however, did not mean the Jew who wanted to write in French could do so without facing problems of "entitlement" such as described by Hélène Cixous as she remembers her "coming to writing": "You want to write? In what language?...I have learned to speak French in a garden where I was about to be expelled because I was a Jew. My race was that of the losers of Paradise. Write in French? By what right? Show us your credentials, give us the passwords, cross yourself, show us your hands, your paws, what about that nose?"[212] Perfect mastery then, of a literary language acquired at school where you were arbitrarily accepted, or rejected, as permitted to learn. But as both Derrida and Cixous remember, for them, the perfect mastery of the French language became an obsession: "...at school I always wanted to beat the French in French, to be the best 'in French' as they say, to honor my father, who had been driven out."[213]

---

211 "Très vite, le juif d'Afrique du Nord eut conscience que sa perception du monde et sa relation active au monde passaient par une rupture par rapport à la langue de la mère. Il allait oublier, renier, réapprendre. La langue dominante allait écraser et remplacer la langue maternelle fragile ; bientôt (et c'est l'un des nœuds de la mystification culturelle), le juif ne la percevait plus comme intruse, mais elle était acceptée, courtisée, respectée au détriment de l'autre." Danielle Levy-Mogelli, "Un cas particulier," 253.
212 "Tu veux écrire? Dans quelle langue?...j'ai appris à parler français dans un jardin d'où j'étais sur le point d'être expulsée parce que juive. J'étais de la race des perdeurs de paradis. Ecrire en français ? De quel droit ? Montre-nous tes lettres de créance, dis-nous les mots de passe, signe-toi, fais voir tes mains, montre tes pattes, qu'est-ce que c'est ce nez-là ?" Cixous, *Entre l'Ecriture*, 22.
213 Cixous, "My Algériance", 275.

"*Ecrivains judéo-maghrébins d'expression française*" (Judeo-Maghrebi writers of French Expression) is itself a somewhat redundant designation since practically all Jewish writers who came from North Africa would only use French as a way to express themselves in writing. The young Jewish women growing up in North Africa during the colonial period and who immigrated to France during and after decolonialization usually spoke French both at home and at school, and even their parents (especially in Algeria) had fully adopted the French language and used Judeo-Arabic only as a means to communicate with the older generation, and Arabic to speak with the general Arab population.

Contrary to their Arab countrymen who were French subjects, the Jews, as we know, did not generally experience either the French language or French culture as imposed but rather a window of opportunity, a way to gain access to greater social mobility and better prospects for their children, often with hopes of pursuing higher education in the *métropole*. Despite their distinction from Arabo-Muslim writers, the Jewish writers who were also formed under colonization and who more or less had to leave and be rediasporized in the 1950s and 1960s, dealt with many of the same issues and problematics in their writing as did their Arab peer immigrants to France. Both groups struggled with marginalization, hybridization, alienation, and of course nostalgia, if for nothing else than the Mediterranean sun, smells, sounds and tastes.

The Arab writers, however, often had a more deeply conflicted relationship to the French language and experienced guilt from writing (literature) in French causing resentment and difficult choices sometimes leading to "excommunication" or forced exile, whereas these dilemmas were less common among Jewish writers. Cultural and geographic dislocation as well as issues relating to memory and identity have become classic preoccupations among all immigrant writers. One significant difference between Jews and Arabo-Muslim writers is that the latter would often only reach their status of writer and intellectual by feeling as if they had betrayed not only their mother tongue but also, by adopting the French language to write, they felt like they had committed a treasonous act against their own people, their own country, as has been expressed by, among other Algerian writers, the late Assia Djebar.

The problem of language does not disappear in post-colonial discourse, since continued use of the language of the absent colonizer remains deeply ingrained in the independent population as a constant reminder of colonial humiliations and indignation. This complex situation of language was even more complicated for the Jews since, with the loss of the homeland of the Maghreb, they lost the basis for their patois, their culturally unique original language, intimately bound to the environment of North Africa. The Arabs however, would be able to reclaim the prominence of their maternal language with the decolonization and through their nationalist movements, although this often proved to be a difficult task for some writers who had come to relate to Arabic only as an oral language, due to the absence of any official education in Arabic during the colonial period. North African writers would later appropriate and use the French language in their struggle for independence as a subversive message to show the world and those who had held the power of discourse and the discourse of power, that it was now time to let go and recognize the rights of self-rule, self-definition, indeed to writing their own life: to "autobiography."

Mary Ellen Wolf notes that "To write in the language of the colonizer was considered an effective weapon, a way to 'dynamite from the inside,' thereby 'breaking at every level…the founding logic of the French language,'"[214] as she refers to the controlled violence of the writing practices of the Souffles movement in the late sixties and early seventies in Morocco. Françoise Lionnet points to what Moroccan literary critic, novelist and playwright Abdelkebir Khatibi showed us when he referred to the use of the French language as a "means of translating into the colonizer's language a different sensibility, a different vision of the world, a means therefore of transforming the dominant conceptions circulated by the more standard idiom."[215] French is thus appropriated by these new and evolving narratives, turned into a vehicle for expressing a hybrid, heteroglot universe, what Lionnet has coined as "linguistic *métissage*."[216]

It can indeed be seen as a creative act of "taking possession" of a language, which then in turn becomes the basis for the development of

---

214   Wolf, "Rethinking the Radical West: Khatibi and Deconstruction." *L'Esprit Créateur* 2 (1994): 61.
215   Lionnet, *Post-colonial Subjects*, 326.
216   Ibid.

a new linguistic *métissage* or hybridity/mish-mash as we see in many francophone texts, and later in French literature by Arab immigrants, laden with expressions and evocations from typically "non-French" fields of reference. In *Maghreb Pluriel*, Khatibi celebrates this untranslatable moment, which Orientalism (having positioned the other's identity so it "remains the good object of knowledge, the docile body of difference, that reproduces a relation of domination") cannot tolerate, and which continually reminds us of the "primordial question of language and representation."[217]

Considering the Jewish North African authors in France, we can bear in mind the observation, that "…one aspect of Jewish literature may well be the 'deterritorialization of language' pointed to by Deleuze and Guattari, the French philosopher and psychiatrist respectively who wrote many critical essays together. The Jewish writer's language may be laden with elements from forgotten tongues, foreign to the land in which he lives."[218] As Jonathan and Daniel Boyarin have suggested, a palimpsest of memory is created by each rediasporization, as it also happens with language in the historic re-territorialization of Jews.[219] In Jewish texts this linguistic *métissage* is seen by the frequent use of Judeo-Arabic, Hebrew, Arabic and even Spanish words and expressions, and became narrative tools pivotal for the Judeo-Maghrebi author.

Through their use, evoking meaningful memories becomes more effective, and simultaneously reminding the reader of how historically rich and complex the Judeo-Maghrebi references are. Focusing on Jewish writers from the Maghreb, Nolden notes: "Certainly, the Sephardic writers of Maghrebi background brought to their writing their love of the French language and their intimate familiarity with French cultural and literary tradition. But they also brought to it the notion that the idioms of their lost homes are worth being introduced into a French literature that hitherto had prided itself on its adherence to the Cartesian ideal of purity and clarity."[220]

---
217   As noted in Wolf, 64-65.
218   Rachel Ertel, "A Minority Literature." Translated by Alan Astro. *Yale French Studies* 85 (1994): 226.
219   See Boyarin, *Powers of Diaspora*.
220   Nolden, *In Lieu of Memory*, 27.

It is this French obsession that continues to be challenged today when first and second generation immigrant narratives are forcing the French literary establishment to reevaluate its own present and future in order to reflect the changes apparent in French society, as seen with the emergence and popularization of the slang *verlan*. It is however important to note the difference that exists between a Jewish and an Arab woman writer using the French language in their writing. For as Lionnet notes, "To bare one's self in the language of the conqueror is at once a form of betrayal and the inescapable consequence of any gesture of female emancipation."[221] Thus, the distinguished translator, novelist and filmmaker Assia Djebar decided to write in French, the language of the colonizer, in order to give a voice to women who had remained without a voice for too long, and in this way she would gain access to writing and to the world of patriarchal personal autonomy.

However, as noted by Caws, Green, Hirsch and Scharfman, this came at the price of severing her ties with the house of her mother, and from her maternal language spoken and chanted by generations of Algerian women before her.[222] A Jewish woman writer of Djebar's generation would suffer fewer such consequences (betrayal, severing of ties) since the French language was not seen as the language of the "conqueror" as much as that of the "liberator," and hence had less of a stigma attached to it. Less an issue, then, of a power-powerless relationship, for the Jewish writer it becomes an issue of maintaining a Jewish specificity despite having to express one's self in a language which is not considered a Jewish language such as Hebrew, Yiddish, Judeo-Arabic or Ladino.

Nolden emphasizes that "...the lingua franca of their childhood homes, Judeo-Arabic or Judeo-Spanish, was hardly known to them as a written language. According to Guy Dugas, the ghetto has hardly ever been a literary space...Thus, these authors perceive French as the epitome of a literary language, cementing a difference between everyday and literary language that is more pronounced than what French-born writers may experience."[223] Since language is one of the primary expressions

---

221   Lionnet, "Logiques Métisses", 333.
222   See Caws, Green, Hirsch and Scharfman, eds. *Ecritures de Femmes. Nouvelles Cartographies*. New Haven: Yale UP, 1996, 5.
223   Nolden, *In Lieu of Memory*, 50-51.

of culture and its specificities, the challenge for Jews as they write, perpetually in exile and in languages not considered specifically Jewish, has always been how not to lose oneself in the other's language, but rather subsist in this language which is simultaneously yours. Similar to other authors of immigrant origins in France, the Jewish author from the Maghreb does not have a choice other than to write in French, since, like her immigrant contemporaries, she is not sufficiently versed in Arabic, Berber, Judeo-Arabic or Judeo-Spanish. Like them, she also uses the languages of the parent generation as linguistic spices added to the main ingredients in the dish of French textual and inter-textual, blended delicacies. Judeo-Arabic, the language spoken historically by most North African Jews, is now about to become extinct. Shmuel Trigano notes that "It will perhaps remain only in a few typically Judeo-Arabic expressions, well felt but completely detached from their linguistic hinterland."[224]

As noted earlier, Cynthia Ozik writes about how literature written by Jews in a diaspora language can survive as Jewish texts, as specific testimonies to Jewish existence and continuity. Her argument is that if you ignore your own culture and choose to only address your reading audience as a universalist voice, you will be lost in history:

We can do what the German Jews did…we can give ourselves over altogether to Gentile culture and be lost in history…or we can do what we have never before dared to do in a Diaspora language: make it our own, our own necessary instrument, understanding ourselves in it while being understood by everyone who cares to listen or read…If we blow into the narrow end of the shofar [ram's horn used during the High Holidays] we will be heard far. But if we choose to be mankind rather than Jewish and blow into the wider part, we will not be heard at all.[225]

Language is intimately associated with identity, then, and the Jews of Eastern Europe had developed a massive literary tradition in Yid-

---

224   "Elle ne subsistera peut-être que dans quelques expressions typiques judéo-arabes bien senties mais complètement coupées de leur hinterland linguistique." Trigano, "La Mémoire du Peuple Disparu," 46.
225   Ozik, "America: Toward Yavneh." In *What is Jewish Literature?* Hanna Wirth-Nesher, ed. Philadelphia: JPS, 1994, 34.

dish whose producers and products were turned into ashes during the Second World War. Judeo-Arabic, on the other hand, had evolved primarily as an oral tradition, and when the Jews had permanently lost their connection to the land, French had became the adopted mother tongue. According to Ozik, maintaining a Jewish specificity in literature is so critical that the generations of diaspora living should not be "in vain." By that she means that Jews, because of their diasporic existence, have a particular need for text to create a sense of continuity in contexts, which in turn will ensure an ongoing affirmation of existence despite the seemingly perpetual threat of arbitrariness of that very existence.

How these contexts are created in contemporary French writing by Sephardic women is one of our concerns here, and we will now look closer at the narrative genre most common for women's voices and of Jewish women's voices. That genre finds its creative source in the self and is inspired by the experiences of a Jewish "I" that has followed a dramatic trajectory in contemporary and post-colonial history, but an "I" that embraces that path as it evolves into distinctively resounding and autobiographically inspired texts.

Modes of Narrating the Personal Experience

What kind of literary narrative is it that has flourished in the post-colonial years? Hand in hand with the greater movements for national independence and the struggles for self-governing, followed, necessarily I would say, the argument for the right to define one's self, for saying, proclaiming, writing one's own identity, rights and views of the world as subjects, as opposed to being imposed certain identities as "other" by those in power. The auto in autonomy is extended to the domain of narrative in post-colonial discourse and literatures, and appropriating the writing of one's "self" has thus been a critical part of movements of independence, both national and personal. The notion itself of "personal independence" separated from the communal has not been a typical way for families, communities and nations to exist, historically speaking, and especially not in countries outside of what we call the "West." The less a community or nation is affected by Western influence, the less prevalent is the idea of the self as an autonomous entity distinct and separated from family, community and society. The "other" that the West has historically viewed as "simply" a static object of passive "strangeness," of "*unheimlichkeit*" as it were, became safely controlled and contained by our vision of them.

Post-colonial autobiography is characterized by the plural, the multiple, the transitory, by fragmentation and collage, to name a few ingredients, but these are not elements that the colonizer had projected in their simplified, homogeneous and static view of the colonized other. So for the author, using the self as the creative source for not only the process of writing but also the content as it evolves into a text referring back to the self, gains a sense of autonomy, in a dynamic relationship not involving externally imposed signifiers. Lionnet sees this as a new ground for self-discovery and empowerment: "Self-writing is thus a strategic move that opens up a space of possibility where the subject to history and the agent of discourse can engage in a dialogue with each other."[226]

In the light of this view of autobiographic writing I have suggested that the Jews have had a particular relationship to self-writing, partly developed as a necessary manual to prevent a dissolution of Jewish identity, always already exiled, always already other. Autobiography, says Algerian Jewish writer Albert Bensoussan "…will trace the outline of a chaotic existence,"[227] and he maintains that in the process it becomes an auto-justification and an auto-satisfaction, since the author "…has built his home which is the book, inscribed his destiny and his lineage, sketched the path [of his journey]. Thus, I will say that he has put down his roots."[228] The autobiographic text thus offers a chance for the writer to become rooted, positively, in exile. This has been a means of survival for Jews who have been exiled and re-exiled throughout generations, and the text and story have become a way to inscribe oneself in history, in one's destiny and in one's identity.

---

226   Lionnet, *Autobiographical Voices*, 193.
227   "…va tracer les grandes lignes d'une existence chaotique." Bensoussan, *L'Echelle Séfarade*, 23.
228   "…a bâti sa maison qui est le livre, inscrit son destin et lignage, dessiné son sillage. Je dirai donc, qu'il enfoncé ses racines." ibid., 24.

When Jews were forced into diaspora in the first century C.E, the Jewish narrative became the archetype of the diasporic text, the matrix of which is represented in the unique example of the mother-source of autobiography: the Torah. Let us consider the traditional definition of autobiography by Philippe Lejeune: "Retrospective prose narrative written by a real person [the Jewish people] concerning his own existence, where the focus is his individual life [origins, events, genealogies, ethics and legacy], in particular the story of his personality."[229] As this supposedly "female" (personal and subjective) form of writing one's story becomes a historically, politically and socially significant text, given its cultural function, the significance of the autobiographical account can and should be revisited. Jewish historian Lucette Valensi aptly observes how autobiography is not necessarily a narcissistic exercise but typically extends beyond the "I" of the text:

> Since the emergence of literary fiction among the Jews of the Maghreb, the genre of autobiographical fiction has flourished, especially since the 1950's. This might have signaled the emergence and affirmation of the "I," access to autonomy by the individual who dares speak in his or her own name. The truth is that, from the first novels of Albert Memmi (born in Tunisia in 1920) to those of Albert Bensoussan (born in Algeria in 1935) and of Marcel Benabou (born in Morocco in 1939), "I" speaks of "we." The novel of the singular individual is in fact the family and ethnic novel, always a novel of collective identity: Jew and Arab, French and Maghreb, secular and Jewish, an identity hyphenate, which may be the mark of modernity but nonetheless fully inscribed in the continuity of Jewish culture in North Africa.[230]

We see this also among non-Jewish writers from the Maghreb, and especially from a woman's perspective, where the "I" in the text speaks for the "we" of all women in that society who endure the same silencing, the same marginalization. The Jewish women authors included in

---

229 Lejeune, *On Autobiography*. Paul John Eakin, ed. Translated by Katherine Leary. Minneapolis: U of Minn. P, 1988, 4.
230 Valensi, "Multicultural Visions", 925.

this study, and indeed most of the published Jewish women authors of North African origin, have written works either clearly autobiographical in nature, or where the fiction has been heavily inspired by autobiographical elements.

The majority of post-colonial Maghrebi authors (including those who began writing during colonial times), Jews and Muslims alike, and most of whom are more or less secular, have written autobiographically inspired works of literature that have played a significant role in the self-fashioning not just for the "subject to history" and the "agent of discourse," but also for the sense of self on a more intimate level. Especially for women, readers and writers alike, the autobiographically inspired narratives have proved to be true "spaces of possibilities," offering dialogue both in and out of the text. This is part of the transgressivness of female writing of the self, which, especially in Arabo-Muslim culture, is perceived as revealing the private domain that should be kept veiled, indeed instigating an offense against the silence that has been historically imposed on women by patriarchal cultures. As aptly described by writers such as Djebar, but also by earlier Jewish women writers in the Maghreb such as Alissa Rhaïs and Elissa Chimenti,[231] the female voice had existed in a single outlet, as oral transmitter of culture to her daughters, but only within the confines of the home, the harem or the hammam, places where women would gather.

Although texts with strong autobiographical elements are predominant in post-colonial writing, I find Albert Memmi's statement to be particularly enlightening concerning the inner workings of literature: "There is no such thing as pure autobiography. It does not exist… And secondly, all literature is in a sense autobiographic. It is an attempt at expressing personal anguish."[232] The opening up of the text that we

---

231 For a comprehensive bibliography of Jewish literature from the Maghreb, see Guy Dugas, *Bibliographie Critique de la Littérature Judéo-Maghrébine d'Expression Française*. Paris: L'Harmattan, 1992. Updated addition: "Trente ans de littérature judéo-maghrébine (1982-2013)." In *Expressions maghrébines*, vol. 13, n° 2, hiver (2014).
232 "Il n'existe pas d'autobiographie pure. Ça n'existe pas…Et deuxièmement, toute littérature en un sens est autobiographique. C'est une tentative d'exprimer des angoisses personnelles." Memmi, *Postcolonialisme et Autobiographie*, 69.

see in the plethora of writing from the margins, in border-writings and migrant narratives, is a particular manifestation of literature as a process that invites dialogue, and although the source is drawn from the auto – or the self – there is a constant tapping into imagination, or vice-versa. The starting place of the narrative can be from imagination, but the author's real historical life is used, consciously or not, as a source of creativity.

To Memmi, then, autobiography is similar to psychoanalysis, since even on the couch or divan you make up stories. He finds that in order to construct a character, real things are needed to refer it to, and since inevitable lacks of facts or gaps in memory of the construct always exist, you invent what is missing. This is where the constant paradox of literature comes from.[233] Although Lejeune's autobiographical pact implies an agreement in the writing of the self, Memmi points to the inevitable fictional element always present in autobiography, as in life.

The French writer Serge Doubrovsky has added another critical element to the concept of self-writing by introducing the genre of "autofiction," a disruption of the lejeunian "*autobiographie*," since in autofiction, the elusive divide separating autobiography from fiction is explored to its fullest potential. Literary critic John Ireland suggests that autofiction "delights in its inventive transgressions," which become "the source of palpable aesthetic pleasure for the writer" as moments of "real" life and "real" characters are turned into art.[234] Doubrovsky maintains that it is through writing that he constructs his own self, and the Doubrovskian autofiction is definable as "a story presenting itself as both fiction and autobiography" as it produces a "fictionalizing of lived experience."[235]

If autofiction is stretching the boundaries of classic autobiography, opening it up to polysemic elements of what the self of the text may be, become, or refer to, this seems a useful approach to what we are seeing in

---

233   Ibid.
234   John Ireland, "Introduction: Monstrous Writing: Serge Doubrvosky's Autofiction." *Genre* 26 (1993): 4.
235   "un récit qui se donne à la fois pour fictive et autobiographique"…"fictionalisation de l'expérience vécue." Alex Hughes, "Recycling and Repetition in Recent French Autofiction: Marc Weitzmann's Doubrovskian Borrowings." *Modern Language Review* 97 (2002): 568.

many post-colonial narratives. The lives of the post-colonial subjects, like all lives perhaps, are indeed filled with "voids and fissures of existential lack," and this is where the autofictional text fills in the gaps. The purpose of autofiction is not to represent life but to redeem it, at least esthetically, notes Ireland, and this is exactly the function of writing as we see it among Judeo-Maghrebian writers and critics: a chaotic life delivered in narratives inspired by life experiences. Since life and literature can no longer simply be seen as heterogeneous and irreconcilably separate entities, as was commonly held by post-war critical theory (e.g. structuralism), existence should not be relegated to the margins of literary analysis but, indeed, come in to the center.[236] The distinction between autobiography and autofiction may be just another example of the difficulty of classification in literature, since autofiction is seen as "an occupation of diverse places, a multiple narrative threading" which thus defies Lejeune's "strict" pact-proposition and in a sense undermines it, since autobiography can be seen as having colonized the referential space that is now also being inhabited by the narrative modality of autofiction.[237]

Another significant observation in the writing of the self, and one which is of particular importance to us, is that of Thomas Nolden in his book on post Holocaust Jewish writing in France, where he observes that the "new" kind of Jewish writing that has emerged since the 1980s can be termed autojudeography: "The proclivity toward the autobiographical (auto) and the self-reflexive preoccupation with the nature of writing (*graphie*) provide the narrative frame within which the notion of Jewishness (judeo) appears."[238] The dynamic change from being imaginary Jews to becoming imaginative ones is a similar appropriation of voice and self-fashioning that we see as Orientalism's imagined people reappropriate their right to self-imagination and become imaginative individuals.

Nolden describes the dynamics of autojudeography along these terms: Leave it to the writers to contemplate what being Jewish could entail for them as imaginative rather than imaginary Jews. The term "imaginary Jews" we will remember, is used here in the way Alain Finkielkraut coined the term as he, in his book *Le Juif Imaginaire*

236	Ireland, "Monsterous Writing," 5
237	Hughes, 567.
238	Nolden, *In Lieu of Memory*, 79.

(1980), criticized the self-fashioning of young post Second World War Jews, mostly children of survivors (including himself), who cast themselves in the tragic role of the victim, the outsider, the persecuted, while living lives devoid of any Jewish content, such as knowledge or meaningful practice of their heritage as self fashioning, creative or imaginative Jews. "[This] essay by the child of survivors [Finkielkraut] accomplished at the level of identity discourse what the Six-Day War had done at the political level: it complicated, if not fractured, tendencies toward a mythologization of the Jew as the victim per se."[239]

Writing, then, is born from a conscious rapport with autobiography. Take for instance the *"juifemme"*[240] of Cixous; exiled, a stranger and a foreigner, trilingual, Cixous forms for herself an entrance into the French language by writing, with pain and jubilation.[241] As Nolden points out, none of the spheres in Hélène Cixous' by now famous neologism *juifemme*, the personal (I; in French *je*), ethnic (Jewish; in French *Juif*), and gender experience (woman; in French *femme*), can be separated from each other; "intricately woven together, they inform the way Jewish women writers look at events in history and experience the present."[242] For Cixous as for many Jewish women leaving the Maghreb behind, coming to France offered a certain freedom from difficult, colonial childhood memories, and a new beginning for expressing their identity in a country that had granted them full equality before the law. But as Cixous points out, it did not mean she stopped being a foreigner. "I left Algeria in 1955. Without grief. With no idea of returning. I removed my bandages. Enough silenced. Enough swallowed. I removed my gag. I began. At last I stopped being the one I wasn't. And I was the foreigner that I was."[243]

The purpose of examining the different kinds of self-writing that are part of the French literary landscape has been to understand how

---

239 Ibid., 20.
240 Cixous plays with the words "juif" (Jew) and "femme" (woman) to represent her identity, using the sound of "juif" which phonetically and in slang sounds like "je suis," hence the "I am a (Jewish) woman" of her expression.
241 Cixous in Mary Ann Caws, Mary Jean Green, Marianne Hirsch and Ronnie Scharfman, eds. *Ecritures de Femmes. Nouvelles Cartographies.* New Haven: Yale UP, 1996, 319.
242 Nolden, *Voices of the Diaspora. Jewish Woman Writing in Contemporary Europe.* Evanston: Northwest UP, 2005, xxviii.
243 Cixous, "Letter to Zora Drif," 193.

and where the Jewish woman writer places herself at the intersections of these various models. As we will see, some of the authors figuring in our analysis have created a text that is clearly autobiographical, in the pact-like definition of Lejeune, such as Gisèle Halimi, Annie Cohen, Annie Goldmann, Nine Moati and to some degree Hélène Cixous. Others have chosen to write a fictional work inspired by their own life as emigrated, exiled Maghrebi Jews, more in the vein of Doubrovsky's autofiction, such as Chochana Boukhobza, Annie Fitoussie and Paule Darmon. All, however, are part of what Thomas Nolden identifies as an emergent French autojudeography, a way for Jews in France to inscribe their Jewish difference in a text drawn from personal experiences of loss, memory and the problematics of identity in exile.

On Loss and Memory

Memory plays an important role in every life, and remembering that which has come to define us is a pivotal part of realizing our own identity, of understanding ourselves, indeed of writing our "self." If we stop remembering, we stop being, in a sense. A people that does not have memory stops being a people, as Yerushalmi has noted. But the evaluation of memory changes with time, and its import is dictated by events that unfold in each generation, or to each individual. Alain Finkielkraut notes, "Memory has never occupied the stage as much as it does today. And never has the field of memory been as reduced. Under the name of obligation of memory, only victims are honored, and only great crimes are commemorated."[244] He is of course referring primarily to the crimes of genocide and the many heinous war crimes we have witnessed in the last century, and the memories of those events as they engrave themselves or become engraved in (mostly) public memory. Authorities on Maghreb literatures in France, professor Charles Bonn and his co-editor Naget Khadda, remind us of the critical func-

---

244   "Jamais la mémoire n'a autant occupé la scène qu'aujourd'hui. Et jamais le champ de la mémoire n'a été aussi réduit. Sous le nom de devoir de mémoire, on n'honore plus que les victimes, on ne commémore plus que les très grands crimes." *Magazine Littéraire*. No. 445, Septembre (2005): 33.

tion of memory: "The exploration of memory outwits the falsifications of History and the unifying pretensions of identity discourse. It (the exploration) is fundamentally subversive."[245]

This statement underlines what Yerushalmi has also noted, pointed to earlier, on the importance of memory vis-à-vis history. In discussing Yerushalmi I mentioned the biblical commandment to "Remember!" – "*zakhor!*" – a concept that has accrued a tremendous cultural value for Jews ever since the first exile from The Holy Land. Jewish tradition defines itself by the transmission of memory, and the rigorous and faithful adherence to religious and cultural traditions that are built around the central tenet of memory has allowed the Jews to survive as a distinct people. Jonathan Boyarin underlines that "for Jews memory has also worked to plaster the ruptures in collective existence caused by repeated catastrophe and dispersal. It has been essential to the everyday continuity of a people who cannot rely on a linkage of blood and soil."[246] Loss becomes not only a source of pain, but also evolves into a spring of creation by the mere virtue of being the only hope for survival. And, as Albert Bensoussan reminds us, "I have lost everything in this collapse [of Jewish life in the Maghreb], but not my memory."[247]

Loss is not a new concept for the Jews, and a distinct modus operandi for survival has evolved from the beginning. It was to become The Book, the Torah, and other oral and written texts where the national yet intimate memory of a people was made portable and not dependent on a homeland. A narrative became the history, and the history was built on memory. But, as Boyarin suggests, care needs to be taken not to romanticize Jewish history; the lingering concept of a universal history that Jews somehow fall outside of, is sustained by the reification of memory and history as fundamentally different modes of relating to the past. In this greater "universal history," Jews have remained a favorite case of a "people of memory."[248] The Jewish experience of losing North Africa, of the suffering that follows deracination

---

245   "L'exploration de la mémoire déjoue les falsifications de l'Histoire et les prétentions unificatrices des discours d'identité. Elle est foncièrement subversive." Bonn and Khadda, *Littérature Maghrébine*, 18.
246   Boyarin, *Storm*, 35.
247   Bensoussan, *L'Echelle Sépharade*, 17.
248   Boyarin, *Storm*, 93.

and displacement, has been managed somehow by the deep-rooted literary traditions, created from loss, that the Jews take with them wherever they go. The experiences of the Jewish women writers from the Maghreb become part of their "resources of autonomous invention," as suggested by Boyarin. The most important of these is perhaps memory, "which offers the possibility of a play of difference transcending the seeming alternatives of hierarchy and of leveling."[249]

Even assimilated, atheist Jews (who may call themselves "cultural Jews") typically sit at a Passover *seder* meal and participate in the remembering of the exodus from Egypt. Jews from Arab lands can rely only on their memory to go back to their lost homelands, and the recording of these memories in the narrative of texts, films, and music helps trace one chapter that came to an end, but that left its imprints on memory and will never cease to be real and to matter. Albert Bensoussan elaborates, "We don't rebuild newness from nothing. It is in memory and faithfulness, in this plurality which makes its rich and complex spirit, that the Jewish people have forged its essence and its originality."[250]

Reina Roffé, a Sephardic writer born in Buenos Aires of parents who immigrated to Argentina from Spanish Morocco, states that writing emerges from ancestral memory: "Despite their different origins, authors who include elements of exodus, diaspora, and emigration in their fictional and poetic works are voicing problems of the Diaspora that have been felt and utilized for centuries by authors of Jewish background. These experiences and themes – like initial memories – represent the raw material for our literature."[251] Writing memory, then, is experienced traditionally as imperative for Jews, and as I have suggested in my discussion above specifically regarding autobiography, the narrative of the Jewish self may be seen as having begun with the Torah, the most vital book of Jewish survival and memory. On the importance of books – any book – Bensoussan further notes: "The book will continue,

---

249 Ibid., 114.
250 "On ne bâtit pas du neuf à partir de rien. C'est dans la mémoire et la fidélité que le peuple juif s'est forgé, dans cette pluralité qui fait sa richesse et son âme complexe, puisant à cette multitude de sources son essence et son originalité." Bensoussan, *L'Echelle Séfarade*, 164.
251 Reina Roffé, "Exotic Birds," in *Voices of the Diaspora*, 13.

will follow us, prolong us, it is in it, in literature, that we will decipher our destiny. For if the bodies return to the earth, and if dust re-covers forgetting, the book on the other hand is a permanent memory, a reservoir of humanity and soil for the roots of the large tree of life."[252] The generation of uprooted Jews carries with them the memories of the land of origin. These are memories of sounds, smells, places, and an atmosphere that they were the last ones to be able to experience directly.

THE ROLE OF JEWISH WOMEN VOICES

As women, the Franco-Maghrebian writers included here as representations of female Jewish identities in contemporary France, have a unique way of contributing to the transmission of "other" Maghreb memories and identities, as well as to the evolving discourse on post-colonial identities. The importance of a woman's voice in any study of historical events and their literary manifestations does not need to be proven here; we can be thankful for two generations of groundbreaking feminist movements and studies, and before them, the now often reexamined proto-feminsists of earlier times.

The subsequent evolution of "women's studies," bringing attention to the indispensable value of acknowledging and including both female and male epistemologies in our quest for improved understanding of both world events and more personal events, have become one of the great contributions of the post-structural period. It was the soul of the woman that Descartes dismissed from the world when he defined subjectivity and the feminine as an epistemological threat. The ensuing flight from the feminine was motivated by both fear of the uncertain, and revulsion of the body's mortality which women had come to represent. Sartori and Cottenet-Hage point to the unique experience of Jewish women within their community as the grounds for yielding a particularly rich narrative:

---

252 "Le livre continuera, nous suivra, nous prolongera, et c'est en lui, dans la littérature, qu'on déchiffrera notre destin. Car si les corps vont à la terre, si la poussière recouvre l'oubli, le livre, lui, est mémoire permanente, réservoir d'humanité et terre de racines pour le grand arbre de vie." Bensoussan, *L'Echelle Séfarade*, 22.

Because according to Jewish law, the mother's religion is determinative, a Jewish women's relationship with her own identity is of a different nature that that of a Jewish man – perhaps more intimate, more visceral. Issues of exogamy or endogamy, survival, persecution, exile and loss, and freedom from tradition may become more threatening, more definitive, more dramatic. In many ways, personal selves are more tightly bound to the existence and the history, past and present of the group. Remembering, caring, celebrating, grieving, and rebelling are personal acts performed by these Jewish women within the community.[253]

Here, it is for the exact opposite Descartes' reason that becomes the feeding-ground for deeper knowledge, since the bodily connection to the woman's sensibility in lived experience becomes the source for writing and understanding.

It has taken some time in modern history to realize that as the subjective and the objective come together we are offered a more dynamic form of knowledge. The gendered specificities offered by women in their narrative texts are needed to counter the predominance of world knowledge as dictated by male narratives and what has been valued as exclusively "of the intellect" or "of the mind." As author, literary critic and art historian Mary Ann Caws and her co-editors note, "one of the principal projects of feminist critique has been the analysis of the norms for literary consecration and of the chronic exclusion of women writers...[since] French literary tradition has always been extremely reticent to the idea of integrating women writers."[254]

Women have been marginalized and silenced, and only with the Nouveau Roman (represented by French writers such as Sarraute et Duras) and the post-structuralists (Cixous, Irigaray and Kristeva) did women begin to become recognized as being an integral part of contemporary French thought, until then an exclusively male domain.[255] The threat of the liberated woman as auto-represented and autonomous to

---

253   Sartori, Eva Martin and Madeleine Cottenet-Hage, eds. *Daughters of Sarah: Anthology of Jewish Women Writers in France.* Teaneck: Holes & Meier, 2006. xxv.
254   Caws et al., *Ecritures de Femmes*, 6.
255   Ibid., 7.

Western white Christian male values can be understood as analogous to the historical view of the Jew as a menace to the (patriarchal) powers of governments. Derrida has asked the following question about the relationship between woman and Jew as a threat: "Women and Jews represent the simulacrum of emasculation, and what is emasculation if not circumcision?"[256] As anti-phallus, woman becomes the foundation of Derrida's analogy between Jew and woman, since in his view the Jew is the femininity of society, a threat to all the virile values reigning in a community, an army, a nation..."[257]

Iraqi American-Jewish writer Loolwa Khazzoom has collected marginalized Jewish women's voices in her collection of essays on identity by women from Islamic lands, and she finds it was her own family's culture of patriarchy that had limited her self-knowledge: "As I entered my adult years, I realized that my relationship to my entire family was filtered – often second hand, through my father's lens. 'Family' as I knew it was essentially a matriarchy, with six aunts and one surviving uncle, I knew nothing about the female version of family life."[258] The experience of exclusion or obscurity expressed here, is thus imposed from within the family and cultural structure as her family was used to it from their Iraqi-Arab cultural heritage. Explaining further the destabilizing effect that the *Sephardi/Mizrahi* women – as represented by the writers collected in her project – pose as they are heard and claim their voices, Khazzoom notes:

> *In a world where Jewish is synonymous with Central and Eastern European, where North African/Middle Eastern is synonymous with Arab Muslim, where "of color" is synonymous with "not Jewish," and where communities are generally represented through their men, our mere existence threatens to destroy the foundations of numerous identity constructs as society knows them today.*[259]

---

256   Derrida, *Eperons*, 54, as cited in Ofrat, *The Jewish Derrida*. Syracuse UP: Syracuse, 2001, 50.
257   Ofrat, *The Jewish Derrida*, Syracuse: Syracuse UP, 2001, 50.
258   Khazzoom, ed. *The Flying Camel. Essays on Identity by Women of North African and Middle Eastern Jewish Heritage*. New York: Seal Press, 2003. x.
259   Ibid., xi.

The editors of the previously cited volume of women's writing *Ecritures de Femmes* (1996) speak of the francophone women writers such as Assia Djebar, Yamina Mechakra and Evelyne Accad as women who are making historical portraits of French colonialism and decolonialism, and of the colonial subject from the point of view of women.[260] They point out that their personal histories are profoundly interlaced with cultural history, and that women's lives always inscribe themselves in the greater historical "story."[261] Strangely, aside from Cixous there are no Jewish women's voices included in their collection of 31 francophone women writers analyzed.

In general, if one looks at books presenting voices from the Maghreb, Albert Memmi may be included, and possibly Edmond Jabès and Amram el Maleh (all francophone Jewish writers from Arab lands), but one is hard pressed to find a (Jewish) woman writer. Similarly, works that portray immigrant or minority voices in France concentrate mainly on the narratives of the second-generation Arab immigrants, known as the *beur*, and other minorities from the francophone world who now have made France their home. Granted, the Jews represent a small percentage as a minority population in France compared to the near six million Muslim immigrants living there, but why the complete exclusion? Although about half of France's approximately 600,000 Jews may not be called immigrants, those who arrived in the years leading up to and following decolonization have endured many of the challenges associated with being a newcomer in a country where you are very much a minority, and we may say even an almost invisible minority. North African Jews have a large success rate educationally, professionally, and financially relative to most Arab immigrants, and they have thereby assimilated easier into the mainstream economic system in society.[262] So much so that to the French government the immigrant Jews are less of a constant reminder of the challenge facing French society, with its diverse and economically unequal immigrant groups.

The success rate among Jews has, paradoxically, led to a certain blindness and unwillingness on the part of French officials to acknowledge

---

260 *Ecritures*, 8.
261 Ibid.
262 On the topic of the difference in integration and assimilation between the two communities, see Katz and Mandel, specifically chapters 5 and 3 respectively.

the increasing anti-Semitic sentiment and instances of violence among Arab immigrants, and of the growing population of "*le Pen-esque*" citizens who seem to need a villainous other to blame for their society's ills. In a study on stereotypes and representations of ethnicity in French society, Mireille Rosello notes that Jewishness continues to remain an elusive signifier in French cultures. "Paradoxically, the challenge here may be to question an absence of representation that is easily confused with an absence of stereotyping. The lack of stereotypes can also be the expression of a stereotype of invisibility."[263] Unlike blacks and Arabs, Jews are not represented as immigrants, even if the myth of the Wandering Jew is still as recognizable as ever.[264] The standpoint of women will illuminate aspects of the social totality previously suppressed with the dominant view, and as a minority woman, in our case Jewish, this elucidation is capable of transforming hitherto limited views as to what it means to be a non-Muslim, non-Arab, non pied-noir and yet deeply rooted in the Maghreb and its cultural, historical and political past.

A Unique Point of View: Sephardic Women in France

Many of the young Jewish women who were born in the Maghreb and who left for France, among whom figure our authors, had lived in families that were fully frenchified, that is, they had a deep and profound sense of feeling and living like the French, both linguistically and culturally. Typically these girls and young women were encouraged to speak only French, to receive an exclusively French education often administered by the Alliance Française or French public school as in Algeria. Because of this, Judeo-Arabic culture was only remotely familiar to most of them by the time they left for France. Their own parents, who lived with one foot in that traditional culture and one in the colonizer's French world, had been the last "bridge" generation between their grandparents who spoke Judeo-Arabic, and for whom the Jewish Maghreb culture had defined their lives and those of their ancestors. All they wanted was for their daughters to succeed and to be able to have a better life, one free from subjugation to Islam as defined by

---

263 Rosello, *Declining the Stereotype: Ethnicity and Representation in French Cultures.* Hanover and London: UP of New England, 1998, 8.
264 Ibid., 9.

dhimmitude and filled with possibilities in a fully democratic and secular society. The result was an increasingly limited transmission of a Jewish heritage. This gradual loss of a Jewish specificity was much more pronounced among girls and young women of the last generation of North African Jews to live in that region, because the ritual and religious training, as well as the Hebrew language was traditionally only transmitted to boys.

Speaking of the women in her family, Tunisian born writer Annie Goldmann points to these gaps in their knowledge of Jewish traditions as well as Arab culture: "Dismissed from Hebrew culture as a girl, from Arab culture as a Jew, it was in French that acculturation took place… Until recently I knew nothing of Oriental Jewish culture. I did not know there are schools of thought having played a role in the culture of the Mediterranean."[265] The result was that once the women became settled in France, aside from having lost their home country and all their familiar surroundings associated with the formative years of their childhood, there was the feeling of an abyss, an emptiness that made the loss all the more ambiguous, difficult even to verbalize and to recover now that the physical place of that culture was gone forever. There is an acute awareness, then, among these Jewish women born in the Maghreb, of being alienated within their own religion and their original culture. This will summons a particular kind of narrative voice in writing. As Nolden notes, "They subtly negotiate the ambiguities inherent in their experiences of displacement and emancipation as Sephardic women in post-colonial France without succumbing to the temptations of acculturation or of nostalgia for the lost world of Maghreb Judaism."[266]

The Jewish women writers of the Maghreb share with their exiled Arabo-Muslim peers many motivations for writing, and they are often similarly thrust between the traditions of their parents, a paternalistic cultural tradition, and the forces of a secular and more modern French society. Whereas Arabo-Muslim women did not begin their true *"prise de parole"* (lit: "the taking-control speech") until the 1970s, Jewish women were generally able to circulate more freely in society, and thereby would be more

---

265 "Ecartée en tant que fille de la culture hébraïque, en tant que juive de la culture arabe, c'est en français que se fait l'acculturation…Jusqu'à ces dernières années j'ai tout ignoré de la culture juive orientale. J'ignorais qu'il existe des écoles de penseurs ayant joué un rôle dans la culture méditerranéenne." Goldmann, *Les Filles de Mardochée: Histoire d'une Emancipation*, 26, 123.
266 Nolden, *Voices of the Diaspora*, xxvi.

easily introduced to the influences of European culture. Thus there were few, but widely read, Jewish women authors who started writing in the Maghreb already in the 1920's. Elissa Rhaïs, Blanche Bendahan, Maximilienne Heller and Elissa Chimenti were among the first Jewish Maghreb women to ever publish novels in French, and their works typically focused on depicting the difficult lives of Jewish women in the ghetto, romantic relationships, and Judeo-Arab relations in general.

Aside from sharing experiences common to many immigrant communities and migrant peoples living in-between cultures, Arab and Jewish women have been motivated by reasons specific to their own communities and cultures. Arab women often write to challenge the *"mutisme"* (silence) imposed on them by both traditionally patriarchal and dogmatic Muslim societies and families, and through their writing they seek autonomy, personal equilibrium, and a valorization of the feminine as an entity independent from the house of the father or the husband. Literally writing their way out of silence, in the process they began to break down walls and barriers. They voice a refusal of the role of victim as often experienced in the family in relation to paternal and fraternal abuse, the role of inferiority, muteness, and submission imposed by their cultural traditions. Immigrant Sephardic women writers are generally fortunate enough not to have to battle such extremely misogynistic attitudes or common occurrences of violence toward women in their families, although they too have had to challenge the often traditional views separating women from men, particularly in the areas of education, marriage, and career choices. Annie Goldmann again provides a telling account:

> *The fact of being a woman in this milieu was an additional handicap. Added to the bourgeois puritan morals was the oriental conception of the woman, even in a milieu as evolved as mine. It was completely expected that the role of a girl should be passive. Every sort of activism was reproved. My father considered my education as important, but only to enrich my personality, not at all to gain any material profit from it.*[267]

---

267   "Le fait d'être femme dans ce milieu était un handicap supplémentaire. A la morale bourgeoise puritaine s'ajoutait la conception orientale de la femme, même dans des milieu aussi évolués que le mien. Il était tout à

Despite this paternalistic hesitance to let daughters fully evolve in society, Jewish women did have much more exposure and were able to make their own choices sooner that their Arab sisters. Consequently, Jewish women have been able to help implement and take advantage of many of the positive social and political changes available to women in industrialized societies sooner that their Arab peers, many of whom still live under the stricter guidelines of traditional Muslim societies.

Whereas the new generation of immigrant-born writers in France have been called "*hommes et femmes frontierères*" (border men and women), since they are educated in French state schools and have thereby internalized the culture of France and now serve as interpreters between the two communities, Jews (whether Ashkenazi or Sephardi) had been such "border people" for many generations already. The balancing act of expressing yourself simultaneously as a person who belongs to where you now live and where you once originated from, yet perhaps not fitting in either place fully, is also shared by both Arab and Jews.

As sociologist Roger Bromley points out, among the diasporic cultural fictions which have come to occupy this "third space," a space of revaluation, there is the woman writer who, doubly exiled, has come to challenge worlds that are "almost exclusively male dominated and designed primarily for the fulfillment in terms of the human as envisaged by men occupying positions of power."[268] In this emergent discourse also called "third scenario," the Jewish woman writer offers a particularly acute experience, since she has been exiled or marginalized in multiple circumstances, and this experience is new neither to her nor to her family but rather an ingrained part of her world view and of her identity. The new condition of belonging which we see expressed in society and reflected in literature is mixed, ambivalent, ambiguous and post-essentialist,[269] and in a positive scenario this *métissage* can be seen as a redemption; a liberation connected to the idea that identity does not necessarily need to be bound to issues of nationality, and this, in turn, may suggest a post-national model of belong-

---

fait admis que le rôle de la fille devait être passif. On reprouvait fermement toute manifestation d'activisme. Mon père considérait que je devais faire des études, mais pour enrichir ma personnalité, non pas pour en tirer un profit quelconque." Goldmann, *Filles de Mardochée*, 126.
268   Bromley, *Narratives for a New Belonging: Diasporic Cultural Fictions*. Edinburgh: Edinburgh UP, 2000, 4.
269   Ibid., 18.

ing, as suggested by the Boyarin and Bromley. This model is one that we may see more and more in the emergent hybrid literatures in France as in all the countries that have large immigrant communities.

The challenge that arises may be how to identify authors so that their works can be classified, if nothing else for practical reasons. This difficulty applies particularly to the Jewish authors in France who are of North African origins, since although they are French citizens, their writing has a deep connection to the Maghreb, and in some way also to the traditional Jewish notion of exile, Diaspora, and the idea of belonging, emotionally, in and/or to the Land of Israel. And society likes to classify. The need and push to label, organize, and catalogue is one way to control and manage knowledge.

Where Do They Fit In? Issues of Classification

This brings us to the question of classification of post-colonial Jewish literature in France. In his study *La Littérature Judéo-Maghrébine d'Expression Française* (1990), Guy Dugas points out that although francophone literature by Arabo-Mulsim authors from the Maghreb has benefited from a great infatuation, two other literary productions have been left largely in the shadows. These two are equally inspired by the North African space and include Western literature with Maghrebi resonances, as well as francophone Judeo-Maghrebi literature.

More than just a simple forgetting or disregard, this disinterest seems to stem from a methodological difficulty inherent in the models of classification adopted, since the most important criterion has been that of ethnicity as inherited from the concept of national literature.[270] Since the Jews who lived in the Maghreb never had the legal status of Moroccan, Algerian or Tunisian nationals, they have not been defined "simply" as Maghreb authors. Being part of a greater Jewish civilization, which in itself has always been an international and migrant phenomenon – as well as defined by diversity – literature produced by Jewish writers have trouble fitting in to the more narrowly defined national literatures.

Alec Hargreaves writes on this inevitable connection between the author and his origin: "The literary community to which a writer belongs is defined far less by the themes which are treated than by the au-

---
[270] Dugas, *La Littérature Judéo-Maghrébine*, 9.

thor's origins and the readership which he or she seeks to address."[271] We may recall the discussion by Michael Kramer evoked earlier on this very topic, and I ask again: what makes literature Jewish? If Jewish literature is defined primarily by its diversity and complexity, and the fact that it is written by a Jew, than we need to recognize the fact that this literary production is not a singular thing. It is unique exactly by its plurality. Just like the "Jewish people," it is an international phenomenon, as heterogeneous and complex in its components as it is diverse in its literature.

Despite the diversity, however, there is a sense of unity. Notwithstanding the vast difference between, for example, a German Jewish text and a Moroccan Jewish text, there is a transcending core and a unifying foundation. Speculating on the existence of a Jewish literature in a non-Jewish language, considering that much of Jewish literature is written neither in Hebrew, Yiddish nor Judeo-Arabic, is tantamount to reflecting upon the existence of the Jewish people itself. According to Rachel Ertel, "If the Jewish people – geographically and linguistically dispersed – exist, so does its literature exist. It is created in the image of the Jewish people: it is diverse."[272] Clara Levy notes that there have been plenty of contradictions in the French press as to the existence of "a Jewish literature" in the French language, and she adds that in one and the same article an author may argue that yes, indeed, it does exist, followed by a reconsideration and a "no, it does not." [273] This attitude of inconsistency does not simply concern one or two journalists but has been a general contradiction for the past thirty years.[274]

In his book *The Jewish Derrida* (2001), Gideon Ofrat analyzes the various Jewish elements in Derrida's biography, evolution, philosophy and theoretical approaches, and I think this text is a perfect example of how what is extracted from a text depends on who reads it. In other words, it is only natural that an analysis of Derrida's work by a non-Jew will yield fewer notes on Jewish influences, especially those not apparent to someone not trained or raised to recognize them. It even poses the interesting question about how the author sees him or herself, since many would ar-

---

[271] Hargraves, "Writers of Maghreb Immigrant Origin in France: French, Francophone, Maghreb or Beur?" in *African Francophone Writing. A Critical Introduction*. Laila Ibnlfassi and Nicki Hitchcott, eds. Oxford: Berg, 1996, 36.
[272] Rachel Ertel, "A Minority Literature," 226.
[273] Clara Levy, *Ecritures de l'identité. Les écrivains juifs après la Shoah*. Paris: PUF, 1998, 123.
[274] Ibid.

gue that Derrida certainly did not identify strongly with his Jewish background until later in life, when his reflections became more personal.

When one reflects on what makes a text Jewish, I would argue that most people would not see Derrida's as "Jewish," although after reading Ofrat's analysis it becomes difficult to ignore all those telling moments of Jewish "*différance*" in the derridean corpus. In any event, when Ofrat quotes Derrida talking about the difficulty of being a Jew, "…which coincides with the difficulty of writing; for Judaism and writing are but the same waiting, the same hope, the same depletion,"[275] we are reminded of a Jewish difference that will always be connected in some way to a writing difference. It may be minute, and barely noticeable, but the difference is there, regardless of how close to or far from Jewish tradition the Jewish writer was formed. But just as it is different, it is also always different from its difference; as diverse and complex as life in all places, impossible to essentialize. As Rachel Ertel notes, "Indeed, because of its complexity (but life itself is complex!), Jewish literature is atypical and cannot be contained within a one-dimensional definition."[276]

French literature, like most "national" literatures, is becoming diverse and increasingly hybrid as the European and world borders are shifting, and immigration as well as migration is a central element of French culture. The migrant lives that are but one component of globalization are clearly affecting production of literature. It too needs to come to terms with the perhaps threatening prospect that all things "French" are about to evolve into a more fluid, less controllable and even knowable "product." Françoise Lionnet suggests that we need to rethink the very idea of literature, rejecting reductive oppositions between French literature and "francophone" literatures. She reminds us of Abdelkebir Khatibi's call for the plural in the French: "Who still appeals to…the unity of the French language? Who today still speaks of THE French literature?"[277]

A visit to a French bookstore will indicate that there is a clear diversification within what is included in the greater corpus of French literature. Categories such as "*Ecritures Arabes,*" "*Voix d'Europe,*" "*Immigration*" or

---

275 Derrida, from *Writing and Differences*, as quoted in Ofrat, 32.
276 Ertel, "A Minority Literature," 226.
277 "Qui se réclame encore…de l'unité de la langue française ? Qui parle encore aujourd'hui de La littérature française?" Lionnet, *Post-colonial Representations,* 169.

"*Littérature Maghrébine*" fill the shelves, but it is also apparent, according the Hargreaves, that booksellers, critics and librarians are often divided and confused on the issue, due to increased literary hybridization. "The real issue we have to confront, therefore, is whether these writers belong more to French or to Maghreb literature, or perhaps to some intermediary or marginal space."[278] I am sure, however, that if we were to designate a shelf or a section for "hybrid, *métissage*, border" literature, this shelf would quickly overflow with far more authors and texts than first expected, and soon become the majority literature, even in a place with such deep and exclusive literary traditions as France. After all, we are living in an explosively hybrid border-crossing age, and we know that the thus far "marginal" and minority literary texts will soon occupy center stage as a major force in the various national contemporary bodies of literary work and "canons." There are too many narratives today that are not purely this or purely that, a natural reflection of the global movement of peoples and cultures. The dilemma we experience is both attempting to situate this scenario and also refusing to confine it to a knowable location.[279] Knowing may imply controlling, but it can also be an important element in learning, in order to understand and to improve relations and rectify perceptions.

We are faced with a difficulty of placing or classifying, and therefore finding texts by authors whose works fit in neither the canonical corpus of French literature, nor in the heterogeneous field of francophone literatures can be complicated (be it Maghrebian, West African, Caribbean, Canadian, Vietnamese or other francophone minority literatures as classified within the French system).

While it is theoretically conceivable that a "minor literature" as defined by Gilles Deleuze and Félix Guattari might one day emerge as a distinct immigrant-based enclave within the language of the former colonial motherland, the corpus which has so far been produced, like the word beur itself, seems more likely to prove a transitional step along the road towards incorporation into the mainstream of French cultural production.[280]

---
278 Hargraves, "Writers of Maghreb Immigrant Origin," 34.
279 As noted by Bromley in *Narratives for a New Belonging*, 6.
280 Hargraves, "Writers of Maghreb Immigrant Origin in France," 43.

I think we need to bear in mind that it may be the "mainstream" that is likely to undergo a radical change as borders become more virtual than real, and that the so called "minor literature" will move into a new kind of mainstream, leaving its old space open to other evolving differences yet unknown.

In our attempt to place the Jewish/Sephardic woman writer within the current literary considerations of post-colonial and contemporary discourse in France, we have seen that the many narrative elements that form an integral part of this discourse are also tantamount to what constitute the reflections of Sephardic women writers. Narrating her difference in French society, as an immigrant, a French national, a Jew, and as a woman, is a multifaceted endeavor, requiring the reader to perform a similarly complex analysis, and a reading open to new ways of understanding another element of diversity within the hybrid literary corpus of modern day France.

As we have observed, the Jewish immigrants from the Maghreb had not, like their French-born contemporaries, been raised under the Jacobin notion of cultural hegemony where one had become accustomed to keeping one's Jewish identity a private matter. Instead, they brought with them a natural sense of hybridity resulting from centuries of living in countries where different ethnic, cultural, religious and linguistic communities had learned to coexist with each other.[281] This in turn inspires a different form of writing, a differentiated view on identity, text and even memory. As the Sephardic woman confidently writes of her experiences of exile, marginality, loss, and hope, her identity is firmly voiced through the (re-) workings of memory. According to the critic Lazare Bitoun (born in 1944 in Casablanca), the works of the newly self-assertive French Jew has removed the self-imposed invisibility of the literature by the Frenchman of the Israelite faith. "There is no more *se faire oublier* (self-imposed forgetting), no more hiding behind *noms de plume* (pennames), no more writing for solely Jewish audiences. The new motto instead is '*se faire entendre*' (to make oneself heard), and to make oneself heard as participant of a highly heterogeneous literary project reflective of the diversity of attitudes among young Jews."[282] We are indeed able to hear the minorities speak out, but it is no good to hear if we don't know how to listen. The art of listening takes practice, and

---

281   Nolden, *In Lieu of Memory*, 24.
282   Ibid., 42.

if we could teach our children and students one valuable lesson, it would be to listen to the other's voice, the other's narrative.

As Edward Said reminds us, the main connection between culture and imperialism is all about the power to narrate, or to block other narratives from forming and emerging.[283] Once the narratives have been "released," these signs of existence become impossible to ignore, and the narrators can, through their texts, help bring about a change in power-relations, both small and great. Thanks to the Sephardic community in France, the reference to the "Jewish community" has changed. Nolden points out that "...as immigrants they feel a friction that sets them apart from French society; as Maghreb Jews, they feel estranged from the official institutions of the established Jewish community; as emigrants, they are separated from their countries of birth; and as members of the younger generation they feel a distance from the Judaism practiced by their ancestors.[284] Hence there are multiple reasons that may bring our authors to writing and many existential paradoxes to understand. With the discussions above, and the textual analysis of selected works by Jewish women writers of Maghreb origins to follow, I hope to contribute to the emerging exploration of what it means to be a French woman writer, considering these notions of difference that distinguish them not only from other immigrant narratives but also from the other and better known narratives by today's European women writers.

---

283   Said, *Culture and Imperialism*, xiii.
284   Nolden, *In Lieu of Memory*, 48.

Part III

Voices

Chapter 5

Mothers, Fathers and Rabbis:
Sephardic Traces in Writing Memory and Identity

So far, the attempt to map out the trajectory of the forgotten Sephardic narratives of North Africa has been a relatively wide-ranging inquiry encompassing a broad spectrum of concerns relating to this often-minimized chapter of Jewish history. It has also been a venture to reach a better understanding as to the reasons why and how memories and voices of these entire communities have been marginalized or unseen in both post-colonial and contemporary discourses on displaced and exiled peoples. These issues, historical, cultural and literary in nature, have enabled us to gain an informative perspective in the arena of "global" studies on silenced and marginalized minorities. We can now begin to appreciate that the Judeo-Maghrebian communities do not in any way present a homogeneous group of Jews who all had the same experiences during their centuries of life as *dhimmi* or for the duration of the colonial experience. Nevertheless, whether as individuals, families, neighborhoods or towns, religious or secular, they identified with a profound sense of Jewish North African belonging, which is always discernible among the recovered testimonies, memoirs and narratives.

The present chapter signals the opening of a more intimate inquiry. Our choice to focus on Jewish women writers has been elaborated upon in the preceding pages, and I would like to open this chapter on specific Sephardic women's voices by quoting one of our authors, Gisèle Halimi, a French lawyer, activist, and co-founder with Simone de Beauvoir of *"Choisir la cause des femmes,"* (Chosing the Women's Cause), a feminist organization lobbying for women's rights. In the concluding pages of her maternal memoir *Fritna* (1999) that I will analyze below, she makes the following statement:

"Freud claims that women do not know how to talk about themselves. That they only express their femininity as psychoanalysts, hence as men. Today Freud would be surprised. They dare, they speak and it is all new. Words, desires, conquests."[285] This is precisely what we will encounter as we look at these Jewish women's texts, all reverberating with traces of their Maghreb heritage and memories of collective frameworks as they were experienced ever so intimately in childhood and beyond.

Living integrated, typically assimilated lives as adults in France, often minimally touched by their Jewish Maghreb heritage during their daily lives, the presence or mourned absence of a mother, or a father, or a rabbi, or a marabout, brings about rediscoveries of a lost origin. In her book on nostalgia, Svetlana Boym notes that, "One becomes aware of the collective frameworks of memories when one distances oneself from one's community or when that community itself enters a moment of twilight. Collective frameworks of memory are rediscovered in mourning."[286] It is a desire for a vision of this collective framework of a Jewish Maghreb, as expressed in individual narratives and on personal and intimate levels, that impels us, the readers, to inquire. The Jewish narratives whose imaginary is thus anchored in the Maghreb will, as Najib Redouane points out, contribute to "the transformation of the modes of structure of knowledge and ideas about the Maghreb…It remains a fact that Sephardism constitutes an essential component, even a fundamental one, of this literary production."[287]

Mothers, fathers and rabbis (and a marabout!): each a powerful cultural symbol that has a central and vital presence in the narratives considered in the following pages. They are indeed complex

---

285 "Freud prétend que les femmes ne savent pas parler d'elles. Qu'elles n'expriment leur fémininité qu'en psychanalystes, donc en hommes. Aujourd' hui Freud serait surpris. Elles osent, elles parlent et c'est tout neuf. Les mots, les désirs, les conquêtes." Gisèle Halimi, *Fritna*. Paris: Plon, 1999, 204.
286 Boym, *The Future of Nostalgia*. New York: Basic Books, 2001, 54-55.
287 "…la transformation des modes de structuration des savoirs et des idées du Maghreb…Il reste que le séphardisme constitue une composante essentielle, voire fondamentale, de cette production Romanesque." Najib Redouane, editorial, *International Journal of Francophone Studies*, 3.

cultural constructs whose meanings change over time and according to place, and whose symbolic significances become modified as they are introduced to the West. They also move beyond mere symbols, acting as catalysts for profound internal turmoil through experiences of nostalgia, mourning, opposition, rebellion, contradictions, and exile. Most significantly, they are catalysts for writing and for change. As such they become channels through which the women writers can let their selves develop and reclaim a space of autonomous subjectivity, a space from where they will be able to make sense of the chaos of complex (Sephardic) memories and hybrid identities.

All the authors who will be discussed spent their formative years of childhood in North Africa. Some were young girls as they left hurriedly and clandestinely on their father's arms; others were young adults eagerly seeking out the French capital for its educational possibilities. Nostalgia (*nostos* – return home, and *algia* – longing) is a common emotion when you know you cannot go home, as it occurs not only for a place such as a home, a town or a country but also for the (lost) parent, especially the mother, who represents our beginning, our origin. It is a longing for a home (or the deceased mother) that no longer exists or that has never existed. Knowing that a return to the homeland or to the safe womb of the mother is impossible, the writer is faced with the reality of inaccessibility of the origin, and reminiscing – sometimes obsessively – about her childhood becomes a means to cope with the eventuality of exile or death.

As Boym points out: "At first glance, nostalgia is a longing for a place, but actually it is a yearning for a different time; the time of our childhood, the slower rhythms of our dreams."[288] For Gisèle Halimi, Annie Cohen, and Nine Moati, the different time is when their mother was alive, as their narratives float between joyous or painful childhood memories and dreams of intimacy with the (m)Other whom they need to let go. The realization that this origin is inaccessible needs time to be digested, as the labor of mourning textually reinvents its maternal legacies.

---

288 Boym, *The Future of Nostalgia*, xiv.

Woman as Mother, Woman as Daughter: Annie Cohen, Nine Moati and Gisèle Halimi

A country is, after all, the presence of a mother.
Nine Moati

We begin by looking at three autobiographically inspired texts that share the theme of remembering the mother, all written as the mother has just died. "*Quand la vie s'éteint, la plume s'avive*" (when a life is extinguished, the pen comes alive) goes a well-known saying, and creation – literary creation in this case – becomes a helpful element in the process of mourning. But it is not just about mourning, for the Jewish women writers of North African origin it is also about affirming a marginalized identity, one that even they have contributed to marginalizing in their own lives after they arrived and became even more acculturated in France than they had already become as children in colonial Maghreb. For as Kristeva notes,

> ...*women's desire for affirmation has emerged as a longing for artistic and especially literary creation. Why the emphasis on literature? Is it because when literature is in conflict with social norms, it diffuses knowledge and occasionally the truth about a repressed, secret, and unconscious universe? Is it because literature intensifies the social contract by exposing the uncanny nature of that which remains unsaid?* [289]

Sometimes that which remains unsaid are the things that the writing subject has not said, perhaps not even to herself, and other times the unsaid can be that which society or the dominant culture does not want to talk about. As the authors "write their mother," the narrative becomes an opportunity for the re-writing of a personal and often intimate personal history of identity formation, closely linked to their shared Maghreb heritage.

---

[289] Kristeva, "New Maladies of the Soul," in *The Portable Kristeva*. Kelly Oliver, ed., New York: Columbia UP, 1983, 364.

Nine Moati's *Mon enfant, ma mère* (1974),[290] Annie Cohen's *Bésame Mucho* (1998),[291] and Gisèle Halimi's *Fritna* (1999),[292] are three very different (m)Other texts, but they share the need and desire to come to terms with the mother, their other, and the irreversibility of this loss. As they write and narrate the mother, the mourning slowly passes with the elapsing of time needed for what Freud termed "the work of grief." We will see that the writers deal with coming to terms not only with the loss of the mother, but also with the mother herself and what she represented, and how she related to her daughter and the world around her. Each mother evokes not only an origin but also a (vanishing) connection to the Jewish Maghreb source, and as Adalgisa Giorgio has noted, "The maternal figure is often a metaphor of origins, encompassing not only kinship but also race, ethnicity, and language. She comes to represent the ethnic roots which the daughter wishes simultaneously to repress in her search for assimilation to the dominant culture, and to preserve in order to remain loyal to the values and memories of her community."[293]

These mother-daughter narratives are produced from within a certain marginal space, which is France's Jewish North African immigrant community, and the narrators are faced with the sometimes agonizing awareness of the contradictions of their chosen assimilated French lifestyles and the Judeo-Maghrebian heritage embodied by the mother, albeit sometimes resented as archaic and problematic. Our three narrators write three Sephardic mothers, all remembered as products of their distinct historical formation as female, Jewish, colonial subjects, rooted in their unique Sephardic culture. How was the Judeo-Maghrebian locus affected by the values of colonial French Catholic bourgeois values? These mothers were raised in a paternalistic colonial universe with a double law – that of the colonizer, that had merely supplanted the discriminatory *dhimmi* law of the Shari'a, and that of the father, whether Jewish, Christian or Muslim. The daughters try to place their mothers within these historical situations, in order to understand the

---

290   Nine Moati. *Mon Enfant, Ma Mère*. Paris: Editions Stock, 1974.
291   Annie Cohen. *Bésame Mucho*. Paris: Gallimard, 1998.
292   Gisèle Halimi. *Fritna*. Paris: Plon, 1999.
293   Adalgisa Giorgio ed., "Writing the Mother-Daughter Relationship," in *Writing Mothers and Daughters*. New York: Berghahn Books, 2002, 32.

desires, secrets and fears that may have guided their actions, inactions or reactions as women and mothers.

There are several models of discourse possible in daughterly narratives, including matricidal, reconciliatory, and recuperative, which represent three of the more "classic" feminist categories. As we look closer at the three daughterly narratives selected here, we need to ask if these texts aim for maternal erasure *à la* feminist theorists Julia Kristeva and Adrienne Rich, or if the narrator is looking to resolve and settle a complicated relationship, or perhaps a recovery or a salvaging is what is sought out.

Alex Hughes suggests that "within a sociocultural system under which the mother is desubjectivized as the disempowered Other, a daughter's relation to her maternal parent will necessarily admit a fear of identity fusion, a desire for a differentiation, and ultimately, a willingness to commit (symbolic) matricide in order to consolidate it."[294] However, as our analysis will reveal, writing (about) the mother is not necessarily always a subconsciously hostile, matricidal act, since daughters also adore their mothers and have experienced intimate and healthy relationships with this elemental other of theirs, who has permitted them to separate, individuate, and assume an adult life. The idea that the daughter can manifest her complete individuation only by effacing the mother she ostensibly sets out to remember and to name is relevant, but not the only mother/daughter paradigm available. The mother text becomes a passage, a process not only of mourning but also of that very individuation the writing daughter craves. Consider Daniel Sibony's concept of the "*entre-deux*," useful to my view of this process: "The in-between of women…is the space between a woman and herself; between a woman and the feminine experienced as her origin; hence as Other. The in-between-women is the passage where a woman has to pass through as her own origin as woman; it is the impasse when she considers herself the origin of the feminine."[295] This

---

[294] Alex Hughes, "Writing Mother-Daughter Relationality in the French Context," *Writing Mothers and Daughters*, 163.
[295] "L'entre-deux femmes…c'est l'espace entre une femme et elle-même ; entre une femme et le féminin ressenti comme son origine [mother] ; donc comme Autre [Other]. L'entre-deux femmes est le passage où une femme doit passer par son origine de femme; c'est l'impasse quand elle s'y prend pour l'origine du féminin." Sibony, *L'Entre-Deux*, 142.

would be similar to a mother-quest where the daughter's search for her self happens through a recuperation of her maternal heritage.

As we look closer at these maternal texts, we also need to ask about the writer's vision of the mother. Is there an all-embracing, invasive maternal presence evoked? Does the daughter's "thralldom" to the maternal admit a resolution (as asked by Alex Hughes)? Is there mother-daughter over identification? Does the text function as a form of matricide, as suggested by Kristeva and Rich, and will this murder of the (dead) mother allow the daughter to achieve complete individuation? Julia Kristeva acknowledges in an interview with Elaine Hoffman Baruch that although there is a community of women, it is important to realize that it should be (and is!) made up of particularities because it is not, and should not be a uniform mass of standardized desires, reactions and needs.[296] This view seems relevant in our approach to the mother-texts here, since the authors' styles in writing their mothers are not uniform, nor do their relationships with the mother seem standardized.

These are three very different views of mothers, indeed three singular mothers, and three unique ways of writing her. What is, however, a common thread in the daughterly narratives is the trace of the Jewish mother's Sephardic whispers, and the memories of the Maghreb origin that defines part of the narrator's identity. Recovering these seems to become an essential part of the narration also, thereby rooting the daughter in the Sephardic heritage she may not have valued or identified with as much during the mother's life. Daniel Sibony talks about the dead mother as that origin which finally "accepts" to be "decomposed" in order for the daughter to live on: "...an origin is needed which 'accepts' to be divided, put into pieces, decomposed, recomposed, in short that consents to be transformed into fertile in-betweens in the form of a living passage rather than fixed messages."[297] Again, it is the mother who gives life, this time to writing – via her own death.

---

296   Julia Kristeva, "Interview with Elaine Hoffman Baruch" in *Julia Kristeva: Interviews,* edited by Ross Mitchel Guberman. New York: Columbia UP, 1996. 113-21.
297   "il faut une origine qui 'accepte' de se laisser démultiplier, mettre en morceaux, décomposer, recomposer, bref qui consente à se reporter en des entre-deux féconds en forme de passage à vivre plutôt que des messages à fixer" Sibony, *L'Entre-Deux,* 65-66.

A Mother to Contend With in Gisèle Halimi's *Fritna*

Gisèle Halimi, lawyer, feminist, and activist, was born in Tunisia in 1927 and immigrated to France in 1944 to begin her university education culminating in her law degree and entry in the French and Tunisian judicial systems in 1948. Known in France first and foremost for fighting for the rights of Algerian freedom fighters/terrorists and representing the FLN during the Algerian War, she occupied a controversial place in French public opinion throughout the 1950s and 1960s. In the 1970s she dedicated much of her time to the cause of women, and allied with Simone de Beauvoir she founded the organization *"Choisir – La cause des femmes,"* as they fought for legalization of abortion and a woman's right to choose. She continues to have a public presence and is known for her activism and for having published texts recounting some of the more controversial cases she has represented, on issues relating to the women's cause both globally and nationally in France, and more recently for her two autobiographical and personal narratives depicting her parents, her upbringing and her formative years.

Fritna, the title of Halimi's maternal text, is also the Judeo-Arabic translation and diminutive of her mother's given name, Fortunée. The text recounts a desperate longing for maternal love, and we discover a sad, disappointed, and resigned woman who, until the last moments of her mother's life, tried, in vain, to experience intimacy with her. "I am afraid of her dying, she will take with her forever the answer that I await"[298] says Halimi, who will recount her last attempts at finding some answers as her mother lay dying, while going back to her childhood to dissect the mother's and daughter's difficult co-existence. The text is presented like a quest; Halimi wants to find out why it is that her mother did not show any signs of love toward the young child as well as toward the woman daughter. "She refused any embrace, any kiss, any contact. This delight…she did not want."[299] She wants to understand her own emotional exile and her mother's rejection so that she

---

[298]   "J'ai peur de sa mort, elle emportera pour toujours la réponse que j'attends." *Fritna*, 77.
[299]   "Elle refusait toute étreinte, tout baiser, tout contact. Cette volupté…elle n'en voulait pas." Ibid., 16.

may rewrite differently the many years of affective wandering: "Her un-love had destabilized me, even uprooted me."[300] The goal is not just to understand, but to try to find, in time, in the mother, in answers, a moment when the childhood can be redeemed. "I hang onto her, I do not want her to leave before we can love one another, without the abolishment of my love-less childhood."[301] We learn about a young girl and woman who experienced a near total lack of maternal affective commitment, and it is this emotional exile that is mourned throughout her book, tellingly subtitled *"Pour l'amour d'une mère"* (For the love of a mother). The text functions as a way for the author to organize her own self, as she says it in the end of the book, after the mother's funeral: "I will write a book about *Fritna*, between confession and complaint. I need to put order in my deepest self."[302]

Halimi identifies her mother's care for her and her sister according to the principle of necessity or responsibility, whereas her father's coaxing and tenderness are referred to as a principle of pleasure, of affectivity. The father called her lovingly *aziza*, sweetheart in Judeo-Arabic, and *doye anaye*, light of my eyes, whereas the mother had no diminutive for her daughter. Edouard, the father, "indulged in the pleasure of having two daughters who were a little crazy but intelligent and in love with him."[303] She admits that the love she felt from her father valorized her and functioned as a substitute for the maternal love she so craved: "Fritna is absence. Absence of all affection, absence of the body, absence of the mother."[304] Halimi points out that she and her younger sister Gaby lived with a deficit that mutilated them: they were girls and not loved by their mother.[305] The daughters' births were not celebrated, and when Gisèle was born, her parents hid the news from the outside world for three weeks, paralyzed by the shame they felt since she was not a coveted son.

---

300 "Son désamour m'avait déstabilisée, je dirais déracinée." Ibid., 59.
301 "Je m'accroche, je ne veux pas qu'elle s'en aille sans que nous nous soyons aimées, sans que soit abolie cette enfance de désamour." Ibid., 122.
302 "J'écrirai un livre sur Fritna, entre confession et plainte. Il faut que je m'ordonne au plus profond de moi." Ibid., 211.
303 "…se laissait aller au plaisir d'avoir deux filles un peu maboula ('folles') mais intelligentes et amoureuses de lui." Ibid., 97.
304 "Fritna est l'absence. Absence de tout calin, absence du corps, absence de la mère." Ibid., 16.
305 Ibid., 19.

As a girl and teenager the parents would recount this story to her, only to symbolically kill her over and over again. The journal young Gisèle sets out to keep is entitled "*Journal d'une mal-aimée*" (*Diary of an Unloved Girl*), something that hurts the adult Halimi as she finds it and reads it later in life. The knowledge of this symbolic killing of baby Gisèle by hiding her presence devastates the girl, and it is only the beginning of many childhood traumas that would underscore the mother's inability of being loving, comforting and soothing. When she was four her little brother died in an accident at home alone with Gisèle and the older brother, a death for which Gisèle was blamed. And although she realizes that her mother must have projected the anger on her daughter as a way to repress her own guilt for having left the children home alone, it left damaging scars.

Throughout her childhood Gisèle was also reminded about what a difficult baby she was (Fritna called herself "*meghbouna*," or cursed, for her misfortunes) and that she almost killed her father since he suffered from an appendicitis that needed emergency surgery after a long night awake with the screaming baby girl in bed with them. The baby had wiggled around so much that the exhausted parents had fallen asleep without blankets, and hence the mother blamed the baby for the father's ills. Another painful memory was from the bed-wetting problems Gisèle had as a child and well into her pre-teen years. One way for the mother to try to get her daughter to stop this "bad habit" was to bring an old Bedouin woman to the house who traumatized the girl with rituals and threats of physical harm. After the public humiliation (family and neighbors were invited to the "ritual"), and sobbing in her mother's arms, Gisèle recalls: "My mother rejected me, blamed me, doubled my desperation. I had tried many times to cry out to her the need I had for her love, for her understanding, for her arms where I hid while sobbing: 'Mom, forgive me, I don't understand how it happens, this, at night'. But Fortunée would push me away…"[306] This humiliation brought the girl to a "pathetic" suicide attempt, as she describes it, as

---

[306] "Ma mère me rejetait, me culpabilisait, redoublait mon désespoir. J'avais tenté plusieurs fois de lui crier le besoin que j'avais de son amour, de sa compréhension, de ses bras dans lesquels je me jetais en sanglotant : 'Maman pardonne-moi, je ne sais comment ça arrive, ça, la nuit'. Mais Fortunée me repoussait…" Ibid., 96.

this act might have finally made the mother love her in death, as she would no longer be the source of Fritna's *malédiction* (curse).

As she grew up, Halimi felt strongly that the traditional gendered upbringing her mother was giving her and her sister was not right. The feminist fire was ignited early on, and the young girl would read everything she could get her hands on, and confront her mother daily since "confronting her was to have a relationship with her."[307] Attempts by the daughter to create situations where she could "harvest a few crumbs of affection" became part of her continued quest for validation, even as an adult. When Halimi first came to France, just as the Second World War was over, her older brother Marcelo was released from a Nazi camp. The family did not know if he was dead or alive, and Fritna had written him off as dead and was already mourning her second son.

But Gisèle became obsessed with finding him, managed to locate him, and promised the parents to find him and return him home safely. This, she hoped, was her one big chance to gain favor in Fritna's eyes: "As the train left I felt a great gratitude toward this unknown brother who had allowed me to stand out in the eyes of my mother, to prove to her, in short, how much I was her."[308] By having located and returned her brother, and spent a few intimate, emotional moments with him before he returned to Tunisia, Gisèle could by osmosis get closer to her mother. The efforts of Gisèle to create situations where manifestations of affection could occur continues throughout her adulthood, up until Fritna is about to die. As the mother grows dependent, Halimi insists that her mother come live with her so that perhaps this closeness in physical space will give them an opportunity to experience a sense of intimacy: "Fritna with me, from morning until night…Fritna in enormous doses, continuous, to catch up on the void, the absence of my childhood…Fritna would realize, in her lifetime, belated, with me, that loving her daughter was perhaps worth it."[309] Despite Gisèle's prom-

---

307   "l'affronter c'était avoir une relation avec elle." Ibid., 18.
308   "Au départ du train, je ressentis une immense reconnaissance pour ce frère méconnu qui m'avait permis de me distinguer auprès de ma mère, de lui prouver, en somme, combien elle, c'était moi." Ibid., 179.
309   "Fritna avec moi, du matin au soir…Fritna à doses énormes, continues, pour rattraper le vide, l'absence de mon enfance…Fritna réaliserait, dans sa vie, sur le tard, avec moi, qu'aimer sa fille, ça valait peut-être le coup." Ibid., 31-32.

ises of hiring a religious Jewish caregiver for her mother that would prepare kosher meals, the mother refuses, and instead tells her that her brother will take care of her. "End of discussion. A dream forever lost,"[310] the narrator concludes bitterly.

Every time Halimi begins to ask her ailing mother a question, she is brushed away by Fritna, who says she is too tired. The mother consistently rejects any of the daughter's attempts at creating situations that might bring them closer to the other, and she childishly tries to "buy" her mother's affection as when she offers her flowers – that she insists Gisèle take home – or a new nightgown that she will not wear. When Fritna, near death, finally holds her daughter's hands and does not let go and even reciprocates kisses, Gisèle feels a strange, dizzying sensation:

At the moment she seems at peace and does not let go of my hands. I feel something completely new come over me, her tenderness, and the fear of a child who discovers the gestures of love. Overwhelmed, I take her hands and kiss her softly. As if by mimicry, she soon takes mine and covers them with kisses. I begin again, a little taken back. Fritna also. She surrounds my face with her hands and gives me quick, jerky kisses on my nose, on my cheeks. Then slower on the lips, "my girl, my darling."[311]

Gisèle knows that this is but a faint trace of the maternal love Fritna must have been capable of, but that she will no longer be able to receive from her mother, now that she is about to die. This "death kiss" is to her a sign that her mother must have had it in her somewhere, if just a spec from her own childhood, the desire for a "mother-daughterly conspiracy" of intimacy:

---

310   "Débat clos. Rêve à jamais perdu." Ibid., 33.
311   "Pour l'heure elle semble apaisée et ne lache pas mes mains. Je sens quelque chose de totalement neuf m'envahir, sa tendresse, et la peur d'un enfant qui découvre les gestes de l'amour. Submergée, je lui prends les mains et les lui embrasse doucement. Comme par mimétisme, elle prend aussitôt les miennes et les couvre de baisers. Je recommence, un peu interdite. Fritna aussi. Elle entoure mon visage de ses paumes et m'embrasse à petits coups rapides, saccadés, le nez, les joues. Et plus longuement, les lèvres, 'ma fille, ma chérie.'" Ibid., 23.

It seemed certain to me in any event, that girls need to receive the keys to this language from their mothers, in order to forge their own complex and ambiguous "destiny". Through love, through a carnal connection, through a type of erotic complicity, the child-daughter becomes aware of herself and learns to love herself as such. With this other self, from herself, emotionality, intelligence, and rational power take shape in her own identity "source". [312]

    Gisèle Halimi's eventual choice of profession can be seen as a direct result of her relationship with her mother. Emotionally and physically excluded from all maternal bonding, she pursues a career that allows her to defend those initially excluded from the right to justice, as she had "a right" to the love that was not granted her: "I have always shared in the battle of the excluded"[313] she says, and she will defend Arabs, Fritna's other (she hated them) and takes on cases like that of a Catholic girl who had been raped and had to have an illegal abortion. According to Fritna all French girls were labeled as "*khabas*," whores. Gisèle's career does nothing else than counter the entire maternal plan of what a daughter should do, and her mother is disgusted by her conquest of public status and authority. Already as a young girl she began this fight against injustice, but realizes that Fritna most likely perceived this "revolt" as a rejection of her and her more primitive North African life and world:

She did not believe in us, in our revolts. She severely condemned our agnosticism…I had already decided to shake this cover of injustice and of discrimination that suffocated me, because I was a girl…Had Fortunée felt this break from everything that was her universe, her education, in short her entire destiny, a total and intimate breaking off from herself?[314]

---

312   "Ce qui me paraît certain dans tout le cas, c'est le besoin de filles de recevoir de leur mère les clefs de ce langage, pour forger leur 'destin' complexe, ambigu. Par l'amour, par le lien charnel, par une sorte de complicité érotique, l'enfant fille s'appréhende et apprend à s'aimer comme telle. Avec l'autre soi-même, à partir de soi-même, se forment dans sa propre 'source' identitaire l'affectivité, l'intelligence, le pouvoir rationnel." Ibid., 204.
313   "J'ai toujours partagé le combat des exclus!" Ibid., 140.
314   "Elle ne croyait pas en nous, en nos révoltes. Elle condamnait très sévèrement notre agnosticisme…J'avais déjà choisi de secouer ce couvercle

Halimi realizes that Fritna, too, was a product of her childhood and the kind of environment she had grown up in. She tries to find excuses for her mother's maternal inadequacies, and the lack of affection and silence: "Is it not 'shameful,' *ahchouma*, to reveal ones feelings?...a love, but one that does not know how to express itself. It existed, then... had my mother loved me?...in a determination of silent education, of secrecy of feelings. I constructed the alibi for Fritna."[315] She notes the mother's ignorance even in Jewish matters, as if this too would explain her lack of the "maternal commandment" to love your daughter: "In fact, she was ignorant of everything, of religious theory and of the history of Judaism, she did not read or understand Hebrew, and her practices were made up more of a mix of traditions and superstitions than reasoned commandments from the Torah."[316] Not finding any rationale behind her mother's absence, Gisèle chooses a very rational and pragmatic path for herself: she became a lawyer. As she speaks of her children's (her three boys') love for their grandmother Fritna, she criticizes how her mother has created a legend for the grandchildren that she had practically raised them, and that their mother had abandoned them, "*pour défendre les Arabes!*" (to defend the Arabs!).

Halimi can see the rationale neither behind these allegations nor behind her children loving Fritna so much, and concludes: "*Pas de rationalité en amour!*" (No rationality in love!). Halimi needs reason, is avid for Reason, since as a child nothing seemed reasonable to her, and this she was excited to find in France as she describes: "...my fascination to 'touch' France, her land, the leaves and the trees, the true one, not the one of the colonizers and of contempt, but that of the books of

---

d'injustice et de discrimination qui m'étouffait, parce que fille...Fortunée avait-elle senti cette rupture d'avec tout ce qui était son univers, son éducation, son destin en somme, somme rupture intime d'avec elle-même?" Ibid., 125.
315   "N'est-il pas 'honteux', ahchouma, de dévoiler ses sentiments?...un amour, mais qui ne sait pas se parler. Qui existait donc....ma mère m'a-t-elle aimée ?...dans le déterminisme de l'éducation au silence, du secret des sentiments. J'ai construit l'alibi de Fritna." Ibid., 136-137.
316   "Elle ignorait tout, en effet, de la théorie religieuse et de l'histoire du judaïsme, elle ne lisait ni ne comprenait l'hébreu, et ses pratiques tenaient plus d'une mélange de traditions et de superstitions que des commandements argumentés de la Thora." Ibid., 50.

Reason."³¹⁷ According to Halimi, Fritna was corrupted by colonial hegemony and she tries persistently to understand her mother, explaining her to others and to herself. As a teenager she begins to read and finds ways to defend her mother's shortcomings: ignorance, religion, strict education, married off at sixteen; a product of her surroundings: "Housewives inaccessible to desire during the day, sensuous and in love at night. Ideal wives for the Oriental male, manufactured in the unspokenness of religion and tradition."³¹⁸

In some ways, Fritna as a mother is caught between several cultural paradigms: she is a descendant of the Spanish Diaspora, the "real" *Sephardim*, and had married below her since the father was of primitive Bedouin Berber stock. She would often play the drama of the Oriental woman, as when Gisèle's younger sister Gaby elopes from home, pregnant with her non-Jewish, communist lover: "'She is dead to me!' screamed my mother transformed into a mourning Tunisian woman, scratching her cheeks and twisting her hands."³¹⁹ Yet at the same time she identified with the French, speaking of the Arabs as helpless without using a collective "us," referring to the typical references/proofs of better bridges, roads and hospitals, which the French had brought to the Maghreb. She would also justify her hatred of the Arabs from a Jewish perspective, evoking pogroms of the past.

As Halimi's children spend summer vacations with their grandparents in Nice, southern France, they are exposed to parts of their heritage that they did not get at home, such as the sounds of Judeo-Arabic, the religious rituals that Fritna maintains, and traditional Tunisian cooking like couscous. At the weekly "tribal" dinner at the Halimi/Faux household (her second husband, a non-Jew, is named Faux), where she gathers with her children and grandchildren, Gisèle will clap her hands rhythmically and chant "*thé ben nana, thé ben nana!*" (mint tea, mint

---
317 "…ma fascination de 'toucher' la France, sa terre, les feuilles de ses arbres, la vraie, pas celle des colonisateurs et du mépris, mais celle des livres et de la Raison." Ibid., 168.
318 "…ménagères inaccessibles au désir le jour, sensuelles et amoureuses la nuit. Epouses idéales du mâle oriental, fabriquées dans le non-dit de la religion et la tradition." Ibid., 64.
319 "'Elle est morte pour moi!' hurlait ma mère transformée en pleureuse tunisienne, se griffant les joues et se tordant les mains…" Ibid., 84.

tea!), and "...with the gestures of my ancestors, holding the teapot up high and then bringing it back down and resuming the up and down, I pour the magically blond beverage."[320] Magical to her, for this was an act that she is repeating from her father, "*Edouard le magicien,*" since pouring the nana tea is a typically male "show," and the only tradition Halimi has taken with her is imitated from her father, the parent who validated and reciprocated the love of the little girl.

The title of the last chapter of Fritna speaks volumes: "A woman becomes a woman only through a woman."[321] Gisèle Halimi is only too aware of the implications of her mother's physical absence in presence: "She denied me the physical contact that all children demand from their mother."[322] Recall Daniel Sibony speaking of "*entre-deux femmes*" (in-between women) which takes us back to the importance of our origin, and how it marks our passages that follow once we lose that origin which must be lost in order that we live "...where a woman who has received 'nothing' from her mother could be neither daughter nor mother, but remained suspended in her woman-being, in her in-between languages, unable to 'read' or 'write' the traces of femininity."[323] Gisèle notes that she was never able to find a time or a place where female-to-female connectivity could be experienced. As Luce Irigaray has noted, such a place is critical to a woman's development into an independent, autonomous, self-loving individual. Our narrator writes, in a psychoanalytically and feminist-ically informed observation:

> *Definitively, this love without reciprocity by a very a-typical mother will have deprived me of knowing myself. It seems to me that a woman cannot complete this knowledge without the closeness – both emotional and sensual – with another woman. The mother is this other, sublime model, simultaneously put on a pedestal and mixed*

---

320   "...avec les gestes de mes aïeux, montant très haut la théière puis la descendant puis recommençant le va-et-vient, je verse le breuvage d'un blond magique." Ibid., 113.
321   "Une femme ne devient femme que par une femme!" Ibid., 199.
322   "Elle m'a refusé ce contact physique que toute enfant exige de sa mère." Ibid.
323   "... où une femme à qui sa mère n'a 'rien donné' ne pourrait être ni fille ni mère, et restait en suspens de son être-femme, dans son entre-deux langues à elle, ne pouvant ni 'lire' ni 'écrire' les traces de la féminité." Sibony, *L'Origine*, 65.

in with your flesh, in your daily life. She is the woman that the daughter will become. It is by maternal love that the relationship to the body is created...I have not had this fundamental experience.[324]

For, as Alex Hughes points out, "...when daughters confront the 'problem' of mother-daughter (non) relationality and make it the focus of their literary endeavors, they may select either to delineate and denounce the mother's damaging imbrication in the daughter's life/identity, or to mourn the unworkability of the mother–daughter connection."[325] It seems that Halimi has selected both these approaches, in that she deplores her mother's inability to manifest a love for her daughter, and also grieves for the hopelessness of changing what has been and continues to be. "Fritna is dead, it's the end of the absence. Of the emptiness, precisely of this lack. Unavoidable scars...I feel different, new. I recover a piece of internal freedom. Curiously, intimately mixed with the pain is a lightness of being."[326] She admits feeling a relief; she is able to accept the inevitability of being scarred. At the funeral, she confuses her mother's death with her own: "...my childhood knots my throat. This childhood of the Goulette ending at Bagneux. A definitive confusion with the death of Fritna."[327] Thus she sees her own image in death, her own casket and her mourning children. "Clearly, the death of the mother or the father clings to ours,"[328] Halimi concludes.

---

324   "En définitive, cet amour sans réciprocité pour une mère très atypique m'aura privé de la connaissance de moi-même. Une femme, me semble-t-il, ne parfait cette connaissance que par l'approche – émotionelle, sensuelle – d'une autre femme. La mère est cette autre, modèle sublime, à la fois mis sur un piédestal et mêlé à votre chair, à votre quotidien. Elle est la femme que sera la fille. C'est par l'amour maternel que se construit le rapport au corps...Cette aventure fondamentale, je ne l'ai pas vécue." *Fritna*, 202.
325   Hughes, "Writing Mother-Daughter Relationality in the French Context," *Writing Mothers and Daughters*, 163.
326   "Fritna est morte, c'est la fin de l'absence. Du vide, de ce manque justement. Avec Fritna disparaît à jamais la force d'un non-amour...Le manque du manque. Cicatrices inévitables...Je me sens différente, neuve. Je récupère une part de liberté intérieure. Curieusement, intimement mêlée au chagrin, une légèreté d'être." *Fritna*, 187.
327   "..mon enfance me noue la gorge. Cette enfance de la Goulette qui finit à Bagneux. Une confusion définitive avec la mort de Fritna." Ibid., 208.
328   "Décidément, la mort de la mère ou du père colle à la nôtre." Ibid., 212.

In the end she reproduces the Rabbi's suggestion by putting out olives and bread on the table as a way of keeping Fritna with them. She wants to perpetuate a tradition after all, and by doing so, maybe she understands what made her mother continue with hers throughout her life. This act is often motivated by love, irrationally and irrevocably. Halimi has written her mother, and thus is able to assume her life as it has been shaped by that very relationship. In writing her mother she has found a way to express her exile from her, to mourn the absence that defined her childhood, and to contemplate the issues of her emotional as well as Judeo-Tunisian heritage. Aware of her own mortality, but surrounded by her children and grandchildren, her mother's legacy, despite the deep scars it left, becomes part of the family story. Halimi will move on, stronger and able to love.

Lyrical Memories of a Sephardic Mother in Annie Cohen's *Bésame Mucho*

Annie Cohen was born in Algeria in 1944 and spent her childhood in Sidi-bel-Abbès, 75 km inland from the Mediterranean Sea. She left Algeria for France in 1962 at the age of 18. Cohen's lyrical memoir *Bésame Mucho* (1998) is as if set to the soothing tune of the well-known Spanish song also entitled *Bésame Mucho*. Words from this passionate song filled with the urgings of a longing lover, child or parent are scattered throughout the text, and we hear it as reminiscent of the lullaby and love song that the narrator's mother, who has just died, used to sing to her daughter when she was a child, and even before she was born. But the song goes farther back, since it becomes a link to the origin, to the Andalusian heritage of the mother:

Bésame, bésame mucho,
Como si fuera esta noche la última vez
Bésame mucho
Que tengo miedo perderte, perderte después
Bésame, bésame mucho
Como si fuera esta noche la última vez
Bésame mucho
Que tengo miedo perderte, perderte después.

Bésame Mucho is Annie Cohen's hymn to her mother and functions as a thread that she picks up from where the mother left it to eternalize the love she is reciprocating. "Is it you, *Bésame* adored, who gives me words from your hand again?"[329] The memories of the deceased mother inspire writing, for the narrator is not just looking to eternalize her love for her mother, but also the mother herself. One of the first images in the text is the daughter groping around at the base of the tombstone, saying "I should have embalmed her, frozen her, to stop the degradation…"[330] Seeking to eternalize the mother, she is also by extension fearing her own decomposition, for as she says, "Should not accept that her heart stops, should not give in. Tomorrow it will be you."[331]

Similar to the daughter in *Fritna*, the awareness of one's own mortality is part of knowing the mother's, and the time it takes to let the mother go – the grieving time – is also in part a way of coming to terms with one's own mortality. As Kristeva notes, if a daughter does not manage to separate from the mother, even after her death, she will carry along her mother's corpse, forever. We see this attachment when the narrator in *Bésame Mucho* says she wants to rent a small room in front of her mother's final resting place, "It becomes an obsession, an illness, a sort of gangrene that eats my insides."[332] *Bésame Mucho* is a process of grief, a gestational period of detachment needed by the daughter in order for her to move on with her life and not feel obsessed by her mother's death. It even begins, subconsciously, nine months before when she has a dream about her mother dying. However, she is also obsessed by the love the mother gave, and even after she has died does the daughter feel the "Immense and unbearable love which still leaves the grave and comes all the way here…"[333] It is no coincidence that nine months go by from the beginning of the book until the end, when the narrator finally can say "I have gotten used to it…I have to distance myself."[334]

---

329 "Est-ce toi, Bésame adorée, qui me donnes encore les mots de la main?" *Bésame Mucho*. Paris : Gallimard, 1998, 14.
330 "J'aurais dû l'embaumer, la congeler, arrêter la dégradation…" Ibid., 11.
331 "Fallait pas accepter que son coeur s'arrête, fallait pas se soumettre. Demain ce sera toi." Ibid.
332 "Ça devient une obsession, une maladie, une sorte de gangrène qui me bouffe les entrailles." Ibid., 13.
333 "Immense amour insoutenable qui sort encore du tombeau et qui arrive jusqu'ici…"Ibid., 16.
334 "J'ai repris l'habitude…il faut que je m'éloigne." Ibid., 173-174.

Like a new life being issued from the maternal body, she is like an infant again, who learns how to breathe outside the womb. When she is with the mother in the hospital, she remembers how they would begin from the beginning, her beginning, the mother's beginning, and their origin together: "We return to zero and we being again. We return to the time of *Bésame*, to the time when she sang *Bésame mucho* when I was in her belly...First the head comes out and we breathe normally. The time in the belly can last forever."[335] Her mother wants to be buried with the daughter's book on her chest, and this the narrator sees as a way for them to be together eternally: "...in this verbal body-to-body. I will belong to her eternally. Like that, in the earth, as the time of gestation...One against the other."[336] The narrative structure of this nine month period of grieving is fragmentary, a *va-et-vient* or coming and going or push-pull of desires of staying, leaving, returning; between childhood memories, the secret Andalusian memories of the mother recalling ancient origins, time spent next to the dying mother, and finally the narrator's trip to Andalusia, as the freeing process comes full circle. "We are going to sing *Bésame mucho*. Both of us. In bed. Now that the path is clear. We won't care about the family, you and me, we'll stay alone in the world, without them, without the others. Don't believe that death unites. It divides."[337]

The song whose words are evoked throughout the text is a reference to the mother's connection to her Andalusian heritage, as she came from a Jewish Algerian family who were exiled from the Iberian Peninsula in 1492. This constant reminder of the quiet whispers of the love and the heritage of the mother becomes a comforting presence for the mourning narrator, and an emotional window that she feels drawn

---

335 "On repart de zéro et on recommence. On revient au temps de Bésame, au temps où elle chantait Bésame mucho quand j'étais dans son ventre...On sort d'abord la tête et on respire normalement. Ça peut durer indéfiniment le temps du ventre." Ibid., 68.
336 "...dans ce corps à corps verbal. Je lui appartiendrai pour l'éternité. Ainsi, dans la terre, comme au temps de gestation...L'une contre l'autre." Ibid., 116.
337 "On va chanter Bésame mucho. Toutes les deux. Dans le lit. Maintenant que la route est dégagée. On s'en fout de la famille, on restera toi et moi, seules dans le monde, sans eux, sans les autres. Faut pas croire que la mort unit. Elle désunit." Ibid., 31.

to: "It makes me want to go into exile, to get lost, in Spain, in Andalusia, in Seville, in the land of the language of *Bésame*."[338]

The narrator wants to retire from the world, as she sits in a quiet corner of her mother's apartment waiting "…to go back to Andalusia and never again speak…I hate memories. I am leaving for the roads of Spain, on the traces of a memory that exceeds us. *Bésame*. Kiss me. *Bésame mucho*."[339] As much as she doesn't want to be hurt by memories, she craves them, as she craves her mother's origins and the one thing that lives on beyond us: memories. With the mother gone, losing her means losing much more: "It is as if there were no more origin, no more roots, identity, family name. As if everything was lost from both heritage and lineage…The disappearance of her initials has drowned mine."[340] As the daughter's desperation mounts she considers escaping it all, and the place she is driven towards, is, naturally, Andalusia, the place of origin. "I have to get the hell out of here and go to Andalusia."[341] As origin of the Sephardic Jews, not just the mother, not just the narrator, but their "tribe," Andalusia symbolizes the arch-origin, a time in Jewish history to which one can never return, just as a return to the womb of the mother is impossible. The Jews, however, have always kept the memories of their other roots, from Jerusalem to Spain, to Tunisia, and now France…The cultural passions remain ingrained, and a palimpsest or layering of memories from different times and different places becomes a natural part of hybrid identities, whose very hybridity unites them.

There were many Jews of Spanish origin in Oran, and with them came the traces, the tastes, the inherent desire to be alive with the heritage of this "*entre-deux*": "More than others, the people from Oran had the taste for Spanish games and parties, for the body and for dancing, for rhythms and

---

338   "Ça me donne envie de m'exiler, de foutre le camp, en Espagne, en Andalousie, à Seville, dans le pays de la langue de Bésame." Ibid., 48.
339   "…rejoindre l 'Andalousie et de ne plus parler…Je hais les souvenirs. Je vais m'en aller sur les routes d'Espagne, sur les traces d'une mémoire qui nous dépasse. Bésame. Embrasse-moi. Bésame mucho." Ibid.
340   "Ça fait comme s'il n'y avait plus d'origine, de racines, d'identité, de nom de famille. Comme si tout se perdait du patrimoine et de la filiation… La disparition de ses initiales a noyé les miennes." Ibid., 54..
341   "…Il faut foutre le camp en Andalousie." Ibid., 60.

for the *chacha*."[342] And "Nothing reminds me more of my mother than her devilish tangos and those stupid *paso doble* that she danced more in her head than with her body and which pulled her heart apart, I knew it well, for mysterious and secret reasons. Painful music from a lost Spain, *Viva España*, or for a lost passion, *Yo ne sé porque te quiero*."[343] Memories of being part of this longing, of becoming an accomplice as she danced the tango with her mother: "She followed with suppleness, not at all surprised, without realizing how much these few steps in my arms were going to torture my memory. We should have spent her life dancing, listening to tangos. Learning to die, *Bésame*, learning to live, *Bésame mucho*."[344] She wonders if her mother was secretly terrified by the fear of living, losing and longing. How could she have known her mother better? And what was behind this passionate woman, who "…sang sensual rhythms with her hoarse voice, repeating unaffectedly the only verses she knew"?[345] She does not know, but wishes she could understand better the things that made her mother live life as she did.

One window into the life of the mother is through the family's cleaning lady, a staple in the Cohen household since the days in Oran. The maid, usually an Arab woman in Algeria, but a Polish woman in France, represents an intimacy with the mother that makes the daughter jealous. The two women even use the same mascara brand, she observes. The narrator thinks about this special relationship between two women who used to clean together, "just like in Algeria" where the mother would never sit down in "*son fauteuil*" (her armchair), but work with the maid, as they shared intimate stories and time together.

---

342 "Les Oranais avaient plus que les autres le goût de ces espagnolades et de la fête, du corps et de la danse, du rythme et de la tchatcha." Ibid., 83.
343 "Rien ne me rappelle autant ma mère que ses tangos de merde et ces paso doble stupides qu'elle dansait dans sa tête plus que dans son corps et qui lui déchiraient le cœur, je le sentais bien, pour des raisons mystérieuses et secrètes. Musique douloureuse d'une Espagne perdue, Viva España, ou d'une passion perdue, Yo no sé porque te quiero." Ibid., 101.
344 "Elle suivait avec souplesse, pas du tout étonnée, sans savoir combien ces quelques pas dans mes bras allaient torturer ma mémoire. On aurait dû passer sa vie à danser, à écouter des tangos. Apprendre à mourir, Bésame, apprendre à vivre, Bésame mucho." Ibid., 101-102.
345 "…chantait de sa voix rauque ces rythmes sensuels, répétant sans manière les seuls couplets qu'elle connaissait." Ibid., 22.

As she realizes that she didn't really know her mother all that well, she fantasizes about disguising herself as the maid, and then she could have observed her secretly. "In front of me she was never relaxed or serene, never, why?"[346]... "I would have wanted to see her through the eyes of her maid..."[347] When the maid, "*La Polonaise*," comes to clean, the dying mother seems to be soothed, and when the daughter cares for her mother she imagines that she is the mother's maid since the chores she does around her mother are those performed by the cleaning lady, and by doing them she feels a certain added intimacy by bringing comfort to the mother. After the mother dies, the daughter finds a great reassurance in the presence of the cleaning lady, since "Through her, mom came back to us, to me, like before."[348] She wants the maid to tell her anecdotes about her mother with as much passion as she folds the laundry. She wants to know what they said to each other, how they spoke to one another. Could it be that the relationship is based on mutual desires? "Perhaps she looked for my mother through me?"[349]... "only the Polish lady manages to soothe me,"[350] and the once a week that she comes to her house to clean becomes the highlight of the narrator's week.

The fascination and special awareness of the maid can be traced back to the narrator's Algerian childhood, as portrayed in Cohen's essay "*Viridiana mon amour*," which appears in a collection of Algerian childhood stories edited by Leila Sebbar,[351] where Cohen speaks fondly of her memories of the maids her family had in her childhood home in Sidi-Bel-Abbès. This childhood essay underlines "...the love of our maids...so dear to us in Algeria, then in France..."[352]

The Arab maids in Algeria conspired with the children to have fun when the parents were away. They represented a certain indulgence

---

346   "Devant moi, elle n'était ni détendue ni sereine, jamais, pourquoi?" Ibid., 34.
347   "j'aurais voulu la voir avec les yeux de sa femme de ménage..." Ibid., 123.
348   "A travers elle, maman est revenue parmi nous, chez moi, comme jamais." Ibid., 18.
349   "Peut-être cherche-t-elle ma mère à travers moi?" Ibid., 19.
350   "seule la Polonaise parvient à m'apaiser." Ibid., 25.
351   *Une Enfance Algérienne*. Paris: Gallimard, 1997, 65-78.
352   " ...l'amour de nos femmes de ménage...si cher en Algérie, puis en France..." Cohen, "Viridiana", 72.

and a connection to the outside world: "We followed her footsteps, climbed onto her back, pulled her braids, we looked under her skirt to see if it looked like us, it did, despite the skirts layered upon one another...With her we learned words in Arabic without knowing that languages could divide people...We could see that our mothers and grandmothers never sat down, but worked just as much."[353] To the young child the maid was like a queen, a ruler of the intimate space of the home. After the house was cleaned to perfection ("...cleanliness, as everyone knows, and order, are always threatened,")[354] the children would be allowed to play cards with them, since only after the house was spic and span and the parents were out did they clear the tabletop in the kitchen and start their illicit card games: "Here's how a maid can simultaneously give you the taste for order and for playing, for sharing and for competition, for things illegal and for transgression."[355]

One of the maids in Cohen's childhood home, Gisia, would confide in the mother about her man-troubles, and the children would hear snippets of "problematic" stories that surely would enrage the father, since "with him, it was best not to go beyond a certain context, necessarily rather strict."[356] The two texts intertwine, as the childhood essay ends with Annie Cohen visiting her mother in the hospital, and all she dreams of is for her mother to get better and thus again be able to control the chaos: "I dream of seeing her handling disorder, yes, doing with others, with one other, everything within her power to dominate the mess, the chaos. Wash again and again. Rinse, suds...I dream of Passover prepared according to the rules of the art. All that. It's finished. *Terminares?*"[357]

---

[353] "On traînait dans ses pattes, on montait sur son dos, on tripotait ses nattes, on regardait sous sa jupe pour voir si c'était comme nous, c'était comme nous, malgré les jupons superposés les uns sur les autres...Avec elle on apprenait des mots en arabe sans savoir que les langues pouvaient diviser les hommes...On voyait bien que nos mères et nos grands-mères ne s'asseyaient jamais et travaillaient tout autant." Ibid.,74.
[354] "...la propreté, comme chacun sait, et l'ordre, sont toujours menacés." Ibid.
[355] "Voilà comment une femme de ménage peut tout à la fois vous donner le goût de l'ordre et du jeu, du partage et de la compétition, de l'illégalité et de la transgression." Ibid., 78.
[356] "avec lui, fallait pas s'écarter d'un certain cadre, forcément rigide..."Ibid., 79.
[357] "...je rêve de la voir s'en prendre au désordre, oui, faire avec les autres, avec une autre, tout son possible pour dominer le bordel, le chaos. Nettoyer encore et encore. Rincer, savonner...Je rêve...de Pâque fait dans les règles de l'art. Tout ça. C'est terminé. Terminares." Ibid., 80.

Another common theme in these mother-daughter narratives is when an inversion occurs in the mother-daughter relationship. As a young mother, the narrator's (m)Other was instinctively savage in her protection of her children: "She had animal manners that worked her depths long after the births and in our eyes they made her instinctive and savage, not to say primitive and bestial."[358] This instinct is revived in the daughter as she fantasizes about protecting her mother from pain, suffering and death by carrying her away like a lioness carries her cubs to safety: "Yes, between my teeth, on my back, against me, she would have learned to look at the other territory!"[359]

The weaker the mother becomes, the more the protective instinct becomes evident: "The closer she comes to death, the more I become a lioness. And I regret not having carried her off into the woods, I have already said it, I repeat myself and I don't give a damn"[360]... and again: "This is when I should have brought her into the woods, chew for her, becoming the mother of the baby whale, savage, savage, prehistoric, archaic."[361] The narrator, in the role of mother and child, recognizes this instinctual drive, the overwhelming power of maternal love, and the pain it brings, naturally: "Mothers are a race unto themselves...We have cells that remember the animal-like time when they looked at us, cradled us like she-wolves. When their body cut in two wavered between separation and fusion. Perhaps they wanted to swallow us yet again?...It makes incredible love stories and irreversible pain."[362]

---

358   "Elle avait des manières animales qui lui travaillaient les entrailles bien après les naissances et qui la rendaient à notre égard instinctive et sauvage, pour ne pas dire primitive et bestiale." *Bésame*, 30.
359   "Oui, entre mes dents, sur mon dos, contre moi, elle aurait appris à regarder l'autre territoire!" Ibid., 24.
360   "Plus elle meurt, d'avantage je deviens une lionne. Et je regrette de ne pas l'avoir entraînée dans la fôret, je l'ai déjà dit, je me répète et je m'en fous." Ibid., 57.
361   "C'est alors qu'il aurait fallu l'entraîner dans la fôret, mâcher pour elle, devenir la mère du baleineau, sauvage, sauvage, préhistorique, archaïque." Ibid., 126.
362   "Les mères sont une race à part ... Nous avons des cellules qui se souviennent du temps animal où elles nous regardaient, nous berçaient comme des louves. Où leur corps coupé en deux oscillait entre la séparation et la fusion. Peut-être avaient-elles le désir de nous avaler de nouveau ?...Ça fait des

As the mother-daughter relationship is reversed, the origin melts together with the end at the gravesite, and death both unites and separates. Just as they are simultaneously united and separated in birth, they are also in death: "She has become my dead child, the dead flesh of my flesh."[363] This blurring of boundaries occurs as the daughters care for their mothers, and realize that they are becoming their mothers as the mothers in turn become the child: "That's when I noticed that she was becoming my child and I started to be scared."[364] Through the last days of her mother's life the narrator feeds her mother sugar water, and the reversal is total. "And a spoonful for the baby!"[365] When the mother returns to her worldly origin as a daughter-child the daughter can forgive herself and her mother, as she is able to understand fully their relationship through a mother's eyes. The cycle is completed and can begin again.

This mother text is obsessed with the survival of roots, and we find the recurring metaphor of flowers and plants representing the various stages of the narrator's emotional status. Winter killed the hibiscus on her balcony so that it too would be in harmony with her heart, shriveled and drained. She then decides that she wants nothing else that is living on her balcony and throws out all her planters. After some time of grief and resignation she again wishes for the hibiscus plant to come back, as she admits that "Some mornings I would wish for a balcony full of greenery…Plant a hibiscus on the ground, in its pot, some young shoots of fuchia, some honeysuckle or some climatis and wait for the roots to take and for a new creation to form."[366] As she is about to leave for Andalusia she notices a small green sprout coming from the presumably dead hibiscus. "But, it's the hibiscus! It's alive!…I trembled from my head to my toes, disconcerted. So,

---

histoires d'amour invraisemblables et des peines irréversibles." Ibid., 152.
363   "Elle est devenue mon enfant mort, la chair morte de ma chair." Ibid., 101.
364   "C'est là que j'ai vu qu'elle devenait mon enfant et que j'ai commencé à prendre peur." Ibid., 22.
365   "Et une cuillère pour le bébé, une!" Ibid., 84.
366   "Certains matins, je souhaiterais un balcon inondé de verdure… Planter sur la terre de l'hibiscus, dans son pot, quelques jeunes pousses de fuchsia, de chevrefeuille ou de clématite et attendre que les racines prennent et qu'un nouvel individu se forme." Ibid., 91-92.

the death of a tree isn't final?...Can we speak of resurrection when it comes to a tree?"[367] This joyful discovery gives her hope that she too can find her dormant roots and find life again, and she takes off on her "roots tour" of Andalusia: "I got back to Andalusia to hear the language of *Bésame* being spoken, and to get as close as possible to her native country..."[368] and "...to hear the language of *Bésame*...to find an answer to the emptiness of her presence."[369]

The emptiness of her presence may refer to the secrets of her dreams, of the mother's longings that the daughter now will experience and perhaps, finally, understand. The narrator is beginning to understand that roots need tending, and although they may seem withered, if we keep watering them they can revive: "Should I plant other roots, like with the hibiscus, water, and water again, and believe, with all my might, believe, *eso es*, without panic..."[370] In Spain the daughter can see the mother's belonging and her memories: "I am certain that you would have loved Grenada! You would have recognized it in your memory of an ancient plant."[371] Again the metaphor of a plant, an old plant whose roots still are alive, a seemingly dead plant, but which will sprout back to life, through new life that only it can bring forth.

Finally, the narrator dreams of returning to her square, to her apartment, "Take roots on the spot, in front of the square, near the hibiscus, and never again begin something anew."[372] As the mother had lost the place of her origin, Andalusia, then her birthplace Algeria, her need to find a rooting was stronger than her desire to travel even the shortest

---
367 "Mais c'est l'hibiscus! Il est vivant !...Je tremblais de la tête aux pieds, interloquée. La mort d'un arbre n'est donc pas définitive ? ...Peut-on parler de résurrection à propos d'un arbre?" Ibid., 161.
368 "J 'ai regagné l'Andalousie pour entendre parler la langue de Bésame et pour me rapprocher au plus près des côtes de sa terre de naissance." Ibid., 165.
369 "...pour entendre la langue de Bésame...pour trouver une réponse au vide de sa présence." Ibid., 167.
370 "Fallait-il comme avec l'hibiscus planter d'autres racines, arroser, arroser encore, et croire, de toutes ses forces, croire, *eso es*, sans affolement..." Ibid., 166.
371 "Je suis sûre que tu aurais aimé Grenada! Tu l'aurais reconnu dans ta mémoire de plante ancienne!" Ibid., 171.
372 "S'enraciner sur place, devant le square, près de l'hibiscus, et ne plus rien entreprendre..." Ibid., 172.

distances, explaining to the daughter her resistance to travel, to moving, to movement: "Perhaps she had already moved too much, other places, in another memory...her mannerisms showed the desire for her to sink in on the spot...Take root to thwart the disturbances of History."[373] Thus we see traces of a Sephardic trajectory, as a mother longs for a lost time, beyond her, but in her, and a daughter assumes this deep connection that, represented as the roots of a plant, and as roots that revive the beauty and appreciation of dormant origins, allowing her to resume a life worth living since it extends beyond her own, limited time.

As the mother becomes weaker, her eyes signal that perhaps she has started to regress to her origins "...she was entering the big and incredible elsewhere, prehistoric and to come. *Viva Espana*."[374] Death in this way can be a possibility of revival: "It grows and it needs water. Don't think that death erases the features, it revives them."[375] But a revival that does not mean an eternal fusion with the mother, on the contrary, since the new shoot on the hibiscus shares only its root with the mother plant: "Life continues...It makes one want to be free...No longer be the one that one has been. No longer be like one's mother."[376] In the end, in this m(Other) text, Cohen works through her mourning and finds that through it, by writing it, a release in a rooting merges in the same lyrical movement (the past of the mother and the future of the daughter), and now she is free to move on in her own identity and memory.

Sephardic Transmission in Birth and Death: Nine Moati's *Mon Enfant, Ma Mère*

Nine Moati was born in Tunisia in 1938 and is a journalist as well as writer living in France since she emigrated there as a young woman. Her mother insisted on her leaving Tunisia in order to find a better life

---

[373] "Peut-être avait-elle trop bougé, déjà, ailleurs, dans une autre mémoire...ses manières exprimaient le désir de s'enfoncer sur place...S'enraciner, contrarier les désordres de l'Histoire." Ibid., 117.
[374] "...elle s'engageait vers le grand ailleurs invraisemblable, préhistorique et à venir. Viva Espana." Ibid., 23.
[375] "Ça pousse et ça demande de l'eau. Faut pas croire que la mort efface les traits, elle les ranime." Ibid., 112.
[376] "La vie continue...Ca donne envie d'être libre...Ne plus être celle que l'on a été...Ne plus ressembler à sa mère." Ibid., 90-91.

for herself in the *métropole*, as many Jewish parents in the Maghreb did in the years leading up to and immediately after decolonization. Her story-writing talent is recognized in France as an invaluable voice for the Sephardic memory of North Africa. She has received literary distinctions for her work, and several of her books are made into films for TV. Her writing passion is the memories and experiences of women with North African roots like herself, and she focuses much of her attention on their interpersonal relationships.

The women in Moati's texts are usually faced with difficult personal situations during critical times in their lives and in history, during wars, exile or as in this story of dying mother's last days in *Mon Enfant, Ma Mère* (1974).[377] This mother-text, the author's first and most autobiographical book, shares many of the elements seen so far regarding daughters writing their mothers as the latter has just died. Moati is about to give birth to her first child, a daughter, and as she experiences the new life growing in her womb, she identifies with her deceased mother, whom she calls *Man* (Mum), a diminutive for the French word *Maman*: "Man, it's strange, but at times I feel as though I am you, pregnant with me."[378]

The identity exchange between mother and daughter is further developed, as when the narrator reflects on how empty it is to be pregnant without the mother there, since grandmothers "…are pregnant with their grandchildren with seriousness and dignity."[379] The presence of the maternal grandmother in a child's life is evoked as being as critical as that of a parent: "He will be like an orphan from his birth on."[380] Throughout the text, the narrator talks to her mother as if she were present, and in some parts of the text we are brought back to a time when the mother and father are still alive, as the narrator remembers episodes from childhood or from the time leading up to her parents' illnesses and deaths (she lost both within months of each other).

Often Moati speaks to her mother as a present spirit, a spirit companion, fatefully holding her daughter's hand through the process of

---
377   *Mon Enfant, Ma Mère*. Paris: Editions Stock, 1974.
378   "Man, c'est bizarre, j'ai, par moments, l'impression que je suis toi, enceinte de moi…" *Mon enfant*, 78.
379   "…sont enceintes de leur petit-enfant avec gravité et dignité." Ibid., 47.
380   "Il sera comme orphelin dès sa naissance." Ibid., 123.

pregnancy, birth and after, but Moati is also painfully aware that Man really is gone forever and that her baby daughter will never be cuddled and spoiled by her tender grandmotherly arms: "I would have so liked to give everything to my child. Most of all your affection. Your warmth. I think I will love him as you loved me. But my love will be useless without yours."[381] The narrator's mother is the incarnation of their Judeo-Arabic heritage, and her impending death evokes a fear of deracination from the Maghreb and inspires an endless loss of responsibility, and fusion of mother, daughter and unborn (grand) child. This is another highly personal and intimate style of portraying the rooting strength of a mother, as the daughter searches through the traces in her mother's life, hoping to understand choices and forgive.

Although Nine Moati's beautifully written text is about the death of a mother, we are introduced to a narrative that seems like a more life affirming approach to death since, compared to the two earlier mother-narratives, the book begins with the birth of the narrator's daughter. "It's a girl!" are the first words, and we are prepared to understand the forthcoming mother-text as the beginning of a continuation. We are made aware of the thread that connects generations by the fact that the genders are the same of the three generations of females, and it can appear as though the new child is directly connected to the grandmother, since the narrator felt like she was her own mother giving birth to her. As the narrator dozes off in the delivery room she says, "My eyes are closing. I can't stay awake anymore and live in you."[382] Just as Moati's baby had to leave the safety of her mother's womb, so is Moati faced with having to stop living in – through – her mother. Now that she has become a mother herself, she can no longer be (in) her mother.

Chapter two begins as the narrator realizes that her mother has stopped breathing, but the text will continue to alternate between life and death in order to suggest the intimate connection of the two. The dead mother holds all the knowledge of generations as she has crossed

---

[381] "J'aurais tellement voulu tout donner à mon enfant. Surtout ton affection. Ta chaleur. Ton amour. Je crois que je l'aimerai comme tu m'as aimée. Mais mon amour sera inutile sans le tien." Ibid., 123.
[382] "Mes yeux se ferment. Je ne peux plus me tenir éveillée et vivre en toi." Ibid., 15.

over to eternity: " Man, I feel stupid. You know everything now, and I know nothing."[383] The moment of death is beautifully evoked, and happens in the childhood home in Tunisia, contrary to the two other mother-deaths in Halimi and Cohen's texts, where the mothers die in the cold and sterile environment of a French hospital.

Opposite of the institutionalization of death and dying common in Western and modern cultures, Moati's mother is fortunate to die at home: "I take you in my arms, I kiss you gently. You choose this moment to die. Thank you Man, for having waited until we are alone, you and me."[384] While Man visits in Paris to get treatment for her metastasized breast cancer, Nine refuses the home visits by a nurse. "No one other than me will take care of you until the end."[385] We can see how different this mother-daughter relationship is compared to that of Halimi and her mother Fritna, the latter having refused this kind of tender love from her daughter. Moati's mother, on the other hand, lets her daughter naturally reciprocate all the loving care that she in turn received as a child, and even enjoyed one last time not long before the mother got too sick. When Nine, by now an adult woman, suffers from a painful ear infection, she delights in her mother curing her and tending to her: "Spoil me, and worry me. Rock me in your arms and spoil me for an eternity…Tell me a story."[386] The mother's last pampering feels particularly valuable as she recounts time spent together in the hammam or in the bomb shelter during the war, where the mother would dance "*en Arabe*" to Andalusian melodies played by the neighbor.

Throughout the text, the daughter evokes moments shared by the two as she speaks to her absent mother. The mother in turn also evokes memories as the narrator remembers her retelling them to her while she was alive. This way the two voices, the two women comfort each other; one comforting the other about to bring forth a

---

383   "Man, je me sens bête. Tu sais tout maintenant, et je ne sais rien." Ibid., 17.
384   "Je te prends dans mes bras, t'embrasse tendrement. Tu en profites pour mourir. Merci Man, d'avoir attendu que nous soyons seules, toi et moi." Ibid., 37.
385   "Personne d'autre que moi s'occupera de toi jusqu'à la fin." Ibid., 41.
386   "Gâte-moi, et inquiète-moi. Berce-moi et pourris-moi pour l'éternité…Raconte-moi une histoire." Ibid.,157.

new life, and the other comforting the body and soul about to depart. Some of the most tender moments in the text is when the mother is resting in her chair, sick and weak, and Nine is sitting by her on the floor, leaning her head on her mother's knees begging her to tell stories from her life, and from the narrator's childhood. "...as usual. I am by your feet, my head resting on your knees, as usual...You caress my hair...My future without you makes me want to cry...Rock me again, Man. Tell me about your life, Man ...Tell me again, Man, how should I be with boys?"[387]

Seemingly trivial questions become a way to fuse to two women's lives in knowledge and traditions passed on to the next generation. Questions like "why do you put sugar in the tomato sauce?" ("It is a Jewish recipe"), or "Is it really necessary to strain the couscous?" ("No, but it will be fluffier it you do"), and "How about the scrambled eggs you made us every day when we were young, is it difficult?" ("No, there is nothing as easy, and it's excellent for all children"). Speaking to her mother about her new baby girl, Moati reassures her that although she is not with them any more, the baby will still be surrounded by the things that are part of their Judeo-Arabic traditions: The house will still smell like couscous and Tunisian cuisine, the baby will still be protected from the evil eye by the amulet of Fatma's hand, and she will hear the tender, affectionate words in Judeo-Arabic of their folklore-home. Orange blossom water will be used to cure certain ills, pieces of sugar slipped into the baby's crib to ensure she has a sweet life.[388]

Just as the narrator promises to continue the legacy of her mother's Judeo-Arabic heritage filled with ancient superstitions, culinary specialties, unique spices and fragrances, she also expresses her feelings of nostalgia for her mother's culture during her pregnancy in Paris, since there is nobody there to offer any of its comforting elements. To satisfy this *"ouarch,"* (which the narrator explains, unable to find a French equivalent that would express the full meaning of the Judeo-Arabic

---

387   "...comme d'habitude. Je suis à tes pieds, ma tête sur tes genoux, comme d'habitude...Tu me caresses les cheveux...Mon avenir sans toi te fait pleurer...Berce-moi encore, Man. Dis-moi ta vie, Man... Dis-moi encore, Man, comment faut-il être avec les garçons?" Ibid., 140-143.
388   Ibid., 46.

word, to be a simultaneous feeling of a lack, a vague sensation in the soul, and an awareness of nostalgia for either a person or a place), she goes to Belleville, the Paris suburb where a large Jewish Tunisian population had settled and created their own more intimate "ghetto"-feeling in the 1960s and 70s, reminiscent of the Tunisian *hara*. "Everything is there: the accent, the curves, the gestures, the familiarity. I would kiss them!"[389]

There, she says, nobody will bother her about being on a diet, which the French worry so much about, and there, she can satisfy her cravings for traditional foods and atmosphere. The narrator about to become a mother for the first time, alone as she is and far away from her now lost mother land and mother, is only too aware of the cultural difference between her native Tunisia, represented by the absent-present mother, and France, where she is particularly sensitive to the exile she feels. The Judeo-Tunisian grandmother represents the anti-(French) establishment in terms of how to raise children and handle infants, and Moati plans to continue the Judeo-Maghrebian way of her mother: "I will put aside, I will throw Doctor Spock far away. I will hold my baby very tight as you did with us."[390]

The feeling of emotional exile is not just something the narrator feels in France; for she is living the "neither here nor there" common to Jews who no longer have anything but graves to come "home" to in the country they left. Since both her parents are buried in Tunisia, and someone else lives in her childhood home, she has nothing but a burial place to return to, only a bench in the shade opposite her mother's tombstone. There she embraces her mother's marble gravestone and waits to be received by her. "I throw myself into your marble arms" anxiously searching for a welcome, for a sign. She realizes that she is loosing her mother's image "I lose you from time to time…I lose your

---

[389] "Tout y est: l'accent, la rondeur, les gestes, la familiarité. Je les embrasserais!" Ibid., 50.
[390] "J'abandonnerai, je jetterai le 'docteur Spock' très loin. Je serrerai mon bébé très fort comme tu nous as serrés. Je lui murmurerai des mot tendres et barbares." Ibid., 129. (Note: As most Western and "liberated" mothers used the Dr. Spock baby book – a "rational" and modern-day approach to child care preaching the virtues of not spoiling the infant by holding it too much and scheduled feedings – this was considered the parenting bible of the 60s)

face, your smile, your gestures, your smell,"[391] and that this is the beginning of the end of her connection to this place. Even at night she does not succeed: "I try to find you again in my dreams."[392]

By the mother's disappearance she feels all the more alienated from her origin, and this is painfully reinforced when she returns to Tunisia and feels like a stranger, now that her parents are no longer there: "It is horrible to come home and feel like a foreigner. No one is waiting for me. Can you imagine me, Man, in Tunis, alone in a hotel room? While our house is used by strangers."[393] During her talks to her absent mother, the reader gets a sense of various historical and cultural elements as they relate to the Jews of Tunisia. We learn about the division between the indigenous Jews and those who arrived from Livorno, the Grana Jews. The hierarchy and differentiation was so profound that even in death they remain segregated, as they are buried in two distinct sections of the Jewish cemetery, itself separated from the Muslim and Christian ones. Moati's father, being of Livornese origin, is buried in that part of the cemetery, and her mother, although indigenous, had taken on the father's traditions by marriage, and hence was permitted to be buried with him.

We also got a sense of this internal hierarchy in the Jewish Maghreb communities in Halimi's text as Fritna grumbled endlessly about having married below her since she, an Algerian Jew of Spanish origins, had married the father Edouard, who was "only" a poor, indigenous Berber Jew. The narrator in *Mon enfant, ma mère* also evokes the difficult time for their family during the Second World War as her father was deported to Germany where he spent time in the Nazi concentration camp, Sachsenhausen, before he escaped to Paris where he remained in hiding until after the war. Similar to Halimi's family who thought the eldest brother Marcelo had died in camp, Moati's family was also touched by what was to become known as an unimaginable human tragedy and defining moment in modern Jewish history, the Shoah.

---

[391] "Je te perds par moments…Je perds ton visage, ton sourire, tes gestes, ton odeur." Ibid., 101.
[392] "J'essaie de te retrouver dans mes rêves." Ibid.
[393] "C'est horrible de retourner chez soi et de se sentir étrangère. Personne ne m'attend. Tu m'imagines, Man, à Tunis, seule dans une chamber d'hôtel? Alors que la maison est occupée par des inconnus…" Ibid., 103-104.

Despite the many Judeo-Tunisian traces in the text, the narrator admits to being ignorant when it comes to Jewish religious traditions. For instance, she does not know what Jews do with their dead. "I don't even know if Jews watch over their dead. Dead Catholics are watched over, all books will tell you. But the Jews…I have never read about them."[394] This is a classic example of what I have noted earlier regarding the Judaic training of the girls of this generation and the lack of knowledge about their religious heritage. All the books they were exposed to were works by French authors from the *métropole* and hence Moati, as Halimi and Cohen, were formed and impressed by exclusively Catholic writers under colonial educational practices. Sitting next to her mother's tomb she feels helpless: "I don't know how to pray, Man. Not in French, nor in Hebrew, nor in Arabic."[395] The mother's last Yom Kippur is sad, and the holiday becomes devoid of sense since the mother is incapable of making it special, of observing its traditions and preparing any of the festival meals. Nine remembers what the awesomeness of this holiday was like when she was a young girl: "You served everyone, you spread your smile, your smell. How our home was filled with warmth!…Me, I was happy to have you. But I didn't know it …"[396]

Full openness, reciprocity and a profound love and respect defines this relationship, however, similar to the relationships Cohen and Halimi had with their mothers in terms of what they knew about their mothers' lives and secrets, Moati's relationship, too, was guided by modesty, privacy and a sense that the most intimate things were not shared. Moati wants her mother to tell her so many things before she dies, but neither one of them dares to break "A thousand-year-old pact of modesty."[397]

---

[394]   "Je ne sais même pas si on veille les morts chez les juifs. Les morts catholiques, on les veille, tous les livres le disent. Mais les juifs…Je n'ai jamais lu sur eux." Ibid., 89.
[395]   "Je ne sais pas prier, Man. Ni en français, ni en hébreu, ni en arabe." Ibid., 98.
[396]   "Tu servais chacun, tu distribuais ton sourire, ton odeur. Comme notre maison était chaude!…Moi, j'étais heureuse de t'avoir. Mais je ne le savais pas…" Ibid., 177.
[397]   "Un pacte de pudeur millénaire." Ibid., 43.

These questions that the daughter does not dare ask her mother are at once intensely personal and revealing in that the answer will give the daughter the answers to her own life as well. It is as if the mother knows this, and the daughter as well, since both hesitate to uncover a reality they both know to be true: no, you will not be happy all the time just like me, and yes, you will, as I do, have regrets…"Me, I am afraid to ask you if you were happy during your entire life, if you have regrets."[398] In this relationship there is a certain unspoken and mutual understanding, or as Moati puts it: "The law of silence is respected."[399] It is possible to posit that missing from modernity is a certain respect for the unspoken, for the things in our lives that are unknown. We want to know it all, both "inwardly" in our relationships with ourselves and those we love, as well as "outwardly" in our relationship to the world around us. There seems to be no room anymore for unoccupied emotional space, or for stillness and positive emptiness, or positive negatives, and thus things left unsaid leave us suspicious and worried. There are cultures that are still marked by a validation of absence, silence and a certain awareness and willingness to see an affirmative value in the negative, as part of the *ying* and *yang* of our relationships to, and in, the world. Many mother-daughter relationships are marked by this dilemma, and it is not always easy letting go of the unknown. Letting go, though, is much of what these relationships are about, since the difficulty of embracing who we are as daughters is so very intimately connected with the art of letting go of our mother's secrets, fears and desires.

Moati ends her emotional mother-text by evoking her own release. The mother dead, she will keep her "*neshama*," or soul, close to her new baby girl by consciously and subconsciously keeping her mother's legacy of love: "And you. You'll never know, Marie. She is there, alive and well. I surround her with words, I cover her with your story, I rock her with your movements, your gentleness…But you will be there, with her, with me…Ever since I felt the weight and the warmth of Marie in my arms, I am no longer an orphan.

---

398   "Moi, je n'ose pas te demander si tu as été heureuse pendant toute ta vie, si tu as des regrets." Ibid..
399   "La loi du silence est respectée." Ibid., 151.

I will never again be orphaned. Is this what one calls release?"⁴⁰⁰ Liberated to become her own individual, and in turn become her daughter's mother.

****

Finally, let me evoke Adalgisa Giorgio's reminder of Irigaray's observation, relevant to the analysis of these three Sephardic mother-daughter texts: During the time immediately after their mothers' deaths the narrators often "find themselves in condition of *'dereliction'* – a state of loss, abandonment, helplessness, and ultimately homelessness – in being unable either to access the symbolic or to return to the original home of their mothers' body"⁴⁰¹ This dereliction becomes a space of in-between, similar to the one experienced by the exiled person who is nostalgic for the safe and childish memory of the motherland. Alienated in this different place, where the various stages of appropriation are symbolic of arriving and of becoming a speaking subject, an actor in history, the narrators have not yet been realized as their own writers.

Giorgio further recalls Irigaray's enterprise which "is about searching for ways of enabling women to create a home for themselves in an alternative symbolic,"⁴⁰² and here I have suggested three ways that Sephardic women have found this "alternative symbolic" in writing intensely personal texts where they give their life meaning and name their suffering and ultimately their own liberation. It is my impression that between the matricidal and the reconciliatory models of discourse in daughterly narratives there is a model of acceptance that does not look to forgive and forget, nor to erase, and perhaps not even to fully understand the mother. Rather, in this paradigm, the daughter receives and acknowledges the difference that was/is the mother, and with that the daughter will in turn be able to begin life in her own path of self

---
400 "Et toi. Tu ne sauras jamais, Marie. Elle est là, bien vivante. Je l'enveloppe de mots, je la recouvre de ton histoire, je la berce avec tes gestes, tes douceurs…Mais tu seras là, avec elle, avec moi…Depuis que je sens le poids et la chaleur de Marie dans mes bras, je ne suis plus orpheline. Je ne serai jamais plus orpheline. Est-ce cela qu'on appelle délivrance?" Ibid., 178-179.
401 Giorgio, *Writing Mothers and Daughters*, 14.
402 Ibid.

affirmation and individuation, knowing that she will always already be and not be her mother.

Let us call this an alternative symbolic, since it is a place of meaning outside of the mother, separated, verbalized and written, where the feminine "I" begins its own liberated journey. By writing their mother-narratives, Gisèle Halimi, Annie Cohen and Nine Moati have embarked on a process of contextualization of the maternal figure in their lives, including in this process elements of their mothers' Judeo-Maghrebian heritage that now will be integrated into their own lives. Mothers, like daughters, come in all varieties, as we have seen in these texts. Just as we cannot gather all mother-daughter relationships under one umbrella of knowing, so are the reactions and the texts resulting from the need to process a mother's death unique. "Writing, often fragmentary and elliptical, acts as therapy aimed at unraveling a variety of mother-daughter knots, mostly after the mother's death, and at integrating the good as well as the bad mother."[403]

Our three Sephardic women authors have succeeded at integrating the good and the bad mother, without leaving themselves debilitated by their (m)Other's absence, presence and eternal motherly influence. Writing the autobiographical mother-daughter narrative with all its Sephardic traces has permitted them to move on as stronger women writers, allowing us to understand some of the complexities in this unique Franco-Judeo-Maghrebian experience.

---

403   Ibid., 31.

Chapter 6

Phantom Rabbis and Marabouts: Catalysts of Memory and Nostalgia in the Texts of Annie Cohen and Annie Fitoussie

In **Annie Fitoussi's** *La mémoire folle de Mouchi Rabbinou* (1985)[404] and Annie Cohen's *Le Marabout de Blida* (1996)[405] we see how the appearance of a certain phantom like rabbi and a marabout stirs emotions in the lives of the characters in these two Franco-Judeo-Maghrebian texts. The appearances of the curious rabbi and the marabout become a way for the characters in the narratives to reconnect with their past, as if the rabbi and marabout were just figments of their imagination, or elements of their subconscious urging them on. They act as a conscience speaking to the emigrated Sephardic individuals, encouraging them to keep their memories alive by refusing to abandon the cultural traces from their heritage or the complexity of their hybrid identities.

A rabbi and a marabout are both symbolically significant characters with a strong spiritual presence in the Maghreb, among Jews and Muslims alike. Many rabbis were held in esteem by Muslims, who sought them out for advice and blessings, and Muslims were also known to be among the pilgrims making yearly visits to pay homage to the deceased rabbis who had reached saintly status through their righteous lives, and miraculous fulfillments of prayers for healing, prosperity, and fertility. A marabout is someone known for his supernatural powers, a Sufi practitioner who is a source of wisdom, medicine, poetry, enlightenment and witticisms. The marabout is more a personal spiritual leader than the leader of a whole community or congregation,

---
[404] Annie Fitoussi, *La mémoire folle de Mouchi Rabbino*. Paris: Mazarine, 1985.
[405] Annie Cohen, *Le Marabout de Blida*. Paris: Gallimard, 1996.

like the rabbi. The marabout is often a scholar of the *Qur'an*, as the rabbi is a scholar of the Torah, and both can actively guide the life of their followers. Both assume a role in the narratives as a destabilizing (but eventually positive) force of "waking to consciousness" for the novels' characters, as they (re-)appear in Paris, France, a western culture and society where religious and spiritual leaders have lost much of their influence since the advent of the Republic and its rigorous tradition of secularization and assimilation.

A rabbi is first and foremost a teacher (the literal translation of the Hebrew "rav"; with the "i" at the end as in rabbi, it becomes "my" rav) and also functions as a personal counselor, in addition to leading a congregation in services and prayers, performing circumcisions (if he is trained as a *mohel*), bar and bat mitzvahs, wedding ceremonies and funerals. In other words, he is a presence at all the major life cycle events in a Jewish life. When a Jew needs help with remembering certain elements of Jewish prayer, history, customs and ethics, the rabbi is there to advise, always willing and able to assist in the never ending Biblical decree of *"zachor!"* – remember! – the vital core of Jewish continuity and survival.

In these two narratives we also see that the rabbi and the marabout function as catalysts of nostalgia and memory as their appearances in the stories, at times discreet and intimate, other times more public and even provocative, evoke a sense of longing as well as reconciliation of two worlds that seem irreconcilable. The way the rabbi and marabout look and sound, as well as the kind of words and expressions they use, opens up emotional doors for the characters that help them face often painful but vague longings. However, Svetlana Boym reminds us that "The alluring object of nostalgia is notoriously elusive,"[406] and just as the object of nostalgia is elusive, so do the two spiritual guides in the stories seem mysterious and sometimes obscure, since they in fact are the embodiments of the longed for childhood time, or place, and also of a lost emotional language. Boym further notes that "Nostalgia tantalizes us with its fundamental ambivalence; it is about the repetition of the unrepeatable, materialization of the immaterial,"[407] and in this way

---

406   Boym, *The Future of Nostalgia*. New York: Basic Books, 2001, xvi.
407   Ibid., xvii.

the rabbi and the marabout have a particular centrality in the texts of Cohen and Fitoussi, because they are the textual representations of the unrepeatable and immaterial toward which the characters yearn. They both help the authors textualize that which no longer has a place in the real world, and they embody that which is no longer spoken, all that the Jews of North Africa have lost.

The Wisdom of the Fool in Annie Fitoussi's *La mémoire folle de Mouchi Rabbinou*

Annie Fitoussi's novel *La mémoire folle de Mouchi Rabbinou* has a subtitle that reads like a long breath and gives the text a feeling of an orally transmitted tale. Without any punctuation it reads: "the poorest rabbi of the ghetto, the most miserable in Tunisia, stronger than Mussolini and even stronger that death."[408] The rabbi, whose "*mémoire folle*" (crazy memory, but also meaning "extreme memory") we are to encounter, has survived the most horrid of circumstances, and yet, like the mythical wandering Jew, he survives and lives to tell the tale and to remind all those who cross his path of the memory that keeps the exiled from despair: the memory of an origin that is always, already lost, but that will always be sought out, in the "*entre-deux*" that Jews know will only end when the Messiah arrives and restores the Temple in Jerusalem, and returns all Jews to the promised land.

The "*mémoire folle*" of Mouchi Rabbinou can refer to his seeming madness, since he often rambles and speaks incomprehensibly, but it just as likely refers to his "tremendous" memory, one that is impressive and immense, carrying with it the memory of all generations. The rabbi's sometimes folly behavior combined with being able to impart great insight, also places him in the literary tradition of the character of the fool (deprived of speech, babbles incoherently, noisy and lacking constraint or discipline) as an ultimate source of wisdom. Considered since the Middle Ages as protected by God, the fool's gibberish was understood as speech imparted by a higher power. In his use of the fool as revealing character, Shakespeare suggests that in order for his ultimate

---

[408] "…le rabbin le plus pauvre du ghetto le plus misérable de Tunis plus fort que Mussolini bien plus fort encore que la mort."

triumph to take place, the fool's wisdom must exceed the limits of time and this world, thus offering a greater understanding for those who are astute enough to listen to him.[409] From Jewish literary tradition we may recall fondly Isaac Beshevis Singer's "Gimpel the Fool," who, though ridiculed as the town fool, comes to represent the only one in the tale with a deep understanding of what matters most in life.

Fitoussi's choice of name for the wandering Jew-bum, *Mouchi Rabbinou*, who appears at the various life cycle events taking place around the Touitou family in the novel, also holds a specific significance. The Hebrew "Moshe Rabbeinu" translates as "Moses our Rabbi/leader," referring to Moses the greatest prophet in the Torah who brought the Jews from slavery in Egypt into freedom. Moses redeemed his people, brought them the Torah as revealed to him on Mount Sinai, and led them to the Promised Land but he, however, was not permitted to enter the Land and died never having put foot there.

Like the Moses of the Torah, Mouchi Rabbinou in this text also seeks to redeem "his" people from the dangerous trap of forgetting who they are and where they come from, and like the Biblical prophet he remains excluded. Remaining the excluded part of a story/history allows a different view of that story/history. This idea is recalled by Hélène Cixous who had the similar experience in her childhood Algeria: "I am on the side of Moses, the one who does not enter."[410] Like the Biblical Moses, the Mouchi Rabbinou in *La mémoire folle* was born and raised under extraordinary circumstances, or so we are told. Similarly, the Pharaoh's daughter rescued biblical Moses from the river Nile and raised him.

In the novel it is the entire Touitou family, who has recently arrived from Tunisia, that is eventually affected by the phantom rabbi, but it is the sensitive and rebellious teenage daughter Simone who develops a particularly acute awareness of his appearances, as she herself goes through a trying time of identity confusion and search for meaning. In the story, we learn that Mouchi Rabbinou was miraculously born in Auschwitz where his mother – also Albert Touitou's sister (and hence

---

409   For a detailed study of the tradition of the wisdom of the fool see Walter Kaiser's seminal work, *Praisers of Folly: Erasmus, Rabelais, Shakespeare*. Cambridge: Harvard UP, 1963.
410   Cixous, "My Algériance." 277.

Simone's aunt) – ended up after having been disowned by the Touitou patriarch for having eloped to France with a non-Jewish lover.

While in captivity, she underwent monstrous medical experiments in order to be allowed to keep her baby. As a survivor of the horrors of the Shoah, she became insane and institutionalized, her memory repressed and forgotten by her family. Mouchi Rabbinou, however, has found the Touitous now arrived in France, and has come to offer them redemption from the emotional exile in which they find themselves. Similar to Moses of the Bible, who is said to have had a speech impediment and did not always seem a confident leader, Mouchi is not a great public speaker. He appears mentally unstable, for he rambles and makes little sense to most people who hear him. Mouchi, too, is refused entry into society: he lives a life of an outcast and a marginalized fool, but is capable of bringing redemption to those who will listen.

The rabbi's name, however, is not his real name, as he informs the ailing and dying Ommi M'Charda, Albert Touitou's mother, and Mouchi's maternal grandmother, as he has come to pay her a visit in Tunisia where she stayed behind. She had been too old to be able to withstand the move to France (often seen with the older generation who stayed behind), and also wanted to remain in the family home in Tunisia to wait for the return of her excommunicated daughter, Lariffa, Mouchi Rabbinou's mother, Albert's sister. We are told by the narrator that only the old and crazy remained in Tunisia after the exodus of the Jews, and those who stayed retreated into their memories, such as Ommi M'Charda, who would never forget her alienated and lost daughter. Mouchi Rabbinou admits to having taken the name as "some kind of social identity." His mother's memory had been repressed from the family since the day she left, and her son has now returned to offer them redemption through the recovery of their memory of her, by aiding in their possibility to open their repressed channels of memory.

As he tells his grandmother about her daughter's terrible fate at the hands of the Germans, Ommi M'Charda dies. The truth is both too much to bear, and what allows her to die. Mouchi's mother Lariffa has lost use of words since her experiences in the death camp: "Her story was so difficult to carry she sought release from it in madness,"[411] and

---

411   *La mémoire folle*, "Son histoire fut si lourde à porter qu'elle en cher-

Mouchi, her son, has since lost his belief in words. We may understand this to be the reason why he confuses words and expressions, sometimes speaking nonsense, and the stories he tells seem incredible and therefore nonsensical. His words are those of survivors: "I am guilty of life."[412] He wonders if he is crazy to have invented a history for his mother, since she has chosen to be unaware of her own, or has chosen to forget it, and thus he seeks to give his own life a bit of humanity, because this way it may remain in someone's memory. We will look closer at the other instances when Mouchi Rabbinou appears, after we have a better sense of the Touitou family's trajectory, their extended family and friends' new life in France, which will in turn allow us to appreciate the rabbi's role as the story and their lives unfold.

This autobiographically-inspired fiction of the Touitou family's arrival in France in the early 60s is written in a familiar and relaxed oral style, as suggested by the subtitle, allowing the characters' speech to be spelled phonetically, thus highlighting their North African background, lack of literary knowledge of the French language, and their low level of education. Many words in the novel are written in transliteration, allowing the reader to hear the words in the way they are pronounced by the Touitous and their entourage, like "*sberrons*" (esperons, or let's hope), "*françaouis*" (français, or French), "*mainant*" (maintenant, or now), and "*Dreifousse*" (Dreyfus) to name a few. Other words are scattered throughout the narrative that also help emphasize their Judeo-Arabic heritage, such as "*Daou Aleya*" (light of my eyes), "*Mektoub*" (it is written), and "*Kmarak*" (may your turn [in marriage] arrive), words that evoke the intimacy, fate and superstitions shared by these Jews of the Maghreb.

Fabric storeowner Albert Moché Touitou, his homemaker wife Reinette, afflicted by "*la rashra*" (the blues), and their children Simone and Alain, arrive in Marseilles, then on to Paris and the Belleville neighborhood, where they stay with family and friends who have arrived before them from their hometown of Bizerte, Tunisia. Their trajectory is one of humble, silenced, and passive movement, typical to many Jewish fates from Arab lands. Albert Touitou is carried off to

---

cha la délivrance dans la folie." 49.
412   "Je suis coupable de vie." Ibid.,50.

France "…by a history that was not his own, our man did not have the time to reflect."[413] The story of the Touitous is strangely familiar, and not at all unique in the real world of Judeo-Maghrebian lives. We learn of illegal departures, loss of all property, difficult living conditions upon arrival in France, and worse transitional issues such as isolation, unemployment, racism – "The French don't like us, don't know us and do not want to know us, they are afraid of us,"[414] alienation – "The anonymity of the street scared him," depression and repression of memories of their lost world.

A feeling of degeneration soon overwhelms the patriarch as he silently suffers from shooting regrets. "Let me suffer in peace, if you take away my pain, what do I have left?"[415] says Albert, who has decided to strip himself of his memory: "A stranger without memory came ashore in Marseille flanked by a wife and two children."[416] He had been raised not to trust the Arabs, nor did he ever feel comfortable in the company of the "*françaouis*," and hence the man that left Tunisia "like a thief" felt "Doubly cheated, doubly victimized."[417] On the contrary, Albert's brother in law, Maxo Zana, a perpetual gambler and street-savvy guy, succeeds in business in Paris. Having learned to trust his instincts in the *hara* – "the most miserable ghetto in Tunisia" – he was better prepared to take on the high speed and the challenges of the *métropole*. After the *hara* had been razed to the ground, the old synagogue destroyed, and when Tunisia's president Bourguiba decided to transform the Jewish cemetery into public gardens, Maxo said to his wife, Reinette's sister: "The deal is done, pack the suitcases, it's decided, we're leaving."[418]

We get an idea of what it was like as this silent exodus took place in the Maghreb, how the Jews were not thrown out but their life made so

---

413   "…par une histoire qui n'était pas la sienne, notre homme n'eut pas le temps de s'interroger." Ibid., 7.
414   "Les Français ne nous aiment pas, ne nous connaissent pas et ne veulent pas nous connaître, ils ont peur de nous." Ibid., 67.
415   "Laisse-moi souffrir en paix, si tu enlèves ma douleur, que me reste-t-il?" Ibid., 10.
416   "Désireux d'oublier un passé encombrant et douloureux…il se dépouilla de ce que nul n'aurait pu lui dérober, de ce qui lui appartenait en propre : sa mémoire, ses souvenirs. Un étranger amnésique flanqué d'une femme et de deux enfants débarqua à Marseille." Ibid., 14.
417   "comme un voleur"…"Doublement trahi, doublement victim." Ibid.
418   "Le compte est bon, fais les valises, c'est décidé, nous partons." Ibid., 35.

unbearable that the only viable solution was to leave: "It was never officially announced that we should leave, but only declared that we were free to do so, and that they would not hold us back. In the end, leaving was our only freedom."[419] And consequently, "As if affected by a deadly hemorrhage Tunisia was emptied of her Jews."[420] The story unfolds as we see how the Touitou's modest living finally secures them a small apartment in the new Sarcelles suburb development outside Paris, where they are optimistic that it will not seem like the old ghetto-feeling as in Belleville. Reinette admits to the social worker that comes to evaluate their eligibility (based on their level of "frenchness") that she is ashamed of the Arab immigrant atmosphere that surrounds them in Belleville.

The scenery in the Sarcelles development town of high rises, however, is made up of construction sites in progress, and the homey feeling of Belleville is non-existent. This results in Reinette feeling alienated, since here the streets are deserted and quiet, and she has no one to share her day with, as Albert goes off to his small fabric store in the Sentier district, and the kids are in school all day. In Belleville she at least had the group of immigrant lady friends and family who all supported each other, gossiped and shared the challenges of their new life in France. She misses the smells of Tunisian cooking, the noise and even the filth of Belleville. In her new sterile environment she cannot find any trace of herself or her past, and as the days repeat themselves her only anchoring is her fear and the regret that "Never again and nowhere would she be at home."[421] Reinette, afflicted by *la rashra* (a Judeo-Arabic expression referring to the strange yet familiar non-treatable and nondescript condition of restlessness, depression, anxiety and nostalgia, brought on by separation and longing for a return), suffers in isolation, and since *la rashra* is a very private affair, it does not speak itself, it is lived.[422]

We see in Reinette's mental state a nostalgia that is painfully lived, since she knows that what she longs for is not something that will return. The kind of nostalgia experienced by the exiled North African

---

[419] "Il n'a jamais été annoncé officiellement que nous devions partir, mais seulement déclaré que nous étions libres de le faire, et qu'on ne nous retiendrait pas. Partir était en fait notre dernière liberté." Ibid., 63.
[420] "Atteint d'une hémorragie mortifière Tunis s'était vidée de ses Juifs." Ibid., 43.
[421] "Plus jamais et nulle part elle ne serait chez elle." Ibid., 80.
[422] Ibid., 81-82.

Jewish population, both in France and elsewhere in the post-colonial era, is a profoundly alienating experience since the hope of recovery of a "*chez-soi*" (at home) simply does not exist. The memory of that life can be both a source of pain and a source of joy, but in order to remember one needs to stop resisting who one is. Reinette would distance herself from the loud, Judeo-Arabic women and their mannerisms in the Belleville neighborhood, striving for a more "French" lifestyle in the new development, but in doing so, she became alienated and depressed. She had repressed a part of her origins that had given her a profound sense of belonging through familiarity, something she only came to realize once removed from it. Her husband too, although working, sinks deeper and deeper into the abyss of hopelessness: "Albert had lost his taste for life. By erasing his past, this man without memory had become a man without a future."[423]

The Touitou family life continues on its alienating path, with the children becoming more and more assimilated, and especially the daughter, Simone, tries her best to dress, act and speak in a way that will differentiate her from her Tunisian family. In her father's eyes she puts them to shame by her indiscreetness. However, as Albert becomes sick with cancer, she is the one who overcompensates in order not to disturb or displease him. Eventually Albert dies, and Mouchi Rabbinou enters the scene. The young rabbi comes out of nowhere, appearing a little crazy, offering to prepare the body for burial, to perform the *tahara*, the ritual cleansing and dressing of the deceased according to Jewish traditions.

Performing the *tahara* is considered the highest form of mitzvah, or good deed, since the deceased will not be able to repay the doer for his kindness, and therefore the act is deemed one of pure selflessness. Having introduced himself, he exclaims: "…I come to this house because in this house you wanted to forget me. I come to wash the dead and remind you of his sufferings, pains and torments which will be yours if you in turn forget."[424] Albert's teenage daughter, Simone, is the

---

423   "Albert avait perdu le goût de vivre. En tirant un trait sur son passé, cet homme sans mémoire est devenu un homme sans avenir." Ibid., 120.
424   "…Je viens en cette maison parce qu'en cette maison on a voulu m'oublier. Je viens laver le mort et rappeler ses souffrances, douleurs et tourments qui seront les vôtres si à votre tour aussi vous oubliez. Je viens vous

only one who approaches the rabbi, – perhaps the only one who sees him? – and he says to her : "Be wary of words and watch out for those you will utter, the veil of forgetting will never recover them."[425] Simone faints and later cries for her father as well as for her grandmother who had died in Tunisia, and whose death she had not yet mourned but instead laughed at in a scornful manner. Since Ommi M'Charda did not speak French, young Simone had despised her. "At the same time as for Albert, she cried, without realizing it, for all the dead for whom she had never cried."[426] A victim of colonialism's dividing forces, Simone had been ashamed of her grandmother because she spoke mostly Judeo-Arabic. Although she did not know he was her uncle, Mouchi Rabbinou appeared to offer Simone a way out of her amnesia and her self-repression.

Through the character of Simone the author includes more personal autobiographical elements, because Annie Fitoussie too arrived in France from Tunisia with her family as a young girl, and like Simone will set out to do, she studied law and practices law in Strasbourg. Albert's daughter begins to rebel against her father even as a pre-teenage girl in Tunisia, where she was forbidden to play outside in case she would be tempted to spend time with boys. Her father, a traditional Mediterranean patriarch, finds it shocking that his wife and pre-adolescent daughter may indeed have thoughts and fantasies that do not include him, and he acts pre-emptively by violently prohibiting his adolescent daughter any contact with the outside world.

As a young student in France, Simone "learns to lie" as she dates boys and uses her mother as an ally. Her avid reading only increases her ammunition: "An inordinate taste for reading contributed to cementing the reasons for her disobedience, to intensifying her disagreeing, to break her fear into revolt."[427] Similar to Gisèle Halimi in *Fritna*, we see a young woman learning to rebel against what she sees

---

dire ici l'immensité de ma peine, l'infini de ma solitude." Ibid., 129.
425   "Méfie-toi des mots et prends garde à tous ceux que tu proféreras, le voile de l'oubli ne les recouvre jamais." Ibid., 130.
426   "En même temps qu'Albert, elle pleura sans s'en douter les morts, tous les morts qu'elle n'avait pas pleurés." Ibid., 131.
427   "Un goût immodéré pour la lecture contribua à cimenter les raisons de sa désobéissance, à fortifier son désaccord, à muer sa peur en révolte." Ibid., 145.

as her domineering and ignorant family, waiting for the day when she can leave home to pursue her higher studies and, perhaps not incidentally, law. She is encouraged to enter a philosophy competition by a supportive female philosophy teacher in high school, and *Le Monde* announces that the winner is a young repatriated woman from North Africa and publishes an excerpt of her thesis. Simone's level of successful acculturation in France only distances her more from her family, and eventually it excludes them from her life altogether. She would flaunt her literary knowledge and expressions as proof of her erudition, as a reassurance of her feelings of superiority that only reinforced her isolation.

In this way she follows the example of her mother with regards to her attitude toward her Jewish and Arab neighbors in Belleville. Simone's family was impressed by her knowledge but she would in turn scorn "their" culture and ridicule their ignorance.[428] "They were Arab Jews, had they never had a cultural or artistic heritage? What were the names of their famous musicians, and their writers? Did they have painters, or poets? she asks herself."[429] When a classmate confronts her, the right-wing son of a pharmacist in Sarcelles during the Algerian war, he calls her a pied-noir who is too involved in the situation to be able to give an objective point of view, and dismisses her as a "*youpin*" (a kike) with whom he does not want to waste his time. "When it came to racist comments, she did not take note of them: they did not concern her. Simone saw herself as French and atheist."[430] Divided, rejected, and profoundly humiliated, she dreams of new beginnings. "Leave, leave again…leave and go far away, far away to a place where she would finally be able to accept herself."[431] So, she goes off to study in Strasbourg, where the ambiance is "muffled and puritan." There she tried her best to fit in with the motto of the city: "work and austerity." She agonizes over her own image that she had thought was tall and blond, but in this northern setting and surrounded by the "*Strasbourgeois de souche*" (native Strasbourgo-

---

428   Ibid., 148.
429   Ibid.
430   "Quant aux propos racistes, elle ne les releva pas: ils ne la concernaient pas. Simone se voulait française et athée." Ibid., 150.
431   "Partir, partir à nouveau…partir loin, très loin pour un endroit où elle pourrait enfin s'accepter." Ibid., 151.

is), she realizes she is rather short, round with darkish hair and even darker eyes: "Exotic despite herself, cut off from her roots, the daughter of Albert Mouché Touitou, the son of Chmouel Touitou…was only an anonymous student, a bit lost, uneasy in her new skin."[432]

Her experience of (internal) exile is made more painful as she visits her mother and her brother, who accuse her of behaving like a colonialist: "You look at us in silence, you spy on us, you pretend to be surprised by what we eat, by what we say, by what we don't say…All you need is the colonial hat on your head and the services of an interpreter."[433] Her younger brother Alain cannot accept her choice to become a judge, for he feels that she has already judged and condemned her own family enough. In an emotional outburst he screams, "Become a judge and I will conceal your profession as a defect, as we have hidden the madness of our aunt. Thief, whore, I would have accepted you, I would have understood, but judge no!"[434] He then expresses the tragic fate that they share; that it is harder for them to live in France than for their parents' generation: "…you and I, we are from nowhere. You live elsewhere because you reject their world; me, I stay with them without managing to find my place."[435] They are the in-between generation; like the Beur writers of their generation, they have one foot in each culture. And although they can manage in both places, they feel marginalized and do not belong fully in either.

Back in Strasbourg, Simone stays intently focused in her first job since it becomes her only anchor, her singular point of reference. When she receives four anonymous chain letters directing her to make copies to send out or "unlucky events will follow," she is overwhelmed by an

---

432   "Exotique malgré elle, coupée de ses racines, la fille d'Albert Mouché Touitou, le fils de Chmouel Touitou…n'était qu'une étudiante anonyme, un peu paumée, mal à l'aise dans sa nouvelle peau." Ibid., 170.
433   "Tu nous observes en silence, tu épies, tu fais mine de t'étonner de ce qu'on mange, de ce qu'on dit, de ce qu'on dit pas…il ne te manque que le casque colonial sur la tête et les service d'un interprète." Ibid., 173.
434   "Deviens juge et je tairai ta profession comme une tare, comme on a tu la folie de notre tante. Voleuse, putain, je t'aurais acceptée, j'aurais compris, mais juge non!" Ibid.
435   "…toi et moi nous ne sommes de nulle part. Tu vis ailleurs parce que tu récuses leur monde, moi je reste avec eux sans parvenir à trouver ma place." Ibid.

unexplainable and irrational fear, fed by archaic childhood superstitions. As this uncontrollable feeling begins to obsess her, she is driven toward deeper fears and questions she cannot answer. The bolted shut doors of her repressed self and her Arabness are beginning to crack open. Having rejected her Jewishness, her African-ness, she had also denied her own womanhood. *"Juifemme"* [I'm-a-Jewish-woman] she says to herself as she frantically searches for meaning in the chain letters she received, and by verbalizing this bottled up fact, she is eventually able to admit to her womanly desires, so far ignored, and she can finally accept who she is and eventually love her despised family for who they are.

While digging around for the old chain letters, she realized she was humming a song that her grandmother – "*M'Charda ignorante et stupide*" (M'Charda, ignorant and stupid) – used to sing when she was looking for things she had lost. She becomes even more confused and afraid as she lets herself drift toward the unknown, toward madness like her aunt, the cursed Lariffa. "The need to explain, to speak, to write overcame her...What had she left behind, over there, that was so precious? What had she left of herself? Write in order to find the trace of that which she had forgotten, the sense of the words that she had silenced. Write to pay for what she had wanted to renounce. Write to reconcile herself."[436]

Simone does begin to write her "self," her origin and her repressed feelings and shreds of memories, confused by her imagination. As the novel comes to an end, Simone is in court for a hearing, when a tramp enters the courtroom and is quickly dismissed by the judge as not having all his faculties. When asked to give the court his name, profession and address, the "exilé" could only admit his misfortune, and Simone is the only person in the courtroom giving him the opportunity to explain himself since she does not hear his insanity, but rather the reverberations of her own marginality and exile. The scene seems unreal like a dream, and Simone addresses the bum directly and passionately, both to her own and her colleague's surprise, since "...such a lack

---

436   "Le besoin d'expliquer, de parler, d'écrire la submergea...Qu'avait-elle laissé derrière elle, là-bas, de si précieux? Qu'avait-elle laissé d'elle ? Ecrire pour retrouver la trace de ce qu'elle avait oublié, le sens des mots qu'elle avait tus. Ecrire pour expier ce qu'elle avait voulu renier. Ecrire pour se réconcilier." Ibid., 194-195.

of restraint on behalf of a magistrate…had never been seen in Strasbourg."[437] Thus in the tradition of the character of the fool, the wandering rabbi displays an inability (or unwillingness?) to follow correct or appropriate behavioral codes. After a long discourse addressing only Simone, the wandering Jew, Mouchi Rabbinou says, "I am the mad memory of The Book… You have nothing to fear from the past, I guarantee its coherence. Speak."[438] Hence Simone receives the permission she needs to write her self; the deep, repressed and forgotten self, made of incoherent streams of consciousness that she had begun to scribble down. This act of writing the past will eventually bring her coherence, helping her accept her present and give her courage to look toward a future. She must bravely take a big step back in order to move forward.

The role of the rabbi in Annie Fitoussie's text as a catalyst to memory becomes more than just a guide showing the young protagonist the way. Aside from appearing at various occasions to preach his "mad and tremendous memory" to the different members of the Tuoitou family and entourage, he becomes the force bringing Simone to self-discovery and self-redemption through writing. As Hélène Cixous notes, she would wake up at night with a desperate need to write down the intensely vivid images being brought to her from "the gallery of the Forgotten in my memory,"[439] feeling an obligation to return to her origins, as will Simone Touitou after seeing Mouchi Rabbinou. On each visit he plants thought-provoking seeds that will eventually take root in her (sub) consciousness until she becomes willing to let them bloom into text, into memories remembered. The protagonist in Fitoussi's novel needs the mad rabbi as Cixous needs the ghost appearing to her at night: "…I wrote without turning a light on so as not to make the ghost flee…,"[440] says Cixous, where the "Venant" (ghost) has the same inspirational but ephemeral role as our Mouchi Rabbinou.

---

[437] "…un tel manque de retenue de la part d'un magistrat…ne s'était jamais vu à Strasbourg." Ibid., 203.
[438] "Je suis la mémoire folle du Livre…Tu n'as plus rien à redouter du passé, j'en garantis la cohérence. Raconte." Ibid., 205.
[439] Cixous, Rêveries, 9.
[440] "…j'avais écrit sans allumer afin de ne pas risquer de faire fuir le Venant…" Ibid.

By drawing from the wealth of memories of her Judeo-Maghrebian heritage, Simone will be able to acknowledge and embrace her Jewish identity firmly and without shame. A writer is thus born, and the autobiographical elements in *La mémoire Folle* let us appreciate the often agonizing path to writing, since the story in the narrative is always, inevitably, a manifestation of the obsessions of its creator; a real life, where memory and imagination intertwine to create a textual difference that we choose to call fiction.

Faucets Unplugged
in Annie Cohen's *Le Marabout de Blida*

Annie Cohen left Algeria for France in 1962 at the age of 18, but returned briefly again in 1967, during the Six Day War in Israel, only to realize that "Algeria no longer belonged to me, but I still cared about her."[441] The country had changed too much, and it was no longer the country without race, open and generous, the "Algeria still possible"[442] that Cohen had known as a child. Now, there was no room for difference; "Independent Algeria made me mute, she blocked the images and the associations…I became a stranger in my land."[443]

After this terrible disillusionment her only mode of survival is to distance herself both physically and emotionally, and *Le Marabout de Blida* was written as a testament to the liberating forces of coming to terms with the chaotic memory of her Algerian heritage and its devastating uprooting. In 1996, when the text was published, Annie Cohen received two prestigous French literary prizes: *Le Grand Prix Thyde-Monnier de la Société des Gens de Lettres* and the *Prix Tropiques*. This story marks a (re)turn for the writer whose earlier works seem to indicate her desire at the time to detach herself from her ancestral roots and her native country. Cohen is similar to the young woman Simone in *Le Marabout de Blida*, and has settled permanently in Paris, nestled into her poplar-filled square where she decides to firmly root herself in her new French soil.

---

441 "L'Algérie n'était plus à moi, mais elle me concernait encore." *Le Marabout de Blida*, 59.
442 "Algérie encore possible." Ibid., 67.
443 "Algérie de l'indépendence me rendait muette, elle me bloquait les images et les associations… Je devenais étrangère à ma terre…" Ibid., 66.

Annie Cohen had become a true Nordic, pine loving, heat intolerant, rational thinking and cool-headed Parisian: "everything which reminded me, up close or from far away, of the meridinal latitudes, made me want to vomit" and "my bones loved the rain, the wind, the gray, the squalls from the west, the storms, and the hurricanes."[444] When a heatwave strikes in the middle of August, the almost empty Paris seems like a Saharian desert, and the oppressive heat confuses and obsesses the narrator: "The persisting heat was irreconcilable with reason, with the city, with measure, it pushed me…"[445]

It is in the midst of this psychosomatic upheaval that the narrator has a chance meeting with the marabout, "a seer in our country, a man who sits on a rug, with a sort of turban on his head, a way of being in his shoes that always makes me recognize people from our country."[446]

The marabout appears out of nowhere, barefoot, and wearing traditional Arab clothing, and once he opens his mouth to speak he becomes a personalization of the narrator's lost and forgotten land and territory. This man, real or imagined, will evoke moments of her life, events lodged deep in her memory, and will eventually authorize her to rediscover her "Southern speech," guiding her toward a truer sense of who she is. Similar to the rabbi in Annie Fitoussi's *Mouchi Rabbinou*, who opened young Simone's eyes, Annie Cohen's marabout is an emissary from the forgotten past, seeking less to make the young woman restore what was, or regress and repent, than to show her how she may move forward toward a life enriched by the ineffable values bestowed by an acknowledged, remembered and incorporated North African Jewish heritage. Through the rabbi and the marabout, the narrators will learn to say "I," to be comfortable with the full meaning of their subjectivity. "When I say 'we,' I mean 'I,' but I do not know how to say it yet, without a doubt because of this adapted coldness that I so wanted

---

[444] "Tout ce qui me rappelait de près ou de loin les latitudes méridionales était à vomir" Ibid., 12, and "mes os aimaient la pluie, le vent, le gris, les bourrasques venues de l'ouest, les orages, les tempêtes." Ibid., 15.
[445] "La chaleur qui persistait était inconciliable avec la raison, la ville, la sagesse, la mesure, elle me poussait…" Ibid., 16.
[446] "Un voyant de chez nous, un homme qui reste assis sur les tapis, une espèce de chechia sur la tête, une façon d'être dans ses souliers qui, toujours, me fait reconnaître les gens de chez nous." Ibid., 11.

to love...My identity has become fractured by opting for the North and my I had become warped."[447]

The marabout offers droplets of deeply desired and much needed evocations, like eagerly awaited raindrops in the desert. She can feel the seeds taking root, and the need to let the sprouting begin: "the Africa of my language is about to take the word, about to force open the door,"[448] referring to the doors of the subconscious, where the repressed language, images, and feelings are protected from oblivion. The marabout brings her back to her true voice, which liberates a hybrid, frank and loud speech, but not overnight and not without difficulty.

The repetitive mantra of the marabout plagues her thoughts: "Drink the wine of your barrel...Which wine and which barrel was he talking about...? Even the inside of my guts had opted for the barrel of another country."[449] As she listens to his accent "making me blush with shame and pleasure,"[450] she is both intrigued and astounded by the uncanny familiarity: is he from her old neighborhood in Sidi bel-Abbès, a childhood friend? "He spoke to me in a language which was not unknown to me, far from it, that I recognized, that I had spoken formerly with others from my tribe."[451] His language and mannerisms release a stream of memories and sensations elicited by the landscape, the colors, the fragrances, the sounds and the foods "of a distant Algeria." The narrator refers to him as "marabout of my nightmares...of my hidden desires...of my questions without answers,"[452] as she begins her emotional journey of remembering the uprooting from Algeria, the arrival in the *métropole*, the difficulty of adaptation and the deliberate choice of detachment from her past. Striving to become more French than the

---

447   "Quand je dis 'on', je veux dire je, mais je ne sais pas encore le dire, sans doute à cause de ce froid d'adaptation que j'ai tant voulu aimer...mon indentité s'est fracturée en optant pour le nord et mon je s'est tordu..." Ibid., 52.
448   "l'Afrique de ma langue est en train de prendre la parole, de forcer la porte..." Ibid., 32.
449   "Bois le vin de ton tonneau"..."de quel vin et de quel tonneau me parlait-il...? L'intérieur même de mes entrailles avait opté pour un tonneau d'un autre pays..." Ibid., 12.
450   "À me faire rougir de honte ou de plaisir." Ibid., 13.
451   "Il me parlait une langue qui ne m'était pas inconnue, loin de là, que je reconnaissais, que j'avais pratiquée jadis avec d'autres de ma tribu." Ibid., 19.
452   "Marabout de mes cauchemars,...de mes désirs cachés...de mes questions sans reponses." Ibid., 25, 30, 31.

French, and stoically (nordically) denying everything African in her life, is a way of rejecting and escaping the mother-source of that life. "I had to become nordic! Learn how to speak the French of France. Cross out old things, accept the cold, the gray, the snow, the mittens and the gloves, change skin, never again look toward the South, for what good, forget the North African geographies and the nourishing wombs."[453] But the "nourishing wombs" are not easily forgotten and her childhood memories are the first to come up, as she remembers traumatic episodes beginning from even before her birth.

Here we again see elements of intertextuality as images that are later evoked in *Bésame Mucho* (published two years later) are also suggested. Inevitably, and as pointed out by Benyaoun-Szmidt, "In this undertaking of identity-acknowledgement, the figure of the mother is omnipresent and labored by the desire for authenticity."[454] The abrupt uprooting from the motherland brings forth the desire and memory of a return to the womb, to a pre-verbal, pre-conscious state of bliss. Her mother was pregnant with her as her father was shipped off to fight in the Second World War, and she evokes her mother singing *Bésame Mucho* to her unborn baby, longingly awaiting the return of her husband. One of her earliest memories is going to the railroad station to meet her father for the first time, at age one and a half, and as her mother let her go from her protective arms in order to embrace her husband, Annie is again separated from her mother, this time by the real and symbolic arrival of the father! Having been eternally banned from the mother (by her act of letting her go) and the native land (after exile), it was eventually her turn to reject them. But the marabout insists: "Drink from the source of the earth, from the fountain of your tribe! You will not escape your mother![455] suggesting that although it is

---

[453] "Fallait devenir nordique! Apprendre à parler le français de France. Tirer un trait sur les vielleries, accepter le froid, le gris, la neige, les mouffles et les mitaines, virer de peau, ne plus du tout regarder vers le sud, à quoi bon, oublier les géographies nord-africaines et les ventres nourricières." Ibid., 51.
[454] "Dans cette entreprise de reconnaissance identitaire, la figure de la mère est omniprésente et travaillée par le désir d'authenticité." Benyaoun-Szmidt, "Annie Cohen: pour une algérianité retrouvée." *International Journal of Francophone Studies* 7 (2004): 25.
[455] "Bois à la source de la terre, à la fontaine de la tribu! Tu n'échapperas pas à ta mère!" *Bésame*, 133.

painful going back to the original expulsion(s) - (from the womb, from mother's arms, from Algeria), it is a necessary, an always and already present part of her Sephardic/North African memory.

Another defining moment in the narrator's memory is the recollection of a traumatic experience at age five, when she had followed a stranger, who offered her pretty picture books, into a building. Her father's version of the story was that he grabbed her and saved her from the hands of an Arab, but she doubts her own memory, which focuses on shame and embarrassment rather than the man. We are reminded of the ambivalent nature of memory, since the event held different truths for father and daughter: "My father told me his story, and I ended up not being sure about the scene in the stairways. Where does it come from, damn it, this bouillabaisse in my head?"[456] Typical of traumatic experiences is their propensity to become blurred with time, so that facts are confused in each of the versions of the stories of the traumatized parties involved. We may recall the earlier discussion of Yerushalmi's consideration of memory: "Memory is always problematic, usually deceptive, sometimes treacherous,"[457] but at the same time he reminds us of its discriminating quality as determining the content of what defines a person, a community or a people. It is eventually our narrator's remembrance and her writing of it that defines her, and not her father's writing-recounting.

The beginning stages of the realizations prompted by the meeting with the marabout are confusing, suggesting the disorientation experienced when a person's understanding of her identity is being unmoored: "The world is upside down, defigured, unrecognizable, what is going to happen, the interior of my Oranian, Spanish or Biblical land demands to surface. Knock, knock, knock! Who is there? Come in! Come in! The marabout has unlocked my doors..."[458] It is as if all her

---

456   "Mon père me racontait son histoire, je finissais par ne plus être sûre de la scène des escaliers. D'où vient, putain de merde, cette bouillabaisse dans le caillou?" Ibid., 179.
457   Yerushalmi, *Zakhor*, 5.
458   "Le monde est sens dessus dessous, défiguré, méconnaissable, que va-t-il arriver, l'intérieur de mes terres oranaises, espagnoles ou bibliques demande à faire surface. Toc toc, toc ! Qui est la ?! Entrez! Le marabout a deverrouillé les portes..." *Bésame*, 33.

origins are surfacing together and demanding to be told. Yvette Benayoun-Szmidt suggests that this *"algérianité retrouvée"* (Algerianness recovered) becomes a rediscovery that memory helps unearth and liberate. The *"algérianité"* of the narrator's childhood has evolved into a new kind of belonging. Earlier in the text, when she asks "How to live on both sides of the bank? How to be inside and outside, in the barrel and out of it?"[459] she is overwhelmed by the prospect of being so open and vulnerable to more than one variety of "barrel of wine." She feels vulnerable since opening up the heart and the mind to all the parts that make up the whole of her will ultimately offer her a fuller understanding of her self. However, it will also make her more exposed to pain and heartbreak, since her sites of belonging, and therefore rejection, have multiplied. Once she has opened up to her Southern speech she realizes that what she so exclusively held dear no longer is enough: "…the cold, the gray…the imprisonment…the mutism…the tongue cut-off…Bach, I feel it, I hate my intellectual flesh."[460]

With the beginning of her "rediscoveries" comes the guilt of having forgotten: "Forgive me, forgive me for not having known how to love the summer, life, movement, disorder, light…Forgive me for living half way, unevenly, in the margins…Forgive me, my first geography, who saw me born, whom I have betrayed, forgotten, relegated, and who has taught me to be ashamed, ashamed of my country, ashamed of our country, the *rachma*…"[461] From being one of her nightmares earlier on, the marabout becomes "a soulmate" whom she adores, and when he doesn't show up for a while, she misses him so much that she makes a tiny box-like a shrine filled with things that remind her of him and secretly hides it under their regular table in the neighborhood bistro, so she can touch it with her foot, as if to remind herself of his presence in absence, a tactile reminder of her memory-recovery. She recognizes

---

[459] "Comment habiter les deux côtés de la rive? Comment être dedans et dehors, dans le tonneau et hors du tonneau?" Ibid., 58.
[460] "…le froid, le gris…la réclusion…le mutisme…la langue coupée…Bach…je le sens, ma chair intellectuelle me fait horreur…" Ibid., 43.
[461] "Pardon, pardon de ne pas avoir su aimer l'été, la vie, le movement, le désordre, la lumière…Pardon de vivre à moitié, de travers, en marge…Pardon à ma géographie première, celle qui m'a vue naître, que j'ai trahie, oubliée, reléguée, et qui m'a appris la honte, la honte de chez moi, la honte de chez nous, la rachma…" Ibid., 48.

that "...the language and the accent of the marabout had opened up the Mediterranean faucet,"[462] and as she rambles on in all the words reminiscent of her southern past, many "impossible to find in French dictionaries,"[463] she experiences the redemptive liberation of memories. Finally, she admits a desire to be reconciled with her country of origin; a reconciliation which is more auto-reflexive than reflective of the rejected "elsewhere" of her origin, since her struggle comes from within, and until now she has been, to use the term coined by Kristeva, a stranger to herself.

Cohen's use in *Bésame Mucho* of plant metaphors to describe her various mental states, her mother's uprooted-history, and also their eventually shared desire for rootedness, is also found in *Le Marabout de Blida*. It is clear that the author has a keen sense of botanics, both an appreciation for the delicate nature of blossoms, and also the robust survival skills of roots. It is in this way she understands the effects of uprooting on the human experience, and can imagine the resilience of her own life and identity. The narrator's obsession with issues relating to uprootings, transplants, rootings, and ultimately the difference between mere survival and thriving, is evident when she notes that not until the roots have been watered and the plant cared for in its entirety will you find a truly fragrant bloom: "...the flowers become fragrant when the roots are tended."[464] This sort of holistic approach to plant-tending becomes a metaphor for the person whose life experience will come to its fullest and most meaningful expression only when all parts of the individual's identity are nurtured. Since true survival is ultimately in the roots and not in the tips of the leaves or the petals of the evanescent blossom, the narrator stresses that one has to "...draw from one's earth, at the bottom of one's roots, the substance of survival"[465] in order to find that life-affirming source and force.

---

462   "...la langue et l'accent du marabout avaient ouvert le robinet méditerranéen." Ibid., 170.
463   "introuvables dans les dictionnaires français." Ibid., 92.
464   "...les fleurs deviennent odorantes quand les racines sont soignées." Ibid., 44.
465   "...puiser dans sa terre, au fond de ses racines, les substances de survie." Ibid., 42.

Since the marabout had told her to stand on the sidewalk and look up at her apartment, and in this way perhaps get a view of her life from a different perspective as if to see the inside from the outside – the façade from an alternative angle – she spends hours in the protective shade of her square's poplar trees gazing upward. As she wants to understand the marabout's intentions, her instinctive thought is to imagine what would have happened to her lilacs if she moved them from her balcony to the sidewalk, and realizes that their branches would turn to face the sunlight, now a completely different light since from a new angle. So what, she asks, is it that the marabout wants her to see, from down there on the sidewalk? "…does the marabout want to exhaust my vital resources by making me perform these cervical rotations?"[466]

His purpose is certainly not only to make her crooked or make her uncomfortable. It is often awkward, however, to look at ourselves from the outside in, as the perspective makes us see a different "I." The effort makes the narrator feel "*tordue*," warped or crazy, not just physically crooked or twisted, the other meaning of the word in French. Being able to see herself from below, from the south, she recognizes how she has metamorphosized in order to fit in to the North. "You ask me to break down the invisible material of my name, you push me into corners of a world unknown to me, unknown to my memory, you want from me what I want from my tree: an eternal existence."[467] Rather than eternal life, the eternity she claims the marabout is looking for in her may be the concept of an eternal connection, a root that does not dry up, a flame that will not be snuffed out, between her and her North African and Sephardic heritage. This trajectory has taken her ancestors from exodus to exodus, exile after exile, uprooting after uprooting: Jerusalem, Seville, Sidi-bel-Abbès, Paris. Where to next? The enrichment she speaks of comes from the memories of the roots, from acknowledging and celebrating her origin, as painful as it may be to look it in the eye and admit, that

---

466   "…le marabout veut-il oui ou non épuiser mes ressources vitales en me contraignant à ces rotations cervicales?" Ibid.
467   "Tu me demandes d'effriter la matière invisible de mon nom, tu me repousses dans les coins d'une terre inconnue à ma conscience, inconnue à ma mémoire, tu veux de moi ce que je veux de mon arbre: une existence d'éternité." Ibid., 118.

no matter how fast or far she runs away, it will always be a part of her, like the mother-origin, always already there, never easily – but forever possibly – a great source of strength to draw from throughout life. Like Cohen expresses it: "The beauty of plants that acclimate themselves, species that become richer, beauty of the one who seeks direction, orientation."[468]

Yvette Benayoun-Szmidt points out that the *"discours romanesque"* (fictional speech) of Le Marabout de Blida has a distinct ideological function: "…it's about proclaiming the truth by returning to the departure and uprooting from the native country in its painful breaking apart."[469] We can say that the ideological function of the kind of discourse that both Annie Fitoussie and Annie Cohen engage in their writing is symbolically suggestive of the idea that, indeed, there is a reality of existence, of pain, of subjectivity in Jewish post-colonial experiences. This truth is critical to those who seek to proclaim it in order to rediscover and reclaim their Sephardic Maghreb identity. This "speech," or narrative, is also eminently valuable to understand the multiplicity and complexity of Maghreb identities. The memories evoked are marked by the departure and uprooting of individuals, families and communities. As personal as these memories are, they are also inseparable from the collective memory of the Algerian Jews, because in the end, as the narrator in Le Marabout declares: "The barrel seemed to have resonances that easily transcend the matters of our immediate and personal lives."[470]

The hybrid identity that our narrator assumes and embraces after a harrowing summer of soul-searching is made up of a multitude of voices: "…the polyphonic voices, what are they saying?"[471] she asks herself as she begins to decipher their messages. The multi-layered, multiple woman emerging is able to let the marabout go on his way as he has helped her realize who she is: "Crooked

---

468   "Beauté des plantes qui s'acclimatent, des espèces qui s'enrichissent, beauté de celui qui cherche le sens, l'orientation." Ibid., 57.
469   "…il s'agit de proclamer la vérité en restituant dans sa douloureuse déchirure le départ et le déracinement du pays natal ." Benayoun-Szmidt, "Annie Cohen : pour une algérianité retrouvée," 21.
470   "Le tonneau semblait avoir des résonances qui dépassent largement nos affaires de vie immédiate et personnelle." *Bésame*, 69.
471   "…les voix polyphoniques. Que disent-t-ils?" Ibid., 33.

pied-noir, the marabout says to me, Frenchman on the outside, Algerian across, Jew on the side, African like nothing, Parisian passing through, Algerian in Paris, Jew from North Africa, Frenchman from Algeria! And so! Why not? You are what you are. A beautiful child of God..."[472] Like her newfound taste for the marabout's language and his way of defining the indefinable, she acknowledges that "I had started to like it a lot, without reserve, to hear him speak this language..."[473] She has taken up his language and made it her own and she can finally speak her own polyphonic language, and delight in her multidimensional identity.

****

Through the analysis of Fitoussi's *La Mémoire Folle de Mouchi Rabbinou* and Cohen's *Le Marabout de Blida*, we have seen how two marginal characters, a crazy wandering Jew disguised as a rabbi and a colorful, odd marabout have both functioned as catalysts of nostalgia and memory, and ultimately a coming to terms with one's past through writing. It was Cixous who said that, in order to write, you have to lose everything once, and the loss of the South, as in the ancient Jewish North African *"patrimoine"* (heritage) gave both authors the impetus to write. Svetlana Boym has noted that reflective (vs. restorative) nostalgia dwells in *algia*, the longing, the imperfect process of remembrance...it lingers on ruins, the patina of time and history, in the dreams of another place or another time.[474]

The elements of the patina that the exiled Jews long for are the elements of their lost world, such as its music and sounds, its perfumes and spices, its warmth and congeniality. In their lost world, people had time for one another and time for life. In France, the authors/charac-

---

[472] "Pied-noir tordue, me dit le marabout, française de l'extérieur, algérienne de travers, juive à côté de la plaque, africaine de rien du tout, parisienne de passage, algérienne de Paris, juive d'Afrique du Nord, Française d'Algérie ! Et alors ! Why not ? Tu es ce que tu es. Un bel enfant de Dieu..." *Le Marabout*, 156-157.
[473] " J'avais pris un goût sans limites, sans réserves, à l'entendre parler cette langue..." Ibid., 157.
[474] Boym, *The Future of Nostalgia*, 41.

ters/narrators of these texts find little such comforts in their early pursuits to be more French than the French. Having chosen the rabbi and the marabout as their inspirations and guides, memories of lost origins find expression in writing. Annie Cohen says it succinctly: "The idea of taking up with the destiny of the Hebrew people never left me: we are born here, we die elsewhere...the habit of wandering the earth was not unknown to us."[475] Diaspora, exile, exodus; all realities that continue to be part of Jewish experience, perhaps suggesting the need to honor collective memory as the defining principles of Jewish identity, rather than "simply" those of national borders. "The tenacity of the seed lets the plant bend in the wind!"[476] is a truism that has become the very image of Jewish survival and continuity. Without the relentlessness, the stubbornness and the strength of "*zakhor!*" – remember! – the ritual and contractual remembrance, and the constant watering and tending to roots and origins, the flame of the Jewish soul would have been snuffed out long ago.

---

[475] "L'idée de renouer avec le destin du peuple hébreu ne me quittait pas: on naît ici, on meurt ailleurs...l'habitude de tourner sur la terre ne nous était pas inconnue." *Le Marabout*, 57.
[476] "La tenacité du germe permet à la plante de plier sous le vent!" Ibid., 31.

Chapter 7

Rebels With a Cause:
Daughters Resisting the Law of the Father
in Narratives by Paule Darmon and Chochana Boukhobza

Je suis étranger. I am a stranger.
Ana barani

For Sephardic authors Chochana Boukhobza and Paule Darmon, one way of narrating the many challenges that face families as they grapple with making sense of their new lives far away from their native lands in North Africa, is by infusing their texts with autobiographic elements, thus giving a sense of the intimacy of personal experience to the stories told. Both authors introduce the reader to fiercely desperate young women who suffer under their fathers' expectations of how they live their lives, and how they define themselves. While one is continually reined in to fulfill family expectations, the other is rebuked by the silence of the father raging against his daughter's choice to separate from his oppression.

The struggles they face by making choices that oppose the law of the father and the patriarchal family values as defined by their Judeo-Maghrebian heritage create family and personal dramas that exemplify some of the most challenging situations faced by the younger generation of Jewish immigrants from North Africa. The daughters know that their choices will inevitably force them into an emotional exile from the father, but they also know that, if they remain immobile and silenced, they will not be able to break the cycle of victimization. Their "*refus*" in the face of their families is expressed as a refusal of being mastered, of accepting subservience, as expressed in the anti-colonial power struggles that so profoundly impacted their families as well as the Maghreb in general. The difficulty in rejecting the law of the father, be it imposed on the daughter by verbal directives or muted gestures of ignorance, only gives emphasis to the emotional complexity of finding redemption. As much as the young, female narrators are worried about losing the connection to their ancestors, to their birthplace, and to their family's unique expressions of Jewishness, they feel an equally visceral need to break free and redefine their lives, unchained from the backwardness of the Orient, and from what represents to them the very crux of the burden of alienation. The Maghrebi-born women writers envision different and complicated emancipatory strategies for their narrators and characters, making them the vehicles for illustrating the realities of living with the dual challenge of at once desiring to distance themselves from the limitations imposed by their cultural heritage, and fearing the inevitable loss of the world of their childhood years, as represented by their dying relatives and the slowly vanishing traces of the Judeo-Maghrebian history. In these two first-person narratives, we will meet two Sarahs, both the oldest sibling in their families. Darmon's Sarah will take us back to her childhood in Morocco to revisit and explain her formative years leading up to her family's exodus, and then take us with her to provincial France, thus illustrating the challenges of transition for both a new immigrant family and for their daughter as she grows into a young adult. Boukhobza's Sarah brings us to Israel for the summer, where the heroine's confrontations with family as well as with the land that she does not find holy, come to demonstrate the trials of exile. Both narratives evoke critical facets of the Sephardic trajectory we have sought to identify in earlier parts of this study.

CULTURAL CLASHES IN AND OUT OF THE FAMILY IN PAULE DARMON'S *BAISSE LES YEUX, SARAH*

Paule Darmon's novel, *Baisse les Yeux, Sarah* (1980)[477] begins with the dedication "*à la mémoire de mon père*" (in memory of my father), and is inspired by many autobiographical elements in the Moroccan Sephardic trajectory of exodus, marginality, memory and identity. Its focus is a young woman's desire to liberate herself from her family's Orient-style oppressive dynamics as she recounts defining moments

---

477   *Baisse les Yeux, Sarah.* Paris: Grasset, 1980.

from her childhood into adulthood. Paule Darmon was born in 1945 in Casablanca, as is her narrator, Sarah, who tells us that she has written this book in order to release herself from her father: "I have written in order to free myself from him."[478] As we will see, what she seeks to be liberated from is not necessarily her father per se, but rather what he represents, which is also mirrored in the family values as maintained by the mother and the maternal grandmother, as well as the expectations of her spouse, a Jew of European Ashkenazi origins.

The desire for redemption is also tied to important questions of gender, as Sarah seeks her femininity without having to give in to the gendered roles her cultural heritage assigns. As a young *garçon manqué*, or tomboy, Sarah has great difficulty fitting in and feels marginalized and differentiated even in her gender, sexuality, and later in her role as wife and mother. These are issues that permeate the text, and her rebellions are a reaction to the cultural expectations laid upon her, and by extension a reflection or metaphor for the colonial relationship of ruler and ruled. The other major theme is that of the oppositions, contrasts and hierarchical perceptions existing between Jewish cultures, both within and outside the Maghreb. Sarah is an amalgam of two different Sephardic cultures, and when she marries an Ashkenazi Jew with Russian origins, the opposition between those two Jewish specificities becomes yet another challenge in her new French life. There she has already been introduced to the trials of being an immigrant identified as the other that she is not, namely as Arab, pied-noir or colonialist. Issues of hybrid identification of the other, and of auto-identity in gender, sexuality, ethnicity, and cultural belonging saturate the narrative and will direct the path as we look closer at this Sephardic daughter's rebellion.

The story begins in a dreary hospital room in Marseilles, where Sarah, the oldest daughter of four grown children, is alone with her dying father: "I refuse to believe, I don't accept that my all powerful god can abruptly disappear from my life, without warning."[479] She further describes her relationship with her father as "a couple made of love, tenderness, hatred, anger, and passions,"[480] and this opening suggests

---

478   "J'ai écrit pour me délivrer de lui." *Baisse les Yeux*, 12.
479   "Je refuse de croire, je n'accepte pas que mon dieu tout puissant puisse disparaître de ma vie brusquement, sans prévenir." Ibid., 10.
480   "un couple d'amour, de tendresse, de haine, de colère, et de passions." Ibid.

the type of relationship she has with the defining personality in her life: complicated, disturbing, but also one of mutual love and respect. But this is perhaps not what makes this book a unique account of a familial relationship, since daughters often feel torn between the deep, visceral love they experience toward their father and the instinctual opposition they go through in the face of his expectations and his demands, in short against The Law of the Father. So the narrator takes us back to the beginning, to try to understand her fight, her flight, her fear, and her anger, as she struggles with all these conflicting feelings as her father is dying. Hers is a story of an exile as experienced in early childhood both at home and as the family emigrates to France, of marginalization and conflicts, and the legacy of her Judeo-Maghrebian heritage is celebrated, as much as it is criticized, as it is central to Sarah's challenges.

We are introduced to a young Sarah who informs the readers of the various nuances of Maghreb Jewish identities as she tells us she is constantly being squeezed between two Sephardic traditions – her mother's and her father's – as experienced in North Africa. "I have lived squeezed between two bosoms: the one of oral civilization, primitive and religious, coming from my mother, and the one of rational western civilization, coming from my father…On the one hand we lived in a European city…on the other, in the *mellah* of Casablanca."[481] Sarah's father, Charles Levy, an Algerian Jew and thereby French citizen, had "committed" an unsuitable match by marrying Sarah's mother, who came from a poor and uneducated Moroccan family, thus "charitably" giving her access to "his noble French nationality."[482] She describes a father who is obsessed with transforming himself into a *"super-quelque chose"* [483](super something). As a lawyer, he wants to exude self-confidence by expressing his belief that "I am a master of my body and of my mind,"[484] yet he often manifests his authority by searing temperamental explosions.

---

481   "J'ai vécu compressée entre deux mamelles: celle de la civilization orale, primitive et religieuse, venant de ma mère, et celle de la civilization rationnelle occidentale, venant de mon père…D'un côté on habitait la ville européenne…et de l'autre le mellah de Casablanca." Ibid., 17.
482   Ibid., 18.
483   Ibid., 19.
484   "je suis maître de mon organisme et de mon esprit." Ibid., 20.

His study is filled with the complete works of Anatole France and Sartre, the Talmud and books on the life of Jesus, various works on philosophy, religion, poetry and history, as well as extensive studies on the human body. He confidently identifies himself as a Jew, exclaiming to his imaginary non-Jewish French audience in North Africa, "I am Jewish, yes, and I piss you off."[485] Thus, although her father teaches her to reflect, to be critical and to question the world around her, he also has an authoritarian parenting style, expecting complete obedience. This way, Sarah, who knows and understands opposition, and learns and yearns for freedom, is at the same time harnessed to the expectations and traditions of her overpowering father by the love she feels for him. Every time he says *"Baisse les yeux, Sarah"* (lower your eyes, Sarah) she concedes, although her father has also taught her that when you have a conversation you should maintain firm eye contact. Thus, she remains paralyzed and fearful of the pain it will cause her father if she were to follow her instincts and his role modeling of self-assertion, and she continues on a path of self-denial, struggling between pleasing and becoming her own individual.

Opposite the father's contradictory "Western/Oriental" style, the narrator informs us of the mother's Moroccan side of the family history complete with a saintly great-great-great grandmother, pilgrimages, healers, exorcists and miracles. Her grandmother lived in a world of traditions, prohibitions and obligations, and, married off at nine years old, is repudiated at fifteen because infertile. "Her imaginary and cultural world was that of Arab story tellers... monsters, evil spirits, marabouts, thieves, God and my father populated her universe with terror."[486] A woman with plenty of authority in the domain of superstitions and family life, but at the same time subservient to patriarchal and religious traditions, she was the product of a civilization about to disappear. She would express herself exclusively in "judeo-hispano-arabic" in order to differentiate herself from the Arabs: "She was not Moroccan, supreme insult, but

---

[485] "Je suis juif, oui, et je vous emmerde." Ibid., 23.
[486] "Son monde imaginaire et culturel était celui des conteurs arabes. .... Aichawas, djnouns, marabouts, voleurs, Dieu et mon père, peuplaient son univers de terreur." Ibid., 36.

a Jew from Morocco, feeling infinitely superior to the Fatmas who worked in her house."[487]

Sarah's mother is described as an energetic, organized, self-taught reader and writer, who, in contrast to the women of her family, became a woman of action: "All I remember of her is a vision of movement."[488] Raised in the Arabic language, Sarah's mother serves as an interpreter for the family, and she insists on raising her own children "*à la française*": frequent cleanings, no breastfeeding, hygienic walks, and pediatricians. Despite her mother's "advanced" lifestyle and Westernized choices, clearly distinguished from the traditional women's roles and preferences in which she was raised, Sarah does not see her as a role model, but rather as a demanding double-edged sword: "she was simply the ambassador for the supreme authority…She demanded from me force, willingness, control, intelligence, courage, dynamism and submission. But how to be submissive when one is strong? How to become strong when one submits oneself?"[489] Complicated relationships mark the narrator in her emotional development into adulthood: "My mother reflected the image of my contradictions, and its imprint engraved itself in me like an act of violence."[490] Thus, referring to the often opposing messages of her mother's and her father's expectations, she admits the full burden of her paradox "I inherited from all this powerful and contradictory amalgam."[491]

When Sarah was born and a girl was announced, Charles Levy thought the midwife was pulling his leg, since he somehow expected the firstborn to be a boy, as most Oriental men would. And so, little Sarah the first born, was raised expecting to act like a "*garçon manqué*," literally a failed boy, since all the attention on her was guided by her parents' repressed gender-identification to fit her into the role of an

---

[487] "Elle n'était pas marocaine, injure suprême, mais juive du Maroc, et se sentait infiniment supérieure aux fatmas qui travaillaient à la maison." Ibid., 39.
[488] "Je ne retiens d'elle qu'une vision de movement." Ibid., 24.
[489] "elle n'était que l'ambassadeur de l'autorité suprême … Elle exigeait de moi force, volonté, maîtrise, intelligence, courage, dynamisme et soumission. Mais comment se soumettre quand on est fort ? Comment devenir fort quand on se soumet?" Ibid., 30.
[490] "Ma mère me renvoyait l'image de mes contradictions et son empreinte s'est gravée en moi comme une violence." Ibid.
[491] "De tout cet amalgame puissant et contradictoire, j'ai herité…" Ibid., 23.

eldest child, culturally desired as a boy. "The least I could do...was to behave like a dangerous tomboy...Turbulent and destructive, I was a curly haired devil with chubby thighs."[492]

She terrorized the maids and the nannies, her heroes were Robin Hood and Ivanhoe, and she climbed trees and ran faster that all the other girls. "I was happy to be treated as a tomboy, I listened to my mother speak delightedly about my exploits."[493] Of course, a major problem that arises is that the relationships that young Sarah forms in early childhood are defined by falsely identified gender-relations. For instance, during the Passover meal, a hard boiled egg displayed on the Seder plate was traditionally intended for the firstborn son, but in Sarah's family she is the recipient of this egg: "...as a desired child, I was considered the first male child, bringing hope and aspirations, the one who deserved the protection and blessings of the Eternal our King. Amen."[494] And so it becomes part of her childhood "mythology" that she is the much desired firstborn son, and the ensuing Oedipal opposition to the father becomes an unavoidable trap.

Although French philosopher and literary theorist Roland Barthes did not have in mind the female writer in his *Pleasure of the Text*, his observation seems relevant: "If there is no longer a father, why tell stories? Doesn't every narrative lead back to Oedipus? Isn't storytelling always a way of searching for one's origin, speaking one's conflicts with the law?"[495] For Sarah, the narrative of her childhood becomes strongly suggestive of such an origin. Clearly we would need to define a narrative quest that replaces Oedipus's anxieties, the motor of male narrativity, with the pleasure of female narratability, since Sarah indeed is female.

The initial confusion in Sarah's life raises some interesting questions regarding the desire, or the pleasure, of such a narration. Sarah is

---

492   "Le moins que je puisse faire...était de me comporter en garçon manqué et dangereux...Turbulente et destructrice, j'étais un diable frisotté à cuisses dodues." Ibid., 44.
493   "J'étais heureuse d'être traitée en garçon manqué, j'écoutais ma mère raconter mes exploits avec ravissement." Ibid., 46.
494   "...en tant qu'enfant desirée, j'étais considérée comme le premier enfant mâle, portant les espoirs et les aspirations, celui sur lequel on appelait la protection et la bénédiction de l'Eternel notre Dieu. Amen." Ibid., 43.
495   Roland Barthes, *The Pleasure of the Text*. Trans. Richard Miller. New York: Hill, 1975, 45.

trapped in a schizophrenic paradigm in more ways than one: between the two different Sephardic traditions as represented by the clashing cultural expectations of her parents; between the gendered expectations and her gendered reality; as well as the demands of *"fémininité"* imposed by her cultural surroundings. These early childhood experiences will shape the narrator's difficulties, as a young adult, to gain confidence in her own ability for self-emancipation. For while she is acutely aware of her emancipatory potential and need, her emotional baggage forces her to surrender her would-be battle.

Sarah was *"l'Unique"*(the One and only) in her role as the much-awaited boy and she wanted to remain just that. However, when her brother Lucien is born, he becomes, to Sarah's shock and great dismay, "The King," whose circumcised penis is carefully and honorably tended to by the doting grandmother. "If my parents called my brother 'the king,' my grandmother, she would kiss his genitals calling him 'Boya'...that is 'my father.' My grandmother, in her adoration of virility, looked at the corkscrew-like genitals of my brother, calling them 'my father'! ...I possessed the moral virility, but he possessed the tangible instruments of power, which gave him dispensation from all other obligations."[496]

This fact only made her difference as a girl even more profoundly felt, since there were no expectations of him as he was not the firstborn. After the brother's arrival, her parents try to involve her in dance and piano to make her more feminine, but as she says "It was easy to see that I had nothing feminine in me. I had moreover come to believe them."[497] Treated like a boy child as a young girl, and then suddenly expected to become more feminine, only to listen to the lamentations of her family that she has not an ounce of femininity in her, she is headed for a teenage period with complex emotional consequences. She feels that her father's violent and angry outbursts are her fault, since she is no longer able to please her parents.

---

496   "Si mes parents appelaient mon frère 'le roi,' ma grand-mère, elle, embrassait ses organs génitaux en l'appelant 'Boya'...c'est-à-dire 'mon père'. Ma grand-mère, dans son adoration de la virilité, regardait le sexe tire-bouchonnant de mon frère et l'appelait 'mon père' ! ...Je possédais la virilité morale, mais lui possédait les instruments tangibles du pouvoir, ce qui le dispensait totalement de toute autre obligation." *Baisse les Yeux*, 49-50.
497   "Il était facile de constater que je n'avais rien de féminin. J'en étais d'ailleurs arrivée à les croire." Ibid., 51.

As typical with teenagers, this is a time of revolt and rebellion, and Sarah goes through a particularly difficult time: "During these years of rage, I began to methodically detest my family."[498] Many pages of the book are hence dedicated to describing everything she despises, each paragraph starting with "I hated my mother who, as if she had nothing better to do in the world, was hellbent on keeping me in a state of a mindless girl...I hated may father, whose only preoccupation was to make me into a perfected double of himself."[499]

Luce Irigaray, the French feminist philosopher and psychoanalyst, put forward the concept of the masculine "logic of the same" as a classic example of the father who seeks to control the development of his children so that they will seamlessly mirror his importance back to himself. Sarah has revealed this aspiration of her father, and will continue to be torn between her desire and revulsion of such a fatherly project. She also abhors her grandmother for her way of pronouncing words in French, for her "*sauvagerie primitive*" (primitive savagery) and her favoritism of her brothers: "I hated this natural right to live taken for granted by men, and I envied it."[500] She hates the Judeo-Moroccan cuisine, and "I couldn't stand the screaming, the drama and the frenzy...the market of Bab-Marrakech...the noisy *souk* where I had to live...this hypocrisy, this fuss over the religious holidays."[501] She basically feels a powerless rage toward all of the things her family and her life in Morocco represent.

Throughout her young life, Sarah's lack of femininity is greatly lamented and becomes a concern for her mother and her entourage of family and friends. Coming into puberty late, her "flaw" becomes the source of further drama and tragedy. But Sarah does not necessarily

---

498   "Pendant ces années de rage, je me mis à détester méthodiquement ma famille." Ibid., 56.
499   "Je détestais ma mère qui s'acharnait, comme si elle n'avait que ça à faire au monde, à me figer dans un état de petite fille bêtifiante...Je détestais mon père, dont la seule préoccupation était de faire de moi un double perfectionné de lui-même." Ibid.
500   "Je détestais ce droit d'existence évident et naturel de l'homme, et je l'enviais." Ibid., 59.
501   "J'avais horreur des cris, du drame et de la frénésie...le marché de Bab-Marrakech...ce souk bruyant dans lequel j'étais obligée de vivre...cette hypocrisie, et ces singeries de fêtes religieuses." Ibid., 60-61.

see it this way: "The oldest, authoritarian, and without breasts: these three advantages gave me virility and replaced the penis."[502]

Finally, after she has reached puberty and things are growing and flowing as expected, the mother decides to bring her daughter to her first gynecological exam. The doctor affirms that she has an unusually small uterus, and again the mother becomes the source of a grotesquely conflicting message: for just as she was hysterical about her daughter's absent breasts and menstruation, she has no qualms about condemning her to a life defined by a decisive womanly deficiency: frigidity: "This had no importance whatsoever, she affirmed, apart from the fact that I would, because of it, be frigid until the end of my days."[503] Sarah detects her mother's apparent pleasure in giving her daughter this misogynistically defined diagnosis: "Would she have been subconsciously satisfied, seeing me kept in a state of childhood by a medical verdict?"[504] but chooses to ignore such a monstrous possibility.

As the text focuses on Sarah's futile attempts at emancipating herself from the domineering nature of the Oriental father and family, it also recounts the young woman's sexual explorations and liberations which must be understood as manifestations of her opposition to the father, as well as her attempts at defining her own womanhood despite the dire verdict of the mother and gynecologist. When she wants to go on a brief vacation with some male friends, her opposition is short lived:

> ...*after heartrending calls for Love and for Obedience, after the threat of an internment of my father in a psychiatric hospital where he surely would die, I abdicated, even before I started the fight, I abdicated before the power of the stormy familial elements, I abdicated in order to prevent the premature death of my father, and the insanity of my mother, I abdicated like a good little girl, a pain in the ass for sure, but a loving one.*[505]

---

[502] "Aînée, autoritaire et sans seins: ces trois atouts me conféraient la virilité et remplaçaient le pénis..." Ibid., 68.
[503] "Cela n'avait aucune importance, m'affirma-t-elle, mis à part le fait que je serais, à cause de cela, frigide jusqu'à la fin de mes journées." Ibid., 135.
[504] "Aurait-elle été inconsciemment satisfaite, me voyant maintenue en état d'enfance par un verdict médical?" Ibid., 136.
[505] "...après des appels déchirants à l'Amour et à l'Obéissance, après la menace d'un internement de mon père en hôpital psychiatrique dans lequel il

The fear of not being a loving daughter, of not living up to the expectations of the firstborn, the one who is the ultimate pleaser becomes overwhelming. Put up against the prospect of not being able to redeem her parents from a life without offspring, and thereby affirming their value in the eyes of their family members and elders, she finds no other way than to lamely renounce her search for individuality. Again, in a vicious circle of eternal battle between desire and duty, the narrator finds herself trapped.

After this failed attempt of teenage separation from the family, and suffering from persisting self doubt inspired by the humiliation experienced at the doctor's office, Sarah finally decides, at age seventeen, that "The future of my sexuality was at stake."[506] Without her parents' knowledge she takes off to Paris, where she buys Simone de Beauvoir's *Les Mémoires d'une Jeune Fille Rangée* and a pack of cigarettes and enjoys a few days of freedom. This is a short lived but huge step for the narrator in her path toward liberation, for she is soon beckoned to return to the province, and when she comes back home her father asks her "Sarah, what did you want to prove?" He asked me this in a kind voice, feeling sorry for me. With this simple question he appealed to my reason, to my adult capacities. But by forcing me to explain my acts, he put me in my place, in the world of the guilty child."[507] Again stuck between her desire for independence and need to please her father, she feels entrapped, but this instant is at least marked in her memory as her "…first attempt of alienation from the family."[508]

Eventually, the time arrives when the Levy family and most of the other Jewish families of the Maghreb begin their exodus. In 1962, Sarah's father decides he can no longer operate a business under the corrupt circumstances that had come to define post-colonial Moroc-

---

trouverait certainement la mort, j'abdiquai, avant même d'avoir livré bataille, j'abdiquai devant la puissance des éléments familiaux déchaînés, j'abdiquai pour prévenir la mort prématurée de mon père, la folie de ma mère, j'abdiquai en bonne petite fille, emmerdeuse certes, mais aimante." Ibid., 134.
506   "L'avenir de ma sexualité était en jeu." Ibid., 137.
507   "Sarah, qu'as-tu voulu prouver? Il me demanda cela d'une voix gentille, désolée pour moi. Par cette simple question il faisait appel à ma raison, à mes capacités d'adulte. Mais en me forçant à expliquer mes actes, il me renvoyait à ma place, dans le monde de l'enfance coupable." Ibid., 143.
508   "…première tentative de désaliénation familiale." Ibid.

co: "We were going to live in a green France, and for this I had no desire whatsoever...The departure became more concrete...like a fateful and inevitable rupture...Brutally I understood that I would never again see the ocean."[509] A deeply melancholic young woman prepares for her departure, not at all as hopeful and optimistic as some of the other scenarios we have seen earlier: "I convinced myself that I was very unhappy, that I was losing my roots...It was Exodus...an Air France Caravelle tore us away from the country that had seen us born and live..."[510] This historic moment in her life is perceived as a forceful and involuntary separation, as if they were dragged away and ripped out from their native land. As they arrive in "FFFFFrance (to be pronounced ecstatically)," the land of liberty, equality, and fraternity, the narrator wants to stress the difference between home and exile:

We were going to leave the song of the muezzins for the call of the church bells on Sunday morning, the sun for the rain, large spaces for small vegetable gardens, the poetry of the hills scattered with white grave stones for flowery graveyards, roughcast by crosses, curly hair and tanned complexions for blond and Aryan tufts of hair, djellabas for full suits, the royalty of the cherifan Empire for the Republic, ignorance for culture, the greatness of Islam for those of Christianity.[511]

Settled in provincial France where Sarah's father has found a humble but promising place for his law practice, they stick out like a sore thumb : "...this new and hostile place, by its brutal affirmation of

---

[509] "Nous allions vivre dans une France verte, et je n'en avais aucune envie...Le départ se concrétisait...comme une rupture fatidique et inévitable...J'ai compris brutalement que je ne verrais plus la mer." Ibid., 115.

[510] " Je me persuadais que j'étais très malheureuse, que je perdais mes racines...C'était l'exode...une Caravelle d'Air France nous arracha du pays qui nous avait vus naître et vivre..." Ibid., 116-118.

[511] "Nous allions abandonner le chant des muezzins pour l'appel des cloches du dimanche matin, le soleil pour la pluie, les grands espaces pour les petits potagers, la poésie des collines clairsemées de blanches pierres funéraires pour les cimetières fleuris, hérissés de croix, les cheveux frisés et les teints basanes pour les touffeurs blondes et aryennes, les djellabas pour les complets vestons, la royauté de l'Empire chérifien pour la République, l'ignorance pour la culture, les grandeurs de l'Islam pour celles de la chrétienté." Ibid. 113.

our origins and our folklore."[512] Throughout the text, Sarah's hybrid and misunderstood identity in this new place define her difficulty in belonging. Back in Morocco, it was not possible to feel that she belonged fully in Islamic society, since the Jews were viewed as "*à part*" (different). While still living in North Africa she had decided to go to the hammam where the walls separated the outside world from that of the intimate inside, where the "real" women could be just that: "By means of the hammam, I had integrated into the world of the Moroccan woman, I intruded myself into the warm places that united them."[513]

However, Zorah, the old and wrinkled Berber attendant, sees Sarah as the other that she is not: "I was 'the French woman who is unaccustomed'... 'Let yourself go, don't be shy, it's only natural!'"[514] Similar to when she was little and her parents projected their desire for a different identity on their daughter, she is again identified as what she is not. Instances of misidentification persist in Sarah's life, as when she arrives in France, where she enters a program for physical education on a scholarship. There she is reprimanded for sleeping uncovered at night, like an undomesticated immigrant, and at the same time one of her instructors questions her: "How could it be that the daughter of a Moroccan lawyer, a daughter of a multimillionaire settler, was able to get a scholarship from the French government? How did I dare take the place of a real French girl of pure blood...?"[515] She, however, is neither the daughter of a *colon* (a colonizer), a pied-noir, or the primitive creature they make her out to be.

When Sarah meets Bruno Rotzenberger, the Ashkenazi Jew who comes to represent many things her family is not, he, "*le premier homme qui me voyait*" (the first man who saw me) immediately captures the nar-

---

512 "...cet espace nouveau et hostile, dans l'affirmation brutale de nos origines et de notre folklore." Ibid., 119.
513 "Par le biais du hammam, j'avais intégré le monde de la femme marocaine, je m'immisçais dans les liens chaleureux qui les unissaient." Ibid., 103.
514 "J'étais 'la Française qui n'a pas l'habitude'... 'Laisse-toi aller, ne sois pas gênée, c'est naturel !'" Ibid., 101.
515 "Comment se faisait-il qu'une fille d'avocat du Maroc, qu'une fille de colon multimilliardaire ait pu obtenir une bourse du gouvernement français? Comment osais-je prendre la place d'une véritable Française pur sang...?" Ibid., 127.

rator's heart, especially as he takes her side in a family discussion during dinner. However, her immaturity shows as she admits that he "…was my father with something more since he had managed to bring him down in his own home… By openly taking my side."[516] The burden of marrying into a family whose fate has been profoundly marked by both the high culture of pre-Second World War Western Europe and the horrors of the Shoah, proves to be no small challenge for Sarah: "I was going to be, me, Sarah Levy, Sephardic Jew and a non-believer, in the noble Ashkenazi family of the Rotzenberger-of-Vilna, honorably and painfully haloed by the still burning memory of the recent Nazi Holocaust."[517]

She continues, "…by marrying Bruno, I also married his clan."[518] Married, Sarah knows too well that the man she has left her father for is indeed his mere replacement: "…I found myself married, irreversibly, to a generous, charming, and tyrannical being."[519] In trying to become the perfect wife, the narrator is eager to follow the advice from the women in her family: "…they were prepared to help me so that I would become transformed, so that I would enter the order of women, so that I would finally be what they had dreamed that I should be…The marriage would introduce me into the kingdom of saints, of perfect women."[520] This does not come with a cheap price tag for Sarah, however, who so far in life has become hyper-aware of demands put on her and her continuous need to repress her own, natural self. But her desire to please her family and her new husband is stronger than she is: "First condition: learn to forget myself a little…I forgot myself, I offered myself like a package. I got rid of myself."[521] Leaving herself behind to fit into yet another role de-

---

516   "C'était mon père avec quelque chose en plus puisqu'il avait réussi à l'abattre à bout portant dans son propre camp…En prenant mon parti ouvertement… [il] était devenu mon nouveau héros." Ibid., 155.
517   "J'allais entrer, moi, Sarah Levy, juive sépharade et mécréante, dans la noble famille ashkénaze des Rotzenberger-de-Vilna, dignement et douloureusement auréolée du souvenir encore cuisant du dernier holocauste nazi." Ibid., 157.
518   "…en épousant Bruno, j'épousais aussi son clan." Ibid., 162.
519   "…je me trouvais mariée, irréversiblement, avec un être généreux, charmeur et tyrannique." Ibid., 171.
520   "…[elles] étaient prêtes à m'aider pour que je me transforme, pour que je rentre dans l'ordre des femmes, pour que je sois enfin ce qu'ils avaient rêvé que je sois…Le mariage allait m'introduire dans le royaume des saintes, des parfaits." Ibid., 160.
521   "Première condition : apprendre un peu l'oubli de moi-même…Je m'abandonnais, je m'offrais comme un paquet. Je me débarrassais de moi." Ibid., 161.

fined by the world around her, she is faced with the added burden of guilt due to the lack of suffering in her family:

> *I felt guilty having escaped the suffering of the Jewish people by my late birth...Worse, my parents, although submitted to the law of numerus clausus, never had to hide, and no member of my family had died during deportations, or was grilled or asphyxiated in the concentration camps and crematoria...I was not a survivor.*[522]

The cultural difference between her own Sephardic family and that of her newly adopted Ashkenazi family becomes the focus during family gatherings, as the narrator sarcastically and bitterly remarks on the pathetic need of one Other to define their own Other:

> *Ashkenazi. So that's what it was. We were part of the under-developed group of Sephardim...We were excluded from the Ashkenazi nobility...As irrefutable proof of our barbaric ways, down there, in Morocco, the Jews did not speak Yiddish but Arabic, worse, Judeo-Arabic...In this degenerate family of North African Zulus, only my father would have deserved to be Ashkenazi...Besides, by looking at them a little closer, what differentiated Moroccan Jews from Arabs?...This awful language, guttural, incomprehensible. Whereas Russian...The language of Tolstoi...It sufficed entering a Sephardic synagogue in order to understand nothing of the Jewish religion....this revolting mix of Arab folklore...these Orientals, these Jewish Arabs, have not even lifted a finger – not them! – for the construction of the State of Israel. Who, then, were the workers, who shed their blood for the Land of Israel? Eh? Who?*[523]

---

522   "Je me sentais coupable d'avoir échappé par ma naissance tardive à la souffrance du peuple juif...Pis, mes parents, bien que soumis à la loi de numerus clausus, n'avaient jamais eu à se cacher, et aucun membre de ma famille n'était mort en déportations, ni grillé, ni asphyxié dans les camp de concentration et les crématoires... Je n'étais pas une rescapée." Ibid., 163.
523   "Ashkenaze. C'était donc ça. Nous faisions partie du groupe sous-développé des sépharadim...Nous étions exclus de la noblesse ashkénaze...Preuve irréfutable de notre barbarie, là-bas, au Maroc, les juifs ne parlent pas yiddish mais arabe, pis, judéo-arabe... Dans cette famille

The *Sephardim* thus perceived as a bunch of invading newcomers and savages, and also feeling this negative identity thrown in their faces, the contradictions continue to surround Sarah. Naturally, her Sephardic family has plenty to say about the shortcomings of the Yiddish snobs, too, both parties unwilling to recognize "the stranger in themselves," or, as psychoanalyst Daniel Sibony has termed it, *"l'origine en partage"* (their shared origin). Caught perpetually in-between, Sarah falls deeper and deeper into depression, eventually sleeping in the fetus position, waiting for better days. Her marriage becomes shaky, and her husband increasingly morphs into her father in that he makes demands upon her, polices her, and tells her she is not behaving according to what is expected of her in her role as wife. She recognizes that she is in the same situation as she was as a child, that nothing has changed, and that she is imprisoned in the same conflicting situation. She cannot be what she is expected to be, and she cannot help but keep trying to fulfill the demands that are set on her; in the end all she can do is lower her eyes and give up the battle that she does not have the strength to begin. "I neglected my marriage. I neglected my husband, my couple. I kept my head down…My status had not changed, I was still a little disobedient girl, difficult and guilty in front of her dad, and this new daddy had even added sexual demands?"[524]

Sarah knows she is not *"une femme aimante, douce et soumise"* (a loving, gentle and submissive wife) like her mother has instructed her to be, and although she is unhappy she does want a child, hoping this would cement her marriage and help make her a more perfect wife and woman. Having struggled to push sufficiently during childbirth, and later not appearing to be as obsessed with the child's safety and

---

dégenerée de Zoulous d'Afrique du Nord, mon père, seul, aurait mérité d'être ashkénaze…D'ailleurs, en y regardant un peu plus près, qu'est-ce qui différenciait les juifs marocains des Arabes ?…Cette langue affreuse, gutturale, incompréhensible, alors que le russe…La langue de Tolstoï…Il suffisait d'entrer dans une synagogue séparade pour ne plus rien comprendre à la religion juive…cet amalgame révoltant de folklore arabe…ces Orientaux, ces juifs arabes, n'ont pas levé le petit doigt, pas ça! pour la construction de l'Etat d'Israel. Qui donc étaient des laboureurs, qui a versé son sang pour la terre d'Israel ? Hein ? Qui ?" Ibid., 173-175.

524   "Je négligeais mon mariage. Je négligeais mon mari, mon couple. Je bassais le nez…je n'avais pas changé de statut, que j'étais toujours une petite fille rétive, difficile et coupable devant son papa, et que ce nouveau papa avait par-dessus le marché des exigences sexuelles ?" Ibid., 195.

comfort as her mother-in-law and husband think she should be, she continues her desperate attempt at doing the right thing: "Convinced of being a bad wife and a denatured mother, I made a fuss of justifying myself, while still pursuing my way on the right path."[525] The idea of the "right path" is of course the telltale expression, since her desire to please those around her who define what she should be like, has become a pattern she has great difficulty in breaking, as she remains deeply entrenched in her childhood and beyond. Unhappily married, she also sees herself as an incompetent mother, an image that those around her reflect back on her.

Finally, the narrative takes us full circle back to the hospital where her father's slow demise is taking place, and we sense that the imminent definitive break that death will bring between father and daughter might give her the courage to break away, find her wings and fly. "In my refusal of femininity, my lack of a prick, my frigidity could be summed up in this: refusal of a permanent rape of my entire being, of my heart, my soul, my body…a fierce and underground resistance against all forms of authoritarian colonization and occupation…I want to exist, me, Sarah, and no longer be conquered land, occupied territory, having to pay tribute to the Master."[526] Sarah thus conceptualizes her "*refus de fémininité*"(refusal of femininity) in the language of decolonialization, "ultimately referring back to the power struggle that impacted so profoundly the fate of her family," as Nolden points out.[527] During the time that her father is dying, Sarah eventually leaves her husband, and finds comfort and freedom in an older lover, an artist and a bit of a "*juif errant*" (wandering Jew), a married man who for this reason has no demands on Sarah other than that they are equals in their love for one another. As he leaves her in his studio, he reminds her why he cannot

---

525 "Convaincue d'être une mauvaise épouse et une mère dénaturée, je renâclais, me justifiais, mais poursuivais ma route dans le droit chemin." Ibid., 205.
526 "Et mon refus de fémininité, mon manque de queue, ma frigidité se résumaient à ça : en refus de viol permanent de toute ma personne, dans mon cœur, mon esprit, mon corps…une résistance acharnée et souterraine contre toute forme de colonisation et d'occupations autoritaires…Je veux exister, moi, Sarah, et ne plus être le terrain conquis, le territoire occupé, qui doit payer tribut au Maître." Ibid., 218.
527 *In Lieu of Memory*, 197.

stay: "...I have made a choice in life, I have responsibilities...Sarah, I love you."[528] No longer a conquered land or occupied territory, she is free to define her own femininity, but that too comes with a price. Her lover, her equal, expects the same freedom. This, however, is a price that the narrator may be willing to pay for not having to be submissive to a Master. She can finally be her own; free to choose her path, and define justice in being true to her self.

Beyond Personal Confession:
Chochana Boukhobza and *Un Eté à Jérusalem*

Chochana Boukhobza, the youngest of the authors included in this study, was born in Tunisia in 1959. Her many novels are critically acclaimed, and although none of her books are announced as autobiographic, they have been recognized as going "beyond" personal confession. Speaking of how her writing is influenced by memories of her childhood in Tunisia and its abrupt end, Boukhobza has said: "I don't know how to tell you about that. I can't. It's erased...I don't know if I write in order to remember, or if I write to create my own memories."[529] Clearly autobiographical elements engender soul-searching and coming to terms with loss and exile in narratives that question the role of the father, the effect of that role on sibling relations, and the legacy of the parents upon the next generation.

The author illustrates that the drama of exile creates not one tragic male hero, the father, but that the entire family is affected, all members facing their own traumas and memories. The main characters are often strong, independent women who have rebelled in one way or another against the father's oppressive silence, but who seek his love without giving up their freedom. Signs of trauma ensuing from the often multiple exiles endured by the families in Boukhobza's early novels

---
528 "...j'ai fait un choix de vie, j'ai des responsabilités...Sarah, je t'aime." *Baisse les yeux*, 239.
529 "Je ne sais pas raconter ça. Je ne peux pas. Ça s'est effacé...Je ne sais pas si j'écris pour me souvenir, ou si j'écris pour me donner des souvenirs." Boukhobza, Chochana, "Rien sur l'enfance." in *Une enfance juive en Méditerranée musulmane,* ed. L. Sebbar, Saint-Pourçain-sur-Sioule: Bleu Autour, 2012, 81.

permeate the narratives. These are manifested in evocations of fading memories, the fear of losing all traces of the original homeland and the unique heritage it represents, and infinitely painful and complicated family relations, marked by resentment, mourning, anger, and rage as brought on by exile, loss and disillusionment. The characters in her narratives of displacement often seek love, comfort and protection in one way or another, but in so doing, they often ignore each other and slip deeper into silence and isolation.

Un Eté à Jérusalem,[530](1986) which received the French literary prize Prix Méditerranée, represents one of Boukhobza's most intimate and raw texts, illustrating the often tormenting aspects of exile as well as many specificities of the Judeo-Maghrebian narrative of that shared human experience. It is the story of 20-year-old Sarah who is returning to Israel for the summer after having left her family there three years earlier. The Promised Land has quickly become a disillusionment as it spirals toward war and political mayhem, and Sarah feels suffocated by her father's oppressive behavior.

Having migrated from Tunisia to France, her family left behind their relative comfort in France because of their daughter's enthusiasm for Zionism and wishes to settle in Israel. But her mother reminds her, the father took Sarah's running away from them and Israel as the ultimate rejection: "…you announced your return to Paris to him… He thought he was going crazy…You were fleeing."[531] In this way, the young character's movement between North Africa, France and Israel, reflects elements of Boukhobza's own experience. The father barely looks up when she arrives "…in front of me, caught short, he remains silent…silence came between us,"[532] his anger still preventing him from speaking, plunging him deeper into silence: "…he stays in his corner, shaking like a fool with his words that lurk in his head…"[533] The mother tries to explain the father's silence and exasperation as the result of

---

530   *Un Eté à Jérusalem*. Paris: Seuil, 1986.
531   "…tu lui annonçais ton retour à Paris…Il a cru devenir fou…Tu fuyais." *Un éte à Jérusalem*, 44.
532   "…face à moi, pris de court, il reste muet…le silence entre nous est tombé." Ibid., 34.
533   "…il reste dans son coin à trembler comme un fou avec ses mots qui rodent dans sa tête…" Ibid., 40.

the uprooting, the disappointment, and the fear of losing his children: "Your father did what he could…He didn't know…from Gabès to Paris…it was too abrupt, you understand? The oldest daughter…he never could hold you in check…He could not follow you…"[534] The young narrator remembers what she perceived as his tyrannical ways and says she had to leave then, since "…he judges with such grotesque seriousness, confusing superstition and faith."[535]

Now that she is back she quickly notices that he never caresses the mother, or even looks at her. All he knows how to do is to give orders to her: "Come, take, give…bring, do"[536] and he has withdrawn completely leaving his spouse in utter isolation as "He sinks into a sordid silence."[537] Danny, Sarah's brother who has come home for a brief leave from the army, knows all too well how their father's feeling of alienation and despair marks the family, and notes "We live with an unbearable silence. No question, no love. Just sadness…"[538] Her brother and mother have come to accept this reality of the father's despondency, whereas it shocks Sarah when she realizes the grimness of his case and how it affects the family.

During Sarah's absence, her mother has been marked by the trials of having her two sons mobilized to Lebanon, and the narrator is upset to see her "…worried eyes, evasive, animated by bursts of madness. All I see is her tired and haggard look that tries to be happy, but that is infinitely desperate."[539] The mother spends her days waiting for her sons to return from the war, fearing as much as yearning for a phone call, never knowing if it will announce their upcoming leave or their death, and for that same reason she chooses not to listen to the radio that reports daily fatalities every hour on the hour. She is desperately

---

534   "Ton père a fait ce qu'il a pu…Il ne savait pas…De Gabès à Paris …C'était trop brusque, tu comprends?... Fille aînée…ne te contenais jamais…Il ne pouvait pas te suivre…" Ibid., 43.
535   "…il juge avec un sérieux grotesque où superstition et foi se confondent." Ibid., 97.
536   Ibid., 95.
537   "Il sombre dans un mutisme sordide." Ibid., 100.
538   "Nous vivons dans un silence insupportable. No question, no love. Just sadness…" Ibid., 122.
539   "…yeux troublés, fuyants, animés d'un éclat de folie. Je ne vois que son égard fatigué et hagard qui se veut joyeux, qui est infiniment désespéré." Ibid., 13.

trying to achieve normalcy, but feels marginalized and lonely. Even the films on TV are in English with Hebrew subtitles, leaving her outside the modes of understanding since her languages are Judeo-Arabic and French. Sarah notices how she has aged unreasonably much in the three short years of her absence, and that she has begun to cover her hair with a kerchief according to religious tradition, but perhaps also a sign of resignation to the efforts of personal grooming.

Soon feeling overwhelmed by the depressing atmosphere in her parents' apartment, Sarah begins to roam the streets of Jerusalem, the city that had so enthralled her some three years ago. The ancient and Holy City has a unique allure as it evokes memories of the lost North Africa. Jerusalem, a city so much more familiar than Paris or Marseilles. As one friend tells Sarah: "There is some of Morocco in Jerusalem, don't forget…"[540] Another friend, also of North African origin, feels the same: "Here I have found the light of Tlemcen, and in some rare alleys, the poetry of Arabic architecture."[541] Now the city is vibrating in the oppressive summer heat, and as she walks by some Arab road workers they pick up the pace of their labor "…to show me that they are not some stray dogs, but the fallen kings of a country where I will always be but a passer-by."[542] She realizes that she does not feel at home here, and that she may never belong anywhere. When she later walks through a religious neighborhood, someone yells at her: "Cover yourself, shameless one. For them, too, I remain an intruder."[543]

Still later, when the taxi driver who has given her a ride mumbles something under his breath in Arabic, a language she does not understand fully since she was only a small girl when her family left Tunisia, a feeling of estrangement stabs her again: "I felt a pinch in my heart: in France as here, I remain a stranger before whom everyone speaks with secret words."[544] The city is "…beyond the limits of my

---
540   " Il y a du Maroc dans Jérusalem, ne l'oublie pas…" Ibid., 78.
541   "J'ai trouvé ici la lumière de Tlemcen, et dans de rares ruelles, la poésie de l'architecture arabe… " Ibid., 145.
542   "…pour m'indiquer qu'ils ne sont pas des chiens de la route, mais les rois déchus d'un pays où je serais toujours une passante." Ibid., 21.
543   "Couvre-toi, impudique. Pour eux, aussi, je reste une intruse." Ibid., 136.
544   "Mon coeur s'est pincé: en France et ici, je reste donc pour tous une étrangère devant laquelle on parle à mots couverts." Ibid., 213.

logic,"[545] and she feels confused; her memory becomes an entangled web of chiaroscuro, an interplay of light and dark, blind spots and illuminations: "I get lost in Jerusalem as I drift in the meanderings of my memory."[546] To Sarah, Israel has become an exile too, where she does not find her peace, and she feels uprooted from the country's hope and promise of sweetness and redemption: "For me, it was the Hebrew exile that transformed me."[547]

While she is visiting Israel her Safta – grandmother – dies, and Sarah fears that without her the family will lose their last attachment to Tunisia. She represents the vivid memories the narrator can still trace as she thinks back to her childhood: "Safta…she knew how to plant and make the seed of elsewhere grow in my memory."[548] Life had not been easy for the family matriarch in the difficult period following the exodus: "Gabès-Paris. A one way ticket without any hope of return. Ripped away from her empire for the two rooms and a kitchen on the rue Chemin-Vert, Safta enclosed herself in her silence."[549] Silence, then, seems to be a way of coping with the pain experienced by the adult members of the uprooted families, since their minds will not soak up the new environment in the same way as their children:

The road was long, a trajectory like the mark of a circumflex accent. First awakening: North Africa. Then the exile to Paris, Marseille, Lyon, with sneezes of nostalgia, pricklings of the sinus, annoying tête-à-têtes with "paradise." Behind the panicking compass, they again packed their bags, a fantasy. Jerusalem. A whim that has its price. Their kids, surely, speak Hebrew and have fun in the open landscape imitating the young sabras. But the parents, they remain renegades, awkwardly managing the language, nursing the Bible as a last recourse.[550]

---

545   "…hors des limites de ma logique." Ibid., 35.
546   "Je me perds dans Jérusalem comme je dérive dans les méandres de ma mémoire." Ibid.
547   "Moi, c'était l'exil hébraïque qui me transformait." Ibid., 166.
548   "Safta…elle avait su planter et faire germer dans ma mémoire la graine de l'ailleurs…" Ibid., 209.
549   "Gabès-Paris. Un aller simple sans aucun espoir de retour. Arrachée de son empire pour les deux-pièces cuisine dans la rue Chemin-Vert, Safta s'enferma dans son mutisme." Ibid., 57.
550   "Le chemin a été long, une trajectoire en accent circonflexe. Premier

Sarah mourns more than just the death of her Safta: "The mourning also carries the exile. The exile which died with her!...Time will erase the scent of her spices, of her songs. I am afraid..."[551] As the parents' home becomes crowded with older people from the extended family who have come to spend the seven days of mourning, or *shiva*, with the father, Sarah only wants to escape the stifling mood. As much as Sarah can't stand their judging her for leaving, for inciting her father against her, and for exhausting her mother who has to serve them and clean for them during the seven days, she also realizes that they are the last survivors of Safta's world. They represent the last living vestiges of centuries of peaceful co-existence with Muslims, and Sarah realizes that it is in Tunisia that they have lived their best days. For them Israel represents the too holy ground, where they have only come to die. "But when they disappear, a fragment of Jewish history will be scattered on the ground, like sand. Go after it, go find the traces!"[552] When she learns that her controlling aunt has thrown out the grand-mother's belongings, except for the jewelry that she is hoarding in a kerchief in her bra, Sarah is devastated: "How will I explain to my children that I come from North Africa if you throw our history in the garbage?"[553]

The young narrator needs to escape the apartment; in the eyes of her family a disrespectful and irreligious provocation during the time of mourning. They see her choice of clothes and makeup as inappropriate, and her refusal to report to her parents about her whereabouts as she is out in the city at night after dark only further enrages her father. He waits up for her at night and reprimands her as she

---

éveil : L'Afrique du Nord. L'exil ensuite vers Paris, Marseille, Lyon, avec des éternuements de nostalgie, des picotements du sinus, des tête-à-tête empoisonnés avec le 'paradis'. Devant la boussole qui s'affole, ils ont à nouveau refait leurs valises, une fantaisie. Jérusalem. Un caprice qui coûte cher. Leurs gosses, certes, parlent hébreu et s'amusent dans les terrains vagues en imitant les manières des jeunes sabras. Mais eux, les parents, restent des transfuges, maniant maladroitement la langue, tétant la Bible comme dernier recours." Ibid., 32.

551   "C'est de l'exil que porte le deuil. L'exil qui est mort avec elle! ...Le temps va effacer le parfum de ses épices, de ses chants. J'ai peur..." Ibid., 158.

552   "Mais lorsqu'ils disparaîtront, un fragment de l'histoire juive s'éparpillera sur le sol, comme du sable. Va après, va retrouver les traces!" Ibid., 193.

553   "Comment expliquerai-je à mes enfants que je viens d'Afrique du Nord si tu livres notre histoire aux poubelles?" Ibid., 208.

comes home: "Lord! You walk around dressed like a whore. Never a word, never an explanation. Who do you think you are? A monster?"[554] Her father is prepared to disown her, but her mother intervenes and soothes him in his anger and desperation, partly fueled by his concern for what the neighbors might say about him because of his daughter's insolent behavior. Sarah, for her part, becomes more and more obsessed with disguising herself: "How was I going to paint myself, to depict myself?…with which madness would I be struck? Which biblical curse would swoop down on me?[555] As if trying to cheat fate by making herself unrecognizable, she exaggerates the makeup she puts on. She invokes the prophesy of Jeremiah that Jerusalem will one day become the whore of the nations, and speaks of an acquaintance she had made there three years ago, a prostitute named Mavrika. "She was the witness or the prophet. Sometimes both."[556] As a witness to the degeneration of the Holy City due to the looming threats of war and the ominous calls of the sons of Israel to enter and die in the battlefield, the perhaps mystical Mavrika offers companionship to Sarah's imagination as she desperately tries to escape the gloomy atmosphere. "I want her to teach me the art of disguise…I want to forget. To finally be happy."[557]

The novel further evokes what Thomas Nolden notes as "the male politics of nationalism that have corrupted Jerusalem"[558] when the narrator is revolted by the apparent resignation of her parents to the war that mercilessly rips sons from their mothers' arms and hurls them into graves: "God said in the Bible: make war, uh? And if children die, it's fate, right? Oh, do I need something else…I hate you all, you hear me?"[559] She can imagine too clearly the deaths of her own two younger brothers, and thinks of all the mothers who lose their sanity in the

---

554   "Adonai ! Tu te balades habillée comme une putain. Jamais un mot, jamais une explication. Mais qui est-tu? Un monstre?" Ibid., 178.
555   "Comment allais-je me peindre, me dépeindre? …de quelle folie serais-je frappée ? Quelle malédiction biblique allait fondre sur moi ?" Ibid., 166.
556   "Elle était le témoin ou le prophète. Parfois les deux." Ibid., 184.
557   "Je veux qu'elle m'enseigne l'art du déguisement… Je veux oublier. Etre enfin heureuse." Ibid., 53.
558   *In Lieu of Memory*, 198.
559   "Dieu a dit dans la Bible: faites la guerre, hein ? Et si des gosses meurent, c'est le Mektoub, n'est-ce pas ? Oh, j'ai besoin d'autre chose…Je vous déteste tous, tu m'entends ?" *Un été à Jérusalem*, 164.

madness provoked by war and the constant tension they live in: "... these young men. We carry them into the earth in the revolt of their mothers who slowly sink into ecstatic madness."[560]

It is when Sarah meets Henry, a pacifist and nomad like herself and whom she sees as her soul mate, that she starts to calm down. She even wants to leave her safe relationship with her Polish-Jewish-French boyfriend and remain in Jerusalem. Regardless of her conflicted feelings about the city, and despite her deep instinctual vision that Henry is but an ephemeral blessing, "On day, inevitably, he will leave,"[561] she has found a way to share with him a vision of the place she thought lost. He is also someone who is not intimidated by her complex and painful past, since he too has experienced the loss of Maghreb and lives as in exile.

Her French boyfriend, on the other hand, is incapable of understanding her, and she tells Henry how this makes her unable to love him: "I don't love him since he did not try to know how to ask me about my past. He never descended into my tunnels, there where it is written 'danger.' He thinks I only existed from the moment we met."[562] With Henry, she is able to experience a deeper relationship and their love for one another enables them to be hopeful for a country that seems engulfed in war, hate, rage, and distrust. From his bedroom window she notices that the neighborhoods in the old city of Jerusalem suggest the possibilities for the future: "Nevertheless, the houses walk arm in arm. The Armenian quarter meshed with the Christian and the Jewish ones."[563] He sees in her the rebel that she is, finding in her too heavily painted face an endearing sign of someone who is afraid, who lives a life of eternal exile: "'You too, you're my kind, a nomad.' He explains with caustic irony the symptoms of exile, the disorder in thoughts, the nostalgia of swallowed up images…It's a fragile thing, a man without his place. A man who cannot point to a street corner, a piece of land and simply say: this is where I grew up."[564]

---

560 "…les jeunes gens. On les porte en terre dans la révolte des mères qui sombrent lentement dans la folie extatique." Ibid., 136.
561 "Un jour, forcément, il partira." Ibid., 174.
562 "Je ne l'aime pas car il n'a pas voulu ou pas su m'interroger sur mon passé. Il n'est pas descendu dans mes tunnels, là où c'est écrit 'danger'. Il croit que je n'existe que depuis le moment où l'on s'est rencontrés." Ibid., 122.
563 "Et pourtant les maisons marchent bras dessus, bras dessous. Quartier arménien confondu aux quartiers chrétien et juifs." Ibid., 203.
564 "Toi aussi, tu es de ma race, une nomade. Il expose avec une ironie

Unfortunately, Sarah's brief period of optimism abruptly ends when Henry goes to Beirut on a peaceful mission to observe the field, and is hit by a stray bullet, killing him. Sarah's soul mate and inspiration to stay in Israel, giving the troubled country another chance, is ripped away suddenly and violently. She slips into insanity identifying with the tormented prostitute Mavrika, roaming the city at night, unrecognizable and filled with self-inflicted wounds, howling, laughing and screaming her hatred against the violence of the country once inhabited by God: "It is said that God inhabits you, Jerusalem! I think he has cursed you! Let all your sons die! One day you will return to your ruins!"[565] Sarah becomes the prostitute's *doppelgänger*, and in her mind's eye Jeremiah's prophecy has been fulfilled. Boukhobza's tormented narrator experiences the push-pull link to Israel, at once drawn toward and repulsed by the country's inexplicable magnetic complexity. Reflecting on this complex relationship, the author has said, "Strange people, really, my people, torn between a lost homeland; a country in which to live, get married and work; and a promised land. Strange people squeezed between the past, the present, and prophesy."[566] In *Un Eté a Jérusalem*, this existential squeeze as felt by the youngest generation of North Africa's exiled Jews, has been acutely evoked through the eyes of a passionate female character adding a gendered, intimate, and honest voice to a shared experience of post-colonial in-betweenness.

✱✱✱✱✱✱✱✱

The two novels, *Baisse les Yeux, Sarah* by Paule Darmon and *Un Eté à Jérusalem* by Chochana Boukhobza, share many elements in that they both intimately narrate from a daughter's perspective the challeng-

---

caustique les symptômes de l'exil, le désordre de la pensée, la nostalgie des images englouties…C'est fragile, un homme qui n'a pas son assise. Un homme qui ne peut montrer un coin de rue, un coin de terre et dire avec simplicité : c'est ici que j'ai grandi." Ibid., 175.
565 "On dit que Dieu t'habite, Jérusalem! Je crois qu'il t'a maudite! Laisse donc mourir tous tes fils! Un jour, tu reviendras à tes ruines!" Ibid., 255.
566 "Étrange people en vérité que le mien, déchiré entre un pays perdu; un pays pour vivre, se marier, travailler; et un pays promis. Étrange people pris en tenaille entre le passé, le present, et la prophétie." Chochana Boukhobza, "Rien sur l'enfance." In Laila Sebbar (Ed.). *Une enfance juive en Méditerranée musulmane*. Saint-Pourçain-sur-Sioule: Bleu Autour, 2012, 85.

es they face in trying to liberate themselves from an oppressive fatherly presence that suffocates and paralyzes them with demands, expectations and prohibitions. These constricting and unreasonable expectations are often reinforced by the mother or the extended family, suggesting the lasting powerful influence of the "Oriental" (Jewish) heritage that the exiled parent generation clings to for an anchor in their own struggle for meaning, despite the fact that their daughters live completely different lives as second generation immigrants. The young narrators' quest for freedom and a space away from their families' view of their conduct takes the form of rebellion infused with gendered, sexual, and political elements, as well as psychological and emotional factors.

Each family member withdraws into silence – as an instinctual mechanism for surviving the various traumas they share – and the effects of this muteness only plunge each one of them further into isolation and insanity. Using a language of victimhood, colonization, and resistance, the narratives outline a unique Sephardic Jewish experience in the twentieth century. This delineates a different offense, a different struggle, and a different rebellion than that lived by Ashkenazi Jews, or, for that matter, by the Arabs of Maghreb. In addition, a distinctly unique encounter with the other is also traced in these female narratives, since as Jewish women the narrators can enter places, make acquaintances and form relationships from which men are traditionally excluded.

Thomas Nolden notes that for these younger Sephardic women writers the principles of *écriture féminine*, which guided the earlier generation of writers as they built on a female legacy of self-assertiveness, have "retreated into the background and given way to reservations about the possibility of their emancipation. Such authors no longer just write from their 'feminine libidinal economy'…but about an economy of desires that…requires the Sephardic woman to change her face, her body as the bearers of her ethnic heritage to enter the libidinal zone of the French diaspora."[567] We have seen examples of such changes in the bodies and faces of the two Sarah narrators as they represent carriers of their unique ethnic heritage by placing themselves firmly within the geography of the "zone of the French diaspora," and of basic human instincts, as relevant to their female Jewish experience.

---

567   *In Lieu of Memory*, 222.

Through the exploration of seven different narratives written by Sephardic women born in Tunisia, Morocco and Algeria, we have been able to glean an understanding of the obsessions, fears, desires and pleasures that mark this specific generation of women exiles and writers. The fact that they all have experienced first hand, as young children, adolescents or young adults the trials of the silent and silenced Jewish exodus from North Africa makes them bearers of a distinct experience within the various exilic narratives that abound today.

Whether the narratives share memories of a recently deceased mother, introduce a rabbi or a marabout to motivate a recovery of a sense of rootedness and a celebration of a North African Jewish identity, or portray rebellious daughters who struggle for their own freedom in a post colonial, post African life, they offer a collective yet hybrid and polyvocal voice of the complex experience of the Jewish exodus from the Maghreb and its aftermath. While history books and official discourses typically outline the general knowledge of larger and smaller historical movements, it is from literary text that we can harvest a deeper awareness and understanding through the intimate accounts of subjective, and in our case female, human experiences. A vanishing world, a home uprooted, a life disrupted and resumed in new surroundings, are experiences that receive a human face in the pages of these novels. Thanks to the autojudeographic narratives considered here and others like them, this chapter of Jewish history is elucidated and validated.

Conclusion

Toute création littéraire, toute penseé, est source d'histoire
Haim Zafrani

RETURNING TO THE STATEMENT BY AMMIEL ALCALAY noted in the introduction, that the works of Jewish writers, thinkers and historical figures from the Arab world have not figured as part of the central narrative of modern Jewish history, I recall the seed of inspiration. Alcalay termed their experiences "messages in bottles, all waiting to be found and put together."[568] This study has considered many different texts by writers from the Maghreb, both historical and literary, and sought to place them and their messages in the greater narrative and context within both the francophone post-colonial field and the trajectory and context of a greater Jewish modern history. Turning to scholars of both Jewish and non-Jewish origin for input and ideas, it has been possible to shed light on valuable resources giving testimony to human experiences that, when placed within and next to other Jewish and/or post-colonial discourses, claim a space that no longer belongs in the margins.

The isolating vacuum of Alcalay's bottle thus begins to release, and the vital messages by "Oriental" Jews place themselves in a larger perspective. Jewish voices from the Arab world may have been silenced at the same time as awareness of other exiled and marginalized groups of people has increased, but they have been able to slowly claim their own rightful and official place in history as they write their own histories, have written themselves into history, and thus have become acting subjects, rather than defined, passive objects in the sparring of narrative control, power and participation. We discover that the Jews from Islamic lands have a message for us, and here women writers from North Africa have spoken. Ultimately, the issue is one of being recognized as participants in history and as rightful, full-fledged citizens of

---
[568] *After Jews and Arabs*, 10.

a world learning to become increasingly concerned with the common fate of its global humanity and the human rights that extend beyond those defined by specific borders and nationalities.

Moroccan historian Haim Zafrani saw the need for recognizing and including his people's unique history and culture, and in his seminal study *Deux mille ans de vie juive au Maroc* (1998) [569] he succinctly states: "It is time, indeed, to bring forth from the shadows these centuries that have remained obscured by history and by the thinking of Oriental Diasporas, an entire sector of the Jewish universe and of its culture that has been left behind by science and of research, excluded from study and from teaching."[570] Ever since the Jews were forced to leave behind their homes and the life they knew in North Africa to embark on yet another diaspora, the layering continues of the memory-traces from Diasporas that are an integral part of Jewish narrative.

The fact that the "Oriental" Jews' narrative has been in the background of modern Jewish history, as well as not included in other "inclusive" histories of exiled and diasporic people, can be considered an insult at the least, and as an outrage at the most. This can be said within Jewish communities around the world specifically and in the perpetuation of the representation of silenced minorities generally. Lives and experiences that represent and transmit historical significance ultimately will have important personal and political consequences in claiming their space, as seen throughout this study.

The standpoints of women have been in focus here since they illuminate aspects of the social totality and reality historically (and culturally) suppressed in the dominant view. As minority women, in our case Jewish in either North Africa or France, this elucidation hopes to contribute to transforming previously limited ideas about what it means to be non-Muslim, non-Arab, non-pied-noir and yet deeply rooted in the Maghreb and in the francophone cultural, historical and

---

569   *Deux mille ans de vie juive au Maroc*. Paris : Maison Neuve & Larose, 1998.
570   "Il est temps, en effet, de faire sortir de l'ombre ces siècles demeurés obscures de l'histoire et de la pensée des diasporas orientales, tout un secteur de l'univers juif et de sa culture laissé à l'écart de la science et de la recherche, exclu de l'étude et de l'enseignement." Zafrani, 306.

political past and present. We have analyzed Jewish women writers' accomplishments in finding a way out of the phallocentric and patriarchal cultural heritage they grew up with, as they break the silence by using their pens and words as tools to explore and define their evolving identities, different from their mothers, but still anchored in their cultural and religious history.

Their nationalities as well as that of their mothers and their mothers again, do not represent anything constant, but rather something always already other and multiple. Hélène Cixous tells us she decided early on in her life to adopt an imaginary nationality, namely a literary nationality, since she experienced first hand how arbitrary and volatile the comforts of a nationality can be. As a Jewish writer, Cixous would not be the first to find a certain promise in the idea of a literary nationality or a literary home, since to her, as to the other Jewish women writers included here, literature and the ideas contained therein become a homeland from where nobody can throw you out or arbitrarily exclude you. When, not if, you leave a geographic location, the values of your home come with you. Egyptian writer André Aciman expresses this well: "I have done then that which all Jews could do, being the people of the book. If I could not bring my Alexandria with me wherever I went in the world, at least I could have a pocket version."[571]

However, leaving behind the roots that have grown in the land where you have lived becomes all the more painful when your parents' graves are there, sometimes in cemeteries leveled to the ground by new governments determined to erase signs of the past existence of a vibrant Jewish community within its borders. Since the establishment of the State of Israel it has not been easy, safe, if even possible for Jews to return as visitors to most Muslim countries, and this has been particularly difficult where family graves are concerned. For many, as for Hélène Cixous, this becomes an upsetting experience of abandonment: "To leave behind the grave of one's father: through dust I acquire a sort of invisible belonging to a land to which I am bound by my atoms without nationality...

---

571   "J'ai fait, alors, ce que pourrait faire tous les Juifs, étant le peuple du livre. Si je ne pouvais pas emporter mon Alexandrie où que j'aille dans le monde, au moins je pourrais en avoir une version de poche." *La mémoire sépharade*, 63.

The abandonment retains my memory on the unvisited heights of Algiers."[572] All the authors included in this study express at some point in their writing an awareness and sorrow for not being able to visit their ancestors' graves, or live near the final resting place of a loved one. A sense of having been forced to leave behind crucial emotional links to their past such as these may indeed be one of the central catalysts for turning to writing. Nine Moati, Gisèle Halimi, Annie Cohen, Chochana Boukobzha, Paule Darmon, Annie Fitoussie and finally Hélène Cixous all find great inspiration in inscribing their relatives' pasts into their own life-work and thus being able to elaborate and define their own identity as linked to their North African ancestors.

One of the initial goals of this book was to open up the floor to the Oriental Jewish experience, and to gain a better understanding of why and how the North African Sephardic history had remained an excluded or poorly recounted chapter from both Jewish modern and post-colonial histories. Inquiries have included a broad look at the historical contexts of Jewish lives in Arab lands going back to the "beginning of" the Jewish diaspora, so as to fully appreciate what is part of each author's personal story as well as the story of her people. How did the fate of the Jewish communities in the Maghreb evolve as it did and what are some of the factors that lead to the actions, reactions or inactions by these communities throughout time, leading up to the crucial dilemma experienced by those very communities during and immediately following colonization? Through my decision to not simply consider literature from within its own realm, nor history as the only source for historical knowledge and understanding, my aim has been to adjust a lens of inquiry by giving more focus on a much-needed subject. In addition, ideas from literary theory have helped to shed light on the many intersections of literature and history, and in this way hopefully bringing the two closer in revealing meaning of ignored relationships, differences and marginalized voices.

Françoise Lionnet points out the value of approaching history and fiction to one another in order to improve our understanding:

---

572   Cixous, "My Algériance," 260.

Since there are no more "grand narratives" to legitimate knowledge, the crumbled past of the post-colonial subject can now be narrated only in stories and histories that convey the fundamental heterogeneity of her experience. The reader is therefore forced to situate each text in relation to a historical context whose function is not to make the novel more "authentic" but to highlight the symbolic interpenetrability of history and fiction, of the real and the mythic.[573]

I would like to suggest an even more necessary relationship between Lionnet's idea of the "symbolic interpenetrability of history and fiction" and call this relationship one of interdependability, for as Y.H. Yerushalmi notes: "The divorce of history from literature has been as calamitous for Jewish as for general historical writing, not only because it widens the breach between the historian and the layman, but because it affects the very image of the past that results. Those who are alienated from the past cannot be drawn to it by explanation alone; they require evocation as well."[574] History and fiction interpenetrate and depend on each other; and the more we are willing to appreciate and realize this relationship, I believe the more our knowledge will become better nuanced understandings of what complex human experiences truly are. Hopefully this small contribution has been one way to open a dialogue between fields that easily see around each other through its effort at insisting on their connectedness. One becomes fuller and better nuanced by the partnering with the other. History, literature, cultural, minority and post-colonial studies are just a few that, when considered in light of each other, rather than separately, offer a chance to gain a deeper understanding of events as they unfold in personal, communal and national histories.

Jewish communities have both been influenced by and themselves have influenced the culture and histories in the various countries in the Arab world where they have existed for centuries, sometimes millennia. The meeting of these cultures and histories has yielded tremendous fruits, and in times of peace the two people – Jews and Arabs

---

573   Lionnet, *Post-colonial Representations*, 174.
574   Yerushalmi, *Zakhor*, 100.

– will agree that they share more values than not. Unfortunately, hateful and ignorant academic discourse and teachings concerning the relationship between Jews and Arabs are not only found in the Middle East, but extend to Universities in the US as well, where professors with a clear and aggressive political agenda against Israel have been found lecturing in and out of the classroom in ways that only increase the misgivings and myopia that already plague the relationship between Jews and Arabs. The David Project at Columbia University is one organization that tries to shed light on these incidents, and to encourage dialogue based on mutual respect and a shared wish to achieve peace both in an outside of the Middle East.

The inclusion or exclusion of the other in a history is always a political matter, from the intimate confines of the family to the various communities and sub-groups making up society, and ultimately to the peoples and nations of the world. It is necessary to continue to look for messages in bottles, not only within one's own culture or religion, but across borders, wherever there are people whose experiences have the potential to alter the way we build on knowledge and increase understanding. And just when we think we have begun to listen to and find meaning in a forgotten or silenced other, we cannot think the job is done. There will always be other "others," and the desire to silence the imagined threat of the other's narrative will never cease, since this desire often stems from a self preserving instinct or fear. As Alain Finkielkraut notes, the desire for a reconciled society is in itself totalitarian, and "…we live in the relative, and must take care to remain there…there are necessary battles but no *telos*, nor harmony on the horizon…Without utopia, any kind of arrogance or inquisition becomes impossible"[575] In this view, as Jews and Arabs yearn for a future of peace, mutual respect and tolerance, the absence of a utopian dream seems necessary, although we know this has proven complicated, perhaps impossible, in national narratives. The goals of a peaceful co-existence must be based on meeting their other in an ongoing and dynamic chain of compromises, the necessary "peaceful" battles that are needed in order to give peace a chance.

---

575   Finkielkraut, *The Imaginary Jew*, 139.

In light of recent violent events in France that have made the Jewish and Muslim communities there even more on edge and aware of the other's difference, there is no better time than the present to call for reactions that can contribute to a deeper understanding of the shared history of Jews and Muslims in North Africa and France. The roughly 600,000 Jews in France today, more than half of who hail from the former French colonies and protectorates in the Maghreb, live in daily fear of random attacks, sometimes thinly veiled as political and anti-Israel in origin, however uncanny in their similarity to the kind of selective and targeted violence seen toward Jews at other times throughout history. Words, expressions and stereotypes echoing the somber mood leading up to the Second World War and Hitler's rascist and fascist agenda, are freely expressed in the democratic society founded on *liberté, égalité,* and *fraternité.* Many French of both Jewish and Muslim persuasions feel bitterly disappointed and deceived. Anti-Semitism, as well as Islamophobia, as experienced by France's approximately 5-6 million Muslims, are on a rapid rise and the Front National party with Marine Le Pen at the helm is making strides at a disconcerting speed.

Recall that Daniel Sibony's concept of *entre-deux,* or in-between, as a place or a process of creative possibilities, is used in psychology and in inter-personal relationships, but also as a metaphor for the place where two people (as in Jews and Arabs) can go, venture and meet, in order to open up to the possibilities of understanding the other. Here the participant has to dare to lose some of his origin, but only to gain more in the meeting of the other. This process can naturally be extended into the realm of academic and political discourse as well. Let the gates of knowledge open up and let leaders in academia and politics dare to enter the *"entre-deux"*! There the risks may be higher, but the gains all the more rewarding. One of my all-time favorite French philosopher and writer, Michel de Montaigne, once pointed out that it is not in reaching the end of a voyage that he finds rewarding, but rather the crossing itself, in the *"entre-deux."* This is also the space in which the Sephardic women voices as revealed in this study have ventured to actively take part and meet other post-colonial narratives and histories, and thus become agents in renegotiating cultural interactions through the repositioning of their hybrid identities, personal memories and marginal history.

Bibliography

A

Abitbol, Michel. "The Integration of North African Jews in France." *Yale French Studies*. 85, Translated by Alan Astro. (1994): 248-261.
---. *The Jews of North Africa during the Second World War*. Detroit: Wayne State UP, 1989.
Abramson, Henry. "A Double Occlusion: Sephardim and the Holocaust." In *Sephardic and Mizrahi Jewry. From the Golden Age of Spain to Modern Times*. Zion Zohar, ed. New York: New York UP, 2005, 285-299.
Afzal-Khan, Fawzia and Kaplana Seshadri-Crooks, eds. *The Pre-Occupation of Post-colonial Studies*. Durham: Duke UP, 2000.
Agosín, Marjory, ed. *House of Memory*. New York: CNY Feminist Press, 1999.
---. *Passion, Memory, Identity*. New York: CNY Feminist Press, 2001.
Alcalay, Ammiel. *After Jews and Arabs. Remaking Levantine Culture*. London: U of Minn. P, 1993.
---. "Intellectual Life". In *The Jews of the Middle East and North Africa of Modern Times*. Reeva Spector Simon, Michael Menachem Laskier and Sara Reguer, eds. New York: Columbia UP, 2003, 85-112.
Ascha, Ghassan. *Du Statut Inférieur de la Femme en Islam*. Paris: Editions l'Harmattan, 1987.
Attias, Ruth Tolédano. "Lumières du passé." *Pardès* 28 (2000): 143-153.
Ayoun, Richard and Haim Vidal Sephiha. *Séfarades d'hier et d'aujourd'hui*. Paris: Liana Levi, 1992.

B

Bahloul, Joëlle. *The Architecture of Memory: A Jewish-Muslim Household in Colonial Algeria 1937-1962*. Cambridge: Cambridge UP, 1996.

---. "La Rentrée en France des Juifs d'Algérie." *Pardés* 28: *La mémoire sépharade*. (2000): 179-186.
Barthes, Roland. *The Pleasure of the Text*. Translated by Richard Miller. New York: Hill, 1975.
Benabou, Marcel. "Genèse d'une Epopée Absente." *Etudes Littéraires* 29 (1997): 95-106.
Benayoun, Chantal. "Entre hier et Aujourd'hui: Regards et Images des Pieds-Noirs." In *Les Juifs dans le regard de l'Autre*. Toulouse: Editeurs, CIREJ, Presses Universitaires du Mirail/Editions Vent Terral, 1988, 127-143.
Benayoun-Szmidt, Yvette. "Annie Cohen: pour une algérianité retrouvée." *International Journal of Francophone Studies* 7 (2004): 19-34.
Benayoun-Szmidt, Yvette and Najib Redouane. *Parcours féminin dans la Littérature Marocaine d'Expression Française*. Toronto: Les Editions la Source, 2000.
Bensimon, Doris and Allouche-Benayoun, Joëlle. *Les Juifs d'Algérie. Mémoires et identités plurielles*. Paris: Editions Stavit, 1999.
Bensoussan, Albert. "L'Algérie des Ecrivains." *L'Arche* Sept-Oct. (1982): 170-172.
---. *L'échelle séfarade*. Paris: L'Harmattan, 1993.
---. "De la confession à l'autobiographie: l'écriture juive actuelle." *Les Nouveaux Cahiers* 77: 11-19.
---. "Le Roman Sépharade de Langue Française Aujourd'hui." *Sens: Juifs et Chrétiens dans le Monde Aujourd'hui*. 10-11 (1981): 242-247.
Benzakour-Chami, Anissa. *Femme Idéale?* Maroc: Editions la Fennec, 1992.
Bessis, Sophie and Souhayr Belhassen. *Femmes du Maghreb: l'enjeu*. Paris: Editions J.-C. Lattes, 1992.
Bhabha, Homi. *The Location of Culture*. London: Routledge, 1994.
---. "The Post-colonial Critic: Homi Bhabha Interviewed by David Bennett and Terry Collits." *Arena* 96 (1991): 47-63.
Biale, David, ed. *Cultures of the Jews: A New History*. New York: Schocken Books, 2002.
Blanchard, Tzvi. "Photographs," in Frédéric Brenner, *Diaspora: Homelands in Exile. Photographs and Voices*. New York: Harper Collins, 2003, viii.

Blot, Jean. "Une littérature Juive Française?" *L'Arche* 153 (1969): 55-57.
Bonn, Charles, Naget Khadda et Abdallah Mdarhi-Alaoui, eds. *Littérature Maghrébine d'Expression Française*. Cedex: EDICEF, 1996.
Bordo, Susan. "The Cartesian Masculinization of Thought." In *From Modernism to Postmodernism*. Malden, Mass.: Blackwell Publishers, 1996, 638-664.
Boukhobza, Chochana. *Pour l'Amour du Père*. Paris: Seuil, 1996.
---. "Rien sur l'enfance." In Laila Sebbar, ed. *Une enfance juive en Méditerranée musulmane*. Saint-Pourçain-sur-Sioule: Bleu Autour, 2012, 85.
---. *Sous les Etoiles*. Paris: Seuil, 2002.
---. *Un Eté à Jérusalem*. Paris: Seuil, 1986.
Boum, Aomar. *Memories of Absence: How Muslims Remember Jews in Morocco*. Stanford, CA: Stanford UP, 2013.
Boyarin, Jonathan and Daniel Boyarin. "Diaspora: Generation and the Ground of Jewish Identity." In *Theorizing Diaspora*. Jana Evans Braziel and Anita Mannur, eds. Malden: Blackwell Publishing, 2003, 85-118.
---. and Daniel Boyarin. *Powers of Diaspora*. Minneapolis: U of Minnesota P, 2002.
---. *Storm from Paradise. The Politics of Jewish Memory*. Minneapolis: U of Minnesota P, 1992.
Boym, Svetlana. *The Future of Nostalgia*. New York: Basic Books, 2001.
Brann, Ross. "Specular Images: Jews and Muslims in Al-Andalus." *Prooftexts* 24 (2004): 206-217.
Braziel, Jana Evans and Anita Mannur, eds. *Theorizing Diaspora*. Malden: Blackwell Publishing, 2003.
Brenner, Frédéric. *Diaspora: Homelands in Exile. Photographs and Voices*. New York: Harper Collins, 2003.
Bromley, Roger. *Narratives for a New Belonging: Diasporic Cultural Fictions*. Edinburgh: Edinburgh UP, 2000.

C

Cairns, Lucille. *Post-War Jewish Women's Writing in French*. Oxford: Legenda, 2011.

Caws, Mary Ann, Mary Jean Green, Marianne Hirsch and Ronnie Scharfman, eds. *Ecritures de Femmes. Nouvelles Cartographies.* New Haven: Yale UP, 1996.

Césaire, Aimé. *Discourse on Colonialism.* Translated by By Joan Pinkham. New York: Monthly Review Press, 2000.

Chetrit, Joseph. "Judeo-Arabic," in *The Jews of the Middle East and North Africa in Modern Times.* Reeva Spector Simon, Michael Menachem Laskier and Sara Reguer, eds. New York: Columbia UP, 2003, 128.

Chouraqui, André. *Histoire des Juifs en Afrique du Nord.* Tome 1: *En Exil au Maghreb.* Monaco: Editions du Rocher, 1998.

---, *Histoire des Juifs en Afrique du Nord.* Tome 2: *Le Retour en Orient.* Monaco: Editions du Rocher, 1998.

Cixous, Hélène. "Algiers, premires douleurs." *Expressions Maghrébines* 2 (2003): 151-161.

---. *Entre l'Ecriture.* Paris: Des Femmes, 1986.

---. *Les Rêveries de la femme sauvage.* Paris: Galilée, 2000.

---. "Letter to Zora Drif." *Parallax* 4 (1998): 189-196.

---. "My Algériance. In other words to Depart not to arrive from Algeria." Translated by Eric Prenowitz. *Tri-quarterly* 100 (1997): 259-279.

---. *Osnabruck.* Paris: Des Femmes, 1999.

---. "Pieds Nus." In *Une Enfance Algérienne.* Paris: Gallimard, 1997, 53-63.

---. *Portrait of Jacques Derrida as a Young Jewish Saint.* New York: Columbia UP, 2004.

---. *Rootprints.* New York: Routledge, 1997.

Cohen, Annie. *Bésame Mucho.* Paris: Gallimard, 1998.

---. *Le Marabout de Blida.* Paris: Gallimard, 1996.

---. "Viridiana mon amour." In *Une Enfance Algérienne.* Paris: Gallimard, 1997, 65-78.

Cohen, David. "Algeria," *The Jews of the Middle East and North Africa of Modern Times.* Reeva Spector Simon, Michael Menachem Laskier and Sara Reguer, eds. New York: Columbia UP, 2003, 458-470.

Cohen, Julia Philips and Sarah Abrevaya Stein, eds. *Sephardi Lives: A Documentary History 1700-1950.* Stanford: Stanford UP, 2014.

Culler, Jonathan. "The Literary in Theory." In *What's Left of Theory?* Judith Butler, John Guillory and Kendall Thomas, eds. New York: Routledge, 2000, 273-292.

D

Darmon, Paule. *Baisse les Yeux, Sarah.* Paris: Grasset, 1980.
Delouya, Arrik. *Les Juifs du Maroc. Bibliographie Générale.* Paris: Société Nouvelle Librairie Orientaliste Paul Geuthner, 2001.
Derrida, Jacques. "Circonfession." In *Jacques Derrida.* In collaboration with Geoffrey Bennington. Chicago: U of Chicago P, 1993, 120-132.
---. *Le Monolinguisme de l'Autre.* Paris: Editions Galilée, 1996.
---. *Monolingualism of the Other.* Translated by Patrick Mensah. Stanford: Stanford UP, 1998.
Dore-Audibert, Andrée and Souad Khodja, eds. *Etre femme au Maghreb et en Méditerranée.* Paris: Editions Karthala, 1998.
Dugas, Guy. "Trente ans de littérature judéo-maghrébine (1982-2013)." In *Expressions maghrébines,* vol. 13, n° 2, hiver (2014).
---. *Bibliographie Critique de la Littérature Judéo-Maghrebine d'Expression Française.* Paris: L'Harmattan, 1992.
---. *La Littérature Judéo-Maghébine d'Expression Française.* Paris: L'Harmattan, 1990.

E

Elbaz, André E. "Influences Arabo-Berbères dans le Conte Populaire des Sephardim Canadiens d'Origine Marocaine." In *Juif du Maroc; identité et dialogue; actes du colloques international sur la Communauté juive marocaine; vie culturelle, histoire sociale et évolution.* Grenoble: Pensée Sauvage, 1980, 61-68.
Ertel, Rachel. "A Minority Literature." Translated by Alan Astro. *Yale French Studies* 85 (1994): 224-226.

F

Fine, Ellen S. "L' Écriture comme mémoire absente." *Les Nouveaux Cahiers* 101 (1990): 50-56.
Finkielkraut, Alain. *The Imaginary Jew.* London: U of Nebraska P, 1994.

Fitoussie, Annie. *La mémoire Folle de Mouchi Rabbinou*. Paris: Mazarine, 1985.

G

Gerber, Jane. *The Jews of Spain: a History of the Sephardic Experience*. New York: Free Press. 1994.

Giorgio, Adalgisa, ed. *Writing Mothers and Daughters*. New York: Berghahn Books, 2002, 11-45.

Goldberg, Harvey, E., ed. S*ephardi and Middle Eastern Jewries. History and Culture in the Modern Era*. Bloomington: Indiana UP, 1996.

Goldmann, Annie. *Les Filles de Mardochée: Histoire d'une émancipation*. Paris: Denoël et Gonthier, 1979.

Gontard, Marc. "Itinéraires Judéo-Maghrébins." *Peuples Méditerranéens. Mediterranean Peoples* 30 (1985): 123-138.

H

Halevi-Wise, Yael (Ed.). *Sephardism: Spanish Jewish History and the Modern Literary Imagination*. Stanford, CA: Stanford UP, 2012.

Halfon, Jaco. "Pied-Noir." www.zlabia.com, 1. 15 January 2006. Web.

Halimi, Gisèle. *Fritna*. Paris: Plon, 1999.

---. *Le Lait de l'Oranger*. Paris: Gallimard, 1988.

Harding, Sandra. "From Feminist Empiricism to Feminist Standpoint Epistemologies." In *From Modernism to Postmodernism*. Lawrence E. Cahoone, ed. Malden, Mass: Wiley/Blackwell Publishers, 2nd ed. 2003, 342-353.

Hargreaves, Alec G. *Immigration, 'Race' and Ethnicity in Contemporary France*. London: Routledge, 1995.

---. and Mark McKinney, eds. *Post-Colonial Cultures in France*. London: Routledge, 1997.

---. and Jeremy Leaman, eds. *Racism, Ethnicity and Politics in Contemporary Europe*. Edward Elgar Publishing Limited, UK, 1995.

---. "Writers of Maghreb Immigrant Origin in France: French, Francophone, Maghreb or Beur?" In *African Francophone Writing. A Critical Introduction*. Laila Ibnlfassi and Nicki Hitchcott, eds. Oxford: Berg, 1996, 33-43.

Honung, Alfred and Ernstpeter Ruhe, eds. *Postcolonialisme & Autobiographie*. Amsterdam – Atlanta: Rodopi B.V., 1998.

Horowitz, Sara. "Jewish Studies as Oppositional? Or Gettin' Mighty Lonely Out Here." In *Styles of Cultural Activism: From Theory and Pedagogy to Women, Indians and Communism*. Philip Goldstein, ed. Newark: U of Delaware P, 1994, 152-164.

Hughes, Alex. "Recycling and Repetition in Recent French Autofiction: Marc Weitzmann's Doubrovskian Borrowings." *Modern Language Review* 97 (2002): 566-576.

---. "Writing Mother-Daughter Relationality in the French Context." *Writing Mothers and Daughters*. Adalgisa Giorgio, ed. New York: Berghahn Books, 2002, 155-184.

Hyman, Paula. *The Jews of Modern France*. Berkeley: U of California P, 1998.

I

Ireland, John. "Introduction: Monstrous Writing: Serge Doubrvosky's Autofiction." *Genre XXVI* (1993), i-ii.

Ireland, Susan and Patrice J. Proulx eds. *Immigrant Narratives in Contemporary France*. Westport, Connecticut: Greenwood Press, 2001.

---. "Writing at the Crossroads: Cultural Conflict in the Work of Beur Women Writers." *The French Review* 68 (1995): 1022-1034.

J

K

Kaiser Walter. *Praisers of Folly: Erasmus, Rabelais, Shakespeare*. Cambridge: Harvard UP, 1963.

Katz, Ethan B. *The Burdens of Brotherhood: Jews and Muslims from North Africa to France*. Cambridge: Harvard UP, 2015.

Kaye/Kantrowitz, Melanie. *The Colors of Jews. Racial Politics and Radical Diasporism*. Bloomington and Indianapolis: Indiana UP, 2007.

Kenbib, Mohammed. *Juifs et Musulmans au Maroc 1859-1948*. Rabat: Publications de la Faculté des Lettres et des Sciences Humaines, 1994.

Khatibi, Abdelkebir. *Maghreb Pluriel*. Paris : Denoël, 1983.

Khazzoom, Loolwa, ed. *The Flying Camel. Essays on Identity by Women of North African and Middle Eastern Jewish Heritage*. New York: Seal Press, 2003.

Kramer, Michael P. "Race, Literary History and the 'Jewish Question.'" *Prooftexts* 21 (2001): 287-349.

Kristeva, Julia. *Strangers to Ourselves*. New York: Columbia UP, 1991.

---. *The Portable Kristeva*. Kelly Oliver, ed. New York: Columbia UP, 1983.

L

Lalagianni, Vassiliki, ed. *Femmes écrivains en Méditerranée*. Paris: Publisud, 1999.

Laskier, Michael, M. *The Alliance Israélite Universelle and the Jewish Communities of Morocco 1862-1962*. Albany: SUNY P, 1983.

---. *North African Jewry in the Twentieth Century. The Jews of Morocco, Tunisia and Algeria*. New York: NYUP, 1994.

Lejeune, Philippe. *Le pacte autobiographique*. Paris: Editions du Seuil, 1975, 1996.

---. *On Autobiography*. Paul John Eakin, ed. Translated by Katherine Leary. Minneapolis: U of Minn. P, 1988.

Levy, Clara. *Ecritures de l'identité. Les écrivains juifs après la Shoah*. Paris: PUF, 1998.

Levy-Mogelli, Danielle. "Un cas particulier d'aliénation culturelle: les Juifs d'Afrique du Nord dans l'Aventure Coloniale Française." In *Juifs du Maroc. Identité et Dialogue*. Grenoble: Sauvage, 1980, 247-255.

Lionnet, Françoise. *Autobiographical Voices: Race, Gender, Self-Portraiture*. Ithaca: Cornell UP, 1989.

---. "Francophonie, Post-colonial Studies, and Transnational Feminisms." In *Post-colonial Theory and Francophone Literary Studies*. Adlai Murdoch and Anne Donadey, eds. Gainsville: UP of Florida, 2005.

---. "Logiques Métisses. Cultural Appropriation and Post-colonial Representations." In *Post-colonial Subjects. Francophone Women Writers*. Mary Jean Green et al, eds. Minneapolis: U of Minn. P, 1996, 321-243.

---. *Post-colonial Representations. Women, Literature and Identity.* Ithaca: Cornell UP, 1995.

M

Mandel, Maud S. *Muslims and Jews in France: History of a Conflict.* Princeton and Oxford: Princeton UP, 2014.

Meddeb, Abdelwahab and Benjamin Stora, eds. *A History of Jewish-Muslim Relations: From the Origins to the Present Day.* Trans. Jane Marie Todd and Michael B. Smith. Princeton: Princeton UP, 2013.

Memmi, Albert. *Juifs et Arabes.* Paris: Gallimard, 1974.

---. *Portrait du Colonisé.* Paris: Gallimard, 1985.

---. "Who is an Arab Jew?" on www.Jimena.org. Official website of Jews Indigenous to the Middle East and North Africa. Source quoted as Israel Academic Committee on the Middle East, February, 1975.

Minces, Juliette. *La Femme voilée.* Paris: Calmann-Levy, 1990.

Moati, Nine. *Deux Femmes à Paris.* Paris: Ramsey, 1998.

---. *La Passagère Sans Etoile.* Paris: Seuil, 1989.

---. *Mon Enfant, Ma Mère.* Paris: Editions Stock, 1974.

N

Nebot, Didier. *Les Tribus Oubliées d'Israel. L'Afrique judéo-berbère, des origines aux Almohades.* Paris: Editions Romillat, 1999.

Nolden, Thomas. *In Lieu of Memory. Contemporary Jewish Writing in France.* New York: Syracuse UP, 2006.

---. and Frances Milano, eds. *Voices of the Diaspora: Jewish Women Writing in Contemporary Europe.* Evanston: Northwest UP, 2005.

O

Ofrat, Gideon. *The Jewish Derrida.* Syracuse: Syracuse UP, 2001.

Ozik, Cynthia. "America: Toward Yavneh." In *What is Jewish Literature?* Hanna Wirth-Nesher, ed. Philadelphia: JPS, 1994, 20-35.

P

Peters, Joan. *From Time Immemorial. The Origins of the Arab-Jewish Conflict over Palestine.* New York: Harper, 1984.

R

Redouane, Najib. *Editorial Introduction to International Journal of Francophone Studies* 7 (2004), 3-4. (Issues dedicated to the literary contributions of Judeo-Maghrebian writers in North African francophone literature).

Reuger, Sara. "The World of Women." In *The Jews of the Middle East and North Africa in Modern Times.* Reeva Spector Simon, Michael Menachem Laskier and Sara Reguer, eds. New York: Columbia UP, 2003, 235-276.

Roffé, Reina, "Exotic Birds," in Thomas Nolden and Frances Milano, eds. *Voices of the Diaspora: Jewish Women Writing in Contemporary Europe.* Evanston: Northwest UP, 2005, 13-20.

Rosello, Mireille. *Declining the Stereotype: Ethnicity and Representation in French Cultures.* Hanover and London: UP of New England, 1998.

---. *Post-colonial Hospitality. The Immigrant as Guest.* California: Stanford UP, 2001.

Rothberg, Michael. *Multidirectional Memory. Remembering the Holocaust in the Age of Decolonialisation.* Stanford: Stanford UP, 2009.

S

Saadoun, Haim. "Tunisia." In *The Jews of the Middle East and North Africa in Modern Times.* Reeva Spector Simon, Michael Menachem Laskier and Sara Reguer, eds. New York: Columbia UP, 2003, 444-457.

Said, Edward. *Culture and Imperialism.* New York: Vintage Books, 1994.

---. *Orientalism.* New York: Vintage Books, 1978.

Sartori, Eva Martin and Madeleine Cottenet-Hage, eds. *Daughters of Sarah. Anthology of Jewish Women Writers in France.* Teaneck: Holes & Meier, 2006.

Shapiro, Susan E. "Ecriture judaïque. Where Are the Jews in Western Discourse?" In *Displacements. Cultural Identities in Question.* Angelika Bammer, ed. Bloomington: Indiana UP, 1994, 182-201.

Scharfman, Ronnie. "Narratives of Internal Exile." *Post-colonial Theory and Francophone Literary Studies.* H. Adlai Murdoch and Anne Donadey, eds. Gainesville: Florida UP, 2005, 87-101.

---. "The Other's Other: The Moroccan Jewish Trajectory of Edmond Amran El Maleh." *Yale French Studies* 82, Volume 1 (1993): 135-145.

Sebbar, Leïla. *Une enfance juive en Méditerranée musulmane*. Saint-Pourçain-sur-Sioule: Bleu Autour, 2012.

Shohat, Ella. "Notes on the 'Post-Colonial.'" *Social Text* 31/32 (1992): 99-113.

---. "Reflections of an Arab Jew," in *The Flying Camel. Essays on Identity by Women of North African and Middle Eastern Jewish Heritage*. Loolwa Khazzoom, ed. New York: Seal Press, 2003, 115-121.

Shulewitz, Malka Hillel. *The Forgotten Millions: The Jewish Exodus from Arab Lands*. New York: Cassell, 1999.

Sibony, Daniel. *L'Énigme Antisémite*. Paris: Seuil, 2004.

---. *L'Entre-Deux. L'Origine en Partage*. Paris: Seuil, 1991.

---. *Marrakech, le Départ*. Paris: Odile Jacob, 2009.

---. *Proche-Orient. Psychanalyse d'un Conflit*. Paris: Seuil, 2003.

---. *Psychanalyse et Judaïsme*. Paris: Flammarion, 2001.

Smith, Roger. *Derrida and Autobiography*. Cambridge: Cambridge UP, 1995.

Smith, Sidonie and Julia Watson. *Reading Autobiography*. Minneapolis: Minnesota UP, 2010.

Spector Simon, Reeva, Michael Menachem Laskier and Sara Reguer, eds. *The Jews of the Middle East and North Africa in Modern Times*. New York: Columbia UP, 2003.

Spivak, Gyatri Chakravorty. "Displacement and the Discourse of Woman." *Displacement: Derrida and After*, Mark Krupnick, ed. Bloomington: Indiana UP, 1983, 169-195.

---. "Translator's Preface." *Of Grammatology*. Baltimore: John Hopkins UP, 1998.

Stavans, Ilan, ed. *The Schocken Book of Modern Sephardic Literature*. New York: Schocken Books, 2005.

Stevens, Christa. "Judéités, à lire dans l'œuvre d'Hélène Cixous." *International Journal of Francophone Studies* 7 (2004): 81-93.

Stillman, Norman, A. *The Jews of Arab Lands. A History and Source Book*. Philadelphia: JPS, 1979.

---. *The Jews of Arab Lands in Modern Times*. Philadelphia: JPS, 1991.

---. "The Judeo-Arabic Heritage." In *Sephardic and Mizrahi Jewry. From the Golden Age of Spain to Modern Times*. Zion Zohar, ed. New York: NYUP, 2005, 40-54.

---. "Middle Eastern and North African Jewries Confront Modernity." In *Sephardi and Middle Eastern Jewries. History and Culture in the Modern Era*. Harvey E. Goldberg, ed. Bloomington: Indiana UP, 1996, 59-72.

Strike, Joëlle. *Albert Memmi Autobiographie et Autographie*. Paris: L'Harmattan, 2003.

Dossier: "La Littérature Juive." *Traces* 3 (1982): 71-103.

T

Taïeb, Jacques. *Etre Juif au Maghreb à la veille de la colonisation*. Paris: Albin Michel, 1994.

Todorov, Tzvetan. *L'Homme dépaysé*. Paris: Editions du Seuil, 1996.

Trigano, Hélène et Shmuel eds. *Pardès* 28: *La mémoire sépharade*. Paris: In Presse Editions, 2000.

Trigano, Shmuel. "La Mémoire du Peuple Disparu." *Pardès* 28: La mémoire sépharade (2000), 11-53.

U

V

Valensi, Lucette. "Multicultural Visions: The Cultural Tapestry of the Jews of North Africa." In *Cultures of the Jews: A New History*. David Biale, ed. New York: Schocken Books, 2002, 887-931.

W

Waldman, Regina. *Address to the U.N. Human Rights Council*. 8 April 2008. YouTube 15 April 2008. Web.

Wirth-Nesher, Hannah, ed. *What is Jewish Literature*? Jerusalem: JPS, 1994.

Wolf, Mary Ellen. "Rethinking the Radical West: Khatibi and Deconstruction." *L'Esprit Créateur* 2 (1994): 58-68.

Wood, David and Robert Bernasconi, eds. *Derrida and Différance*. Evanston: Northwest UP, 1988.

Wood, Nancy. "Remembering the Jews of Algeria." *Parallax* 4 (1998): 169-183.

Wurmser, Meyrav. "Post-Zionism and the Sephardi Question." *Middle East Quarterly Online*, Volume XII, Number 2, (Spring 2005): 21-30.

X

Y

Yassif, Eli. "The 'Other' Israel." In *Cultures of the Jews: A New History*. David Biale, ed. New York: Schocken Books, 2002, 1063-1096.

Ye'or, Bat, Miriam Kochan and David Littman. *Islam and Dhimmitude: Where Civilizations Collide*. Madison: Fairleigh Dickinson UP, December 2001.

---. *The Dhimmi. Jews and Christians under Islam*. London: Associated UP, 1985.

Yerushalmi, Yosef Hayim. *Zakhor: Jewish History and Jewish Memory*. Seattle: U of Washington P, 1982.

Z

Zafrani, Haim. *Deux mille ans de vie juive au Maroc*. Paris: Maison Neuve & Larose, 1998.

Zohar, Zion. "Sephardim and Oriental Jews in Israel." In *Sephardic and Mizrahi Jewry. From the Golden Age of Spain to Modern Times*. Zion Zohar, ed. New York: NYUP, 2005, 300-327.

Films

Being Jewish in France. Yves Jeuland. France, 2007.
Hélène Cixous. Films for the Humanities and Sciences. Princeton, NJ, 2003.
Jews and Muslims: Intimate Strangers. Karim Miské. France, 2013.
Remembering Memory: Cixous on Cixous. By Lara Fitzgerald. Princeton, New Jersey: Films for the Humanities and Sciences, c 2000.
The Forgotten Refugees. Michael Grynszpan and Tommy Schwarcz. A documentary produced by the David Project, a non-profit educational initiative, 2005.
The Rabbi's Cat. Joann Sfar, 2011.
The Silent Exodus. Pierre Rochav, c 2002.
Va, Viens et Deviens/Live and Become. Radu Mihâileanu, 2005.

Websites

www.dafina.net Website for Moroccan Jews
www.diarna.org Online Geo-Museum of North African and Middle Eastern Jewish Life
www.harissa.com Website for Tunisian Jews
www.zlabia.com Website for Algerian Jews
www.jimena.org Website for Jews Indigenous to the Middle East and North Africa
www.tellthechildrenthetruth.com Website explaining the Nazi Roots of today's Jihad.
www.memri.org The Middle East Media Research Institute

About the Author

Nina Boug Lichtenstein is a writer, teacher, blogger and public speaker. A native of Oslo, Norway, she received her Ph.D. in French literature from the University of Connecticut, where she currently teaches literature and writing. She is also a Research Associate at the Hadassah Brandeis Institute at Brandeis University. She has recently translated a novel into English by the Jewish French-Tunisian writer Chochana Boukhobza, and her research interests and publications concern literature and film by and about Francophone Jewish women from North Africa, Sephardic Jews and the Holocaust, and Jews from Islamic Lands in general.

Index

A

Abitbol 14, 50, 63, 65, 67, 68, 70, 71, 73, 81, 82, 88, 107, 247
AIU 41, 51-54, 58, 84
Alain Finkielkraut 14, 24, 93, 127, 129, 244
Al-Andalus 30, 36, 249
Albert Bensoussan 79, 112, 113, 123, 124, 130, 131
Albert Memmi 14, 29, 35, 37, 72, 111, 124, 125, 135, 258
Alcalay 11, 32, 33, 61, 73, 85, 239, 247
Algeria 13, 14, 17, 18, 23, 27, 29, 31, 39, 41, 42, 45, 47, 49, 50, 51, 54-56, 58, 59, 61, 62, 64, 65, 68-70, 73, 74, 79, 82, 83, 88-90, 110, 113, 117, 124, 128, 136, 164, 168, 169, 170, 174, 188, 199, 201-203, 208, 238, 247, 250, 254, 258
Algerian war 66, 72, 82, 195
Al-Husayni 67
Alissa Rhaïs 125
Aliyah 5, 83
Alliance Israélite Universelle 39, 51, 254
Ammiel Alcalay 11, 61, 239
Annie Cohen 6, 47, 129, 149-151, 164, 165, 170, 184, 185, 199, 200, 202, 207, 209, 242, 248
Annie Fitoussi 6, 185, 187, 200
Anti-Semitism 35, 51, 52, 55, 58, 62, 67, 89, 92
Arab Jew 14, 29, 35, 72, 75, 86, 255, 257
Arabo-Muslim 34, 36, 75, 103, 105, 117, 125, 137
Arabophone 53
Autofiction 126, 127, 129
Autojudeography 127, 129

B

Bahloul 64, 65, 75, 247
Benabou 124, 248
Bensoussan 79, 112, 113, 123, 124, 130, 131, 132, 248
Berber 28-30, 72, 84, 121, 161, 180, 223
Bésame Mucho 6, 47, 151, 164, 165, 202, 205, 250
Bhabha 13, 56, 104, 110, 114, 115, 248
Biale 34, 248, 258
Boukhobza 6, 9, 129, 211, 212, 228, 229, 236, 237, 249, 261

Boyarin 16, 86, 110, 112, 119, 130, 131, 249
Brenner 19, 111, 248, 249

C

Chetrit 32, 250
Chimenti 37, 125, 138
Chochana Boukhobza 6, 9, 129, 211, 228, 236, 237, 261
Cixous 17, 18, 23, 42, 47, 49, 58, 60-62, 69, 80, 89, 90, 110, 111, 113, 116, 128, 129, 133, 135, 188, 198, 208, 241, 242, 250, 257, 260
Cohen 6, 37, 47, 55, 73, 83, 108, 129, 149, 150, 151, 164, 165, 168, 169, 170, 174, 177, 181, 184, 185, 187, 199, 200, 202, 205, 207-209, 242, 248, 250, 251
Crémieux decree 17, 35, 40, 54, 65, 69

D

Danielle Levy-Mongelli 57, 105
Daniel Sibony 19, 48, 86, 110, 152, 153, 162, 226, 245
Darmon 6, 129, 211, 212, 237, 242, 251
David Biale 34, 258
Decolonialization 117, 227
Deconstructionist philosophy 93
Derrida 60, 61, 93, 104, 116, 134, 141, 142, 250, 251, 255, 257, 258
Dhimmi 33, 34, 36, 40, 46, 47, 50-52, 55, 105, 147, 151
Dhimmitude 33, 35, 45, 51, 137
Diasporic 18
Diasporic Jewry 98
Dreyfus 35, 58, 190

E

Edward Said 19, 103, 104, 145
Elissa Chimenti 37, 125, 138
Entre-deux 19, 48, 74, 110, 152, 153, 162, 167, 187, 245
European Jews 16, 26, 32, 92, 94
Exilic 19, 85, 109, 111, 238

F

Final Solution 70
Finkielkraut 14, 24, 93, 94, 127, 129, 244, 251
Fitoussie 6, 129, 185, 194, 198, 207, 242, 251
Frédéric Brenner 19, 111, 248
Frenchified 58, 64, 73, 74, 86, 88, 136
Fritna 6, 147, 148, 151, 154-165, 177, 180, 195, 252

G

Gideon Ofrat 60, 93, 141
Gina Waldman 15
Gisèle Halimi 6, 89, 129, 147-151, 154, 159, 162, 184, 194, 242
Grand Mufti of Jerusalem 67

H

Haim Zafrani 71
Hajj Amin al-Husayni 67
Halimi 6, 89, 90, 129, 147-151, 154-164, 177, 180, 181, 184, 194, 242, 252
Hélène Cixous 17, 18, 23, 42, 47, 58, 62, 80, 89, 113, 116, 128, 129, 188, 198, 241, 242, 257, 260
Homi Bhabha 13, 56, 104, 110, 248
Human rights 40, 89, 100, 240
Hybridity 114, 115, 119, 144, 167

I

Irigaray 133, 162, 183, 219

J

Jewish Maghrebi literature 105
Jewish-Muslim 67, 79, 80, 95, 247
Jews of Algeria 55, 58, 62, 258
Jews of North Africa 12, 14, 20, 24, 27, 31, 34, 51, 57, 63, 68, 70, 71, 74, 103, 107, 187, 247, 258
Jews of the Islamic world 16
JIMENA 15, 94, 95
Joëlle Bahloul 64
Jonathan Boyarin 16, 86, 110, 112, 130
Joseph Chetrit 32
Judeo-Berber 28, 29
Judeo-Maghrebi 119, 140
Juifemme 18, 128

K

Kahena 29
Khazzoom 75, 86, 134, 253, 257

L

Laskier 26, 27, 32, 33, 40, 43, 52, 53, 84, 88, 247, 250, 254, 256, 257

Levy-Mongelli 57, 105
Loolwa Khazzoom 75, 86, 134, 257
Luce Irigaray 162, 219

M

Maghreb 5, 11, 12, 14-16, 19, 22-32, 34, 36, 38, 39, 41, 45-48, 50-53, 59, 60, 63, 67, 70-76, 81, 83, 84, 88, 91, 93, 98, 101, 105-108, 110, 111, 113, 118, 119, 121, 124, 125, 128-131, 135-138, 140, 141, 143-145, 148, 150, 151, 153, 161, 175, 176, 180, 185, 190, 191, 207, 211, 213, 214, 221, 235, 237-240, 242, 245, 248, 250,-253, 258
Maghrebi literature 105, 106, 140
Marabout 148, 185-187, 200-206, 208, 209, 238
Marcel Benabou 124
Mashreq 15, 28, 38, 48, 66, 67, 84, 96
Mellah 53, 71
Memmi 14, 29, 35, 37, 72, 111, 124-126, 135, 255, 258
Métropole 58, 59, 64, 83, 92, 106, 117, 175, 181, 191, 202
Michael M. Laskier 26, 52, 84, 88
Michel Abitbol 14, 50, 63, 67, 68, 81, 88, 107
Mizrahi 16, 31, 37, 70, 85-88, 95, 102, 134, 247, 257, 259
Mizrahim 26, 87
Moati 6, 129, 149, 150, 151, 175-182, 184, 242, 255
Morocco 13, 14, 25, 27, 30-32, 34, 35, 39-41, 45-47, 50, 51, 54, 55, 59, 62, 68, 69-71, 73-75, 82-84, 108, 110, 118, 124, 131, 212, 216, 219, 222, 223, 225, 231, 238, 249, 254

N

Nine Moati 6, 129, 149-151, 175, 176, 184, 242
Norman Stillman 26, 33, 66, 67

O

Ofrat 60, 93, 134, 141, 142, 255
Oriental Jewish 14, 95, 137, 242

P

Patriarchal 211
Paule Darmon 6, 129, 211, 212, 237, 242
Pied-noir 63-65, 67, 88, 136, 195, 208, 213, 223, 240
Post-colonial 11-5, 17, 20, 24, 27, 56, 76, 90, 93, 98-104, 111, 114, 115, 118, 122, 125, 126, 132, 137, 140, 144, 147, 193, 207, 221, 237, 239, 242, 243, 245
Post-Shoah 94

R

Rediasporization 110, 119
Reina Roffé 131
Rhaïs 125, 138
Ronnie Scharfman 75, 128, 250

S

Said 19, 103, 104, 105, 109, 145, 256
Scharfman 75, 120, 128, 250, 256
Sephardic women's writings 11
Sephardim 4, 14, 26, 30, 31, 70, 85, 87, 100, 108, 161, 225, 226, 247, 251, 259
Shmuel Trigano 50, 84, 91, 121
Sibony 19, 48, 86, 110, 111, 152, 153, 162, 226, 245, 257
State of Israel 15, 24, 33, 37, 72, 82, 84, 225, 241
Stillman 9, 26, 33, 66, 67, 68, 73, 257

T

Teshuva 108
Trigano 50, 84, 91, 92, 100, 121, 258
Tunisia 9, 13, 14, 27, 31, 32, 35, 39, 41, 45, 46, 50, 51, 54, 55, 59, 68, 69, 70, 73, 74, 79, 82, 90, 108, 110, 124, 154, 157, 167, 175, 177, 179, 180, 187, 188, 189, 190, 191, 192, 194, 228, 229, 231, 232, 233, 238, 254, 256

V

Vichy 17, 68, 69, 70, 71, 92

W

Waldman 15, 94, 103, 258

Y

Yerushalmi 25, 37, 38, 101, 129, 130, 203, 243, 259
Yosef H. Yerushalmi 25

Z

Zachor 186
Zafrani 71, 240

Gaon Books
Sephardic Heritage Collection

Non-Fiction

Nina B. Lichtenstein. 2016. *Sephardic Women's Voices: Out of North Africa.*

Ron D. Hart. 2016. *Sephardic Jews: History, Religion and People.*

Orit Rabkin. Forthcoming 2017. *Emma Lazarus: Sephardic Woman of Letters.*

Silvia Hamui Sutton.
- Forthcoming 2017. *Lyrical Eroticism in Judeo-Spanish Songs.*
- 2009. *Cantos judeo-españoles: simbología poética y visión del mundo.*

Judah Halevi. 2015. *Kuzari.*

Susana Weich-Shahak. 2014. *Moroccan Sephardic Romancero: Anthology of an Oral Tradition.* (Winner of the European Folklore Prize, 2014).

William Samelson. 2013. *Sephardic Legacy: Stories and Songs from Jewish Spain.*

Raphael David Elmaleh and **George Ricketts**. 2012. *Jews under Moroccan Skies: Two Thousand Years of Jewish Life.*

Estrella Jalfón de Bentolila. 2012. *Haketía: A Memoir of Judeo-Spanish Language & Culture in Morocco.*

Fiction

Sandra K. Toro.
- 2014. *Secrets Behind Adobe Walls.*
- 2013. *Princes, Popes and Pirates*
- 2012. *By Fire Possessed.*

Isabelle Medina Sandoval.
- 2012. *Hidden Shabbat.*
- 2009. *Guardians of Hidden Traditions.*

Mario Martinez. 2009. *Converso.*

Young Adult Readers

Sandra K. Toro. 2016. *Doña Gracia: Beacon of Hope*

Mario Martinez. 2015. *Abran and Isabella's Hidden Faith.*

Angelina Muñiz-Huberman. 2014. *Dreaming of Safed.*

Vanessa Paloma. 2012. *The Mountain, the Desert and the Pomegranate: Stories from Morocco and Beyond.*

CPSIA information can be obtained
at www.ICGtesting.com
Printed in the USA
BVOW11s1437140518
516179BV00003B/400/P